RECOLLECTIONS OF
FULL YEARS

BY

MRS. WILLIAM HOWARD TAFT

1914

Get more great reading from BIG BYTE BOOKS

Contents

ACKNOWLEDGEMENTS

I wish to express my grateful acknowledgment to Eleanor Franklin Egan and my daughter for their valued assistance in the preparation for publication of these Recollections.

HELEN HERRON TAFT.

2014 PREFACE

Written at the immediate end of William Howard Taft's only term as president, this memoir by Nellie Taft is rather remarkable for its scope and its personal nature. She writes with a warm, disarming style of her youthful years, her marriage, and Will Taft's rapid rise in public life.

A particular focus of the book concerns their travels and their time in the Philippines. Nellie Taft seems to have had a talent for cross-cultural friendship and clearly a tremendous curiosity about the world. She writes with intelligence and humor, revealing indirectly to the reader why she was so important to Will Taft's success. In the White House, Nellie was not stuffy and served alcohol to guests at a time when prohibition was being sought.

After the presidency, Taft was a law professor and then became the only president to serve as Chief Justice of the Supreme Court. He eventually had to step down due to health problems and he died in 1930. Nellie Taft survived him by 13 years, dying on May 22, 1943. She is buried next to her husband, one of only two presidents buried at Arlington National Cemetery (the other being John F. Kennedy, beside whom is buried Jacqueline Bouvier Kennedy Onassis).

INTRODUCTION

CINCINNATI, the city of my birth and early memories, was, in the sixties, about as begrimed and noisy and altogether unattractive as any place well could be; yet it possessed certain attributes which really entitled it to the proud designation of "The Queen City of the West."

It was prosperous; it had hardly yet been surpassed in prosperity by Chicago; Cleveland was not even spoken of as a rival; and in many ways it was the most important centre west of New York and east of the Mississippi.

It owed its early development principally to its advantageous location. It lay on the great central route from the East to the West, which runs from Baltimore and Washington to Cumberland and over the Alleghenies to Pittsburg, thence by the Ohio River to Cincinnati and on west to St. Louis and south to New Orleans. It had an important trade with New Orleans and drew commerce from a large territory to the north. But whatever else may be said of it, its most devoted citizen could not claim that Cincinnati was beautiful. Its buildings were unlovely; its streets were badly paved and as badly kept; and it lay under a pall of soft coal smoke which left its sooty mark upon every-thing—inhabitants included.

Yet, ugly as it was, the city boasted an unusual society. During the first half of the nineteenth century many young men of good stock and great ability, drawn by the promise of rapid advancement, had moved to Cincinnati from all parts of the East and South; New Jersey, New England, Virginia and Kentucky contributing, perhaps, the greatest number. There were many families of wealth and culture which, without parade or display, maintained fine homes and dispensed a generous hospitality. The suburbs, East Walnut Hills, Mt. Auburn and Clifton, on the heights to the north and east, were famous for their beautiful country places.

Then there was a large population of the best class of Germans, many of whom were university men who left their own country after the Revolution of 1848 and came to Cincinnati to settle. Of these,

Frederick Hassaurek, General Willich and Judge Stallo, who came to Cincinnati when Carl Schurz went to St. Louis, are perhaps the most prominent. The German influence upon the community was marked. It made for a more liberal Sunday; it brought the study of German into the public schools; and it developed a strong taste for good music. Indeed, the musical advantages of Cincinnati in my girlhood were better than those of any city in the United States, with the exception of New York or Boston. Theodore Thomas was president of the Conservatory of Music and he organised a symphony orchestra which he continued to direct until he went to Chicago along about 1890.

Cincinnati in those days, with her educated, wealthy and public-spirited society, was much in advance of any other city in the Mississippi Valley in culture and refinement. There was great interest in schools of all sorts and in every kind of intellectual activity. Away back in 1848 the Literary Club of Cincinnati was formed by a company of men among whom were both Mr. Taft's father and mine, as well as Rutherford B. Hayes [future Civil War veteran and 19th President of the United States], Stanley Matthews, Manning F. Force and Mr. Spofford, later Librarian of Congress. This club continues to be a cherished institution and in my girlhood it was the centre of all interest in literature and intellectual pursuits.

My father, John Williamson Herron, was a graduate of Miami University at Oxford, Ohio, and was in college with Benjamin Harrison. He was for fifty years a trustee of that institution and was devoted to its interests. My husband's father, Judge Alphonse Taft, was one of the Yale class of 1833, was for many years a member of the Yale Corporation, and had five sons who graduated at that university. My mother's brother, Judge Isaac Clinton Collins, and one of my two brothers also graduated at Yale, while my other brother graduated at Harvard, so it will be seen that both my husband and I grew up in the midst of strong collegiate traditions.

To write about one's childhood is not easy. Memories by the score come flocking up, but, dear as they are, upon examination they turn out to be quite commonplace and hardly worth relating. My memories are not sufficiently "early" to have any special value. The first thing that I dimly remember is sitting on the front steps of my home watching some sort of parade in which there were many soldiers, but I was too young then to know that it was a peace celebration I was witnessing at the close of the Civil War.

My father was a lawyer who came to the bar of Ohio in the 'forties. He was United States Attorney under President Harrison, was a State Senator, and twice declined appointments to the Bench because the salary attached to these positions was not enough to support his large family. I was the fourth in a family of eleven, eight girls and three boys. One boy and two girls died before I can remember.

Our house was one of a block of grey brick houses in Pike Street, at the east end of Cincinnati, which, at that time, was the fashionable residence section of the city. Pike Street runs down to the river on a rather steep incline and, as it was paved with cobblestones, my early memories are somewhat marred by an impression of the frequent clatter and clang of heavy wagons pulling their way up the hill from the river landing.

While our house was not particularly distinguished, being much like those on either side of it, across the street from us there were two very striking and imposing residences which lent distinction to the neighbourhood, and in which, as I grew up, were formed the pleasantest associations of my life. The one directly opposite was a large, square, red brick house which had an air of great dignity. It was the home of Mr. Larz Anderson. There were ten boys in the Anderson family and, though they were all much older than I and most of them had gone away before I grew up, I remember that it was a very lively household always. In my later girlhood we were specially linked to this family by the marriage of one of the boys, Charles, to my sister Jennie.

The house next to Mr. Anderson's, on the north, I knew as the Sinton home. A low, colonial structure, well set in a garden of green lawns and finely kept shrubbery, it is still one of the most beautiful residences in Cincinnati, and, indeed, in the whole country. Its architecture suggests that of the White House and it was, as a matter of fact, designed by the same architect, an Irishman named Hoban.

10

The Sinton house is lower than the White House, being only one story high with a basement, but it has the same classic outlines and it bears, moreover, the stamp of time, which gives it a character all its own.

It was built about 1800 by a Mr. Martin Baum, but was purchased by the first Nicholas Longworth in the early part of the century and was the home of the Longworth family for a generation. Long before I can remember, it was bought by Mr. David Sinton, one of the most successful business men in Ohio, and to me it was always the Sinton home. When I was about twelve years old, Mr. Sinton's daughter Annie married my husband's brother, Charles P. Taft, and as they have always lived in this old house it has come to be known, since Mr. Sinton's death in 1901, as the Taft house. It is the only Taft house in Cincinnati now, the house where my husband was born having been sold after his father's death, and it has been the scene of many of the most important events of my life. It was there that my husband received the announcement of his nomination for the Presidency; it was there, in front of the house, that he made his speech of acceptance; and it was there that Charles Taft gathered a large party of friends on the night of November 6, 1908, to receive with us the election returns. And it is now to this house, where my husband's brother Charles and his wife dispense a generous hospitality, that we always go when we return to Cincinnati.

My girlhood days were spent quite placidly in Miss Nourse's school, which was known in Cincinnati as "The Nursery," and where all the girls of the Herron family, as well as Mr. Taft's only sister, Fanny, received their education. Miss Nourse was a Maine woman with a thorough New England education and with a thoroughly New England idea of imparting it. She insisted, especially, upon languages and literature. Much of my time, outside of that taken up in regular school work, I devoted to the study of music, and I practised my scales on the family piano with such persistence that I wonder the whole neighbourhood did not rebel. Music was the absorbing interest of my life in those days, the inspiration of all my dreams and ambitions.

Our house was none too large for the family, but as there was a wide difference in our ages it happened that my oldest sister was married while my youngest sister was still a baby in long clothes. Then, the boys went away to college and were gone the better part of each year, so it was not often that we were all at home together. Nevertheless, we had our share of the happy-go-lucky and somewhat crowded existence of a large family on a moderate income.

My mother was Harriet Collins, and when she was seventeen years old she came with her mother to Cincinnati, from Lowville, New York, to live with her brother, Judge Collins, who was my father's law partner and continued to be so for more than forty years. Her father, Eli Collins, was a Member of Congress from the Lowville district of New York. My mother was in many ways a remarkable, as well as a most attractive, woman. She had an exceedingly keen wit and a mind alert to the humour in every situation. With so many children to nurse, to scold, to sew for and, sometimes, to cook for— in a word, to bring up on a small income—she would seem to have had little time for outside interests; but she was very popular in society and I remember that in her busiest years she went out a great deal. She had a stimulating personality and I do know that she made her family circle a very amusing and interesting one in which to grow up.

The only incident of my girlhood which was in any way unusual was my first visit to the White House as a guest of President and Mrs. Hayes. Mr. and Mrs. Hayes and my father and mother had been lifelong friends. Mr. Hayes was, at one time, a partner in my father's law firm. They had been closely associated for a great many years and had a very warm regard for each other. My youngest sister was born shortly after the election of Mr. Hayes, was named Lucy Hayes Herron, after Mrs. Hayes, and was taken to the White House to be christened. My mother paid several visits to the White House and after my sister Jennie was married Mrs. Hayes invited her and Mr. Anderson to stay a week with her and, to my intense excitement, she added that she would like to have me accompany them. I was seventeen years old; I had never been to Washington and to me it was a very important event. I was not "out," so I couldn't spend my time in the White House as I would have liked, in going to brilliant parties and meeting all manner of charming people, but, fortunately for my peace of mind, the Hayes lived very quietly, so it was not so trying to have to devote myself to seeing the sights of the Capital like any other tourist.

I didn't meet my husband until I was eighteen years old. We had been born and brought up in the same town; our fathers were warm friends and had practised law at the same bar for more than forty years; during that time our mothers had exchanged visits, and my sister Maria and Fanny Taft were schoolmates and close companions at Miss Nourse's, but the Tafts lived at Mt. Auburn, a hill suburb of Cincinnati, and after Will finished Woodward High School he went for four years to Yale, so it is not at all surprising that we did not meet.

Judge Alphonso Taft was Secretary of War, and later Attorney-General, in Grant's Cabinet while his son Will was at college, but before the latter graduated, the family had returned to Cincinnati, so he came straight home and entered at once upon a law course in the Cincinnati Law School. It was at that time, when he was still a student and working as a law reporter on the Cincinnati *Commercial,* that I met him. It was at a coasting party one winter's night, I remember very well, when I went with a party of young people, including the Charles Tafts, to coast down a fine steep hill in Mt. Auburn. Will Taft was there, and after being introduced to me he took me down the hill on his big bobsled. After that we met very frequently.

A small circle of us went in for amateur theatricals with much enthusiasm and great earnestness. We launched ourselves in our histrionic careers in "She Stoops to Conquer" which we gave at the house of one of the company. Then came "A Scrap of Paper" in Mrs. Charles Taft's drawing-room, in which both Will and I took part. We had become very ambitious by this time and sent all the way to New York for a professional stage-manager to help us with the production. But it turned out a most nervous occasion. We were all over trained, I suppose. One thing after another went wrong until at the crisis of the play, where the hero is supposed to find in the barrel of a gun the scrap of paper upon which the whole plot hinges, the amateur hero looked pretty foolish when he discovered there wasn't any gun. Another one of the company, in a fit of absentmindedness, no doubt due to overwrought nerves, had carried it off the stage, and just when the situation was getting tragic for the hero the culprit came creeping back with it and carefully put it where it belonged, for all the world as if he thought he were making himself invisible to the audience.

But our ardour was not dampened. I remember Mr. Taft especially in a burlesque of "The Sleeping Beauty," which, in its legitimate form, had been produced for charity at Pike's Opera House. The Unity Club, a most respectable organization of the young men of the Unitarian Church, decided to give their version of the same story, and it was a huge success. Mr. Taft played the title role and his brother Horace, who is six feet four in his stocking feet, shared with the Beauty the honours of the evening as a most enchanting Puck.

Then we had parties in the country, too. Many of our friends had country places that spread along the Madison Road and the Grandin Road on East Walnut Hills, and two of my closest friends lived out there in a great house, looking down over the majestic but tawny Ohio River, above the point where the sweeping curve begins that carries it by the amphitheatre in which the business part of the city is built. It was a long distance to East Walnut Hills and in my girlhood we had to go the greater part of the way in a clumsy old omnibus that clumped along over the unpaved roads at the rate of about three miles an hour. But such little inconveniences didn't trouble us, and many were the vaudeville and charade parties that we had, there being enough "talent" among us to get up an amusing performance at a moment's notice.

But in spite of all this gaiety, Mr. Taft was making very satisfactory progress in his career. As a law reporter he showed his growing interest in the public welfare by meeting certain elements in Cincinnati politics with vigorous denunciation. There was a man named Tom Campbell, a clever criminal lawyer, who had something more than a suspicion against him of bribery and corruption of both witnesses and juries, and he had succeeded in organising a political machine that was running the town according to his directions.

Campbell was counsel for the defence in what was known as the Hoffman case and was strongly suspected of tampering with the jury, and Mr. Taft in reporting the case, took special pains to bring out all the fine points in the lawyer's character and methods, telling the truth as he saw it.

This brought him into association with Mr. Miller Outcalt, the Assistant Prosecuting Attorney, who represented the State in the Hoffman case, and when Mr. Outcalt succeeded by election to the position of prosecuting attorney he offered the place of assistant to Mr. Taft, although he had been at the bar not more than seven months. Mr. Taft served in this office for fourteen months and the experience he had in the rough-and-ready practice in criminal trials, in preparing cases for trial, in examining witnesses, in making arguments to the court and in summing up to the jury, was the most valuable experience he could possibly have in fitting him for trial work at the bar.

But this experience was shortened by a circumstance not of his seeking. Major Benjamin Butterworth was the Congressman from one of the Cincinnati districts in President Arthur's administration, and the President being anxious to relieve the Collector of Internal Revenue, called on Major Butterworth to suggest the name of another man.

Major Butterworth had been for a long time a warm friend of Mr. Taft, thought he had a good family name and was too young in politics to have many political enemies, so he suggested him and wrote to urge him to accept the appointment which the President immediately offered to him. He accepted the place and held it for a year, but it proved a serious interruption in his legal career. He resigned as soon as it was possible and began practice with Major H. P. Lloyd who had been his father's partner before he went to Vienna.

Mr. Taft went abroad in the summer of 1883 to visit Judge and Mrs. Taft in Vienna, and it was about this time, when we had all spent several years in frivolities, that several of us became very serious-minded and decided that we must have something by way of occupation more satisfying than dancing and amateur theatricals. I secured a position as school teacher and taught for two years, first at Madame Fredin's and then at White and Sykes, both private schools out, on Walnut Hills. Then, with two of my intimate friends, I decided to start a "salon." We called it a "salon" because we planned to receive a company who were to engage in what we considered brilliant discussion of topics intellectual and economic, and we decided that our gathering should include only specially invited guests. Among these were the two Taft brothers, Will and Horace, and other men common friends of us all.

In view of the fact that two marriages resulted from this salon, Mr. Taft has suggested ulterior motives on the part of those who got it up, but there was no truth in the charge. We were simply bent on "improving our minds" in the most congenial atmosphere we could create, and if our discussions at the salon usually turned upon subjects of immediate personal interest, to the neglect of the abstruse topics we had selected for debate, it was because those subjects were just then claiming the attention of the whole community.

Cincinnati, thanks to the activities of Tom Campbell and his followers, was then in a tangle of political mismanagement of a particularly vicious character, and our little circle developed a civic spirit which kept us alive to local interests to the exclusion, for the time being, of everything else. Mr. Taft was intimately connected with the reform movement, and in all its phases, through comedy and tragedy, disappointment and elation, we fought it out at our salon meetings with such high feeling and enthusiasm that its history became the history of our lives during that period.

Then came the famous Berner case. This was in 1884. Berner had committed a deliberate murder of an unusually appalling nature and with robbery as the motive, and there was great excitement about it. Campbell became his counsel and, in a trial which held the attention of the community while it lasted, he succeeded in getting the man off for manslaughter when the unanimous opinion was that he should have been hanged. Nobody could see how an honest jury could have rendered any other verdict. There was intense indignation throughout the city and a meeting was called to denounce Campbell as an embracer of juries and a suborner of perjury.

On the evening when the meeting to denounce Campbell was called we were having a session of the salon and our whole discussion was of the possible developments which might grow out of the infamous Berner trial. We were greatly excited about it. I remember the evening distinctly because of the terrible things that happened. We were disturbed by a great commotion in the street and we sallied forth in a body to see what it was all about.

The mass meeting was held at Music Hall and was presided over by Dr. Kemper, a very effective speaker. The crowd was angry and quickly passed the condemnatory resolutions which were framed. But with all the indignation and resentment everything might have been carried out quite calmly had not the match been applied to the powder. Just as the meeting was breaking up somebody shouted:

"Let's go down to the jail and take Berner out!"

It was an appeal to the mob spirit which responds so readily in an angry crowd; they went; and of course the worst elements immediately came to the top. They attacked the jail, which was in the rear of the court house, but were held back until the militia, which had been instantly summoned, arrived. Then they went around to the front and set fire to the court house. With the streets packed with raging humanity it was not possible to fight the fire and the building was completely destroyed.

The militia charged the mob and this inspired somebody with the idea of raiding a gun store and seizing arms and ammunition with which to make a resistance. The idea caught on and spread rapidly. One place attacked was Powell's gun shop near Fourth and Main. But Powell, either forewarned or foreseeing some such development, had quietly made preparations to meet it. He lighted up the front of the store as brightly as he could, then, with two or three other men who were expert shots, he put himself behind a barricade in the rear. The mob came on and as the ringleaders broke into the shop they were picked off by the men behind the barricade and killed in their tracks. Four or five of them went down in a heap and the crowd behind them, not expecting such a reception, instantly was brought to its senses. This was in April, 1884.

Such an outbreak was a disgrace to the city of Cincinnati, but it had the effect of bringing the Campbell controversy to a head. A bar committee of ten men, of which both my father and Mr. Taft were members, was formed to see what could be done to rid the community of the evil reputation it had acquired. This committee made a thorough investigation of Campbell's character and record, prepared charges against him and, with my father as chairman, presented them, in June, 1884, to the district court of three judges, and asked a hearing and Campbell's disbarment if the charges were proved.

Campbell had been indicted on a criminal charge of attempting to bribe a man called on the Berner jury and the prosecutor in this case was our intimate friend and associate, Mr. Rufus Smith, who had been in Europe with Mr. Taft the year before. The jury hung, eight to four, although the evidence was strong against the defendant. This fanned the flames of popular resentment and I don't suppose our little salon was the only place in Cincinnati where Campbell was carefully retried and convicted. In this criminal case Mr. Foraker, who shortly afterward became Governor of Ohio, was counsel for Campbell.

The disbarment hearing was set for the following November and some six months was thus given for taking the depositions of non-resident witnesses. Mr. Kittredge and Mr. Ramsey, leaders of the bar, were retained as senior counsel for the committee, and Mr. Taft and Mr. John Holmes, a warm friend of ours, were junior counsel and were directed to prepare the evidence. In this work Mr. Taft and Mr. Holmes went all over the country taking depositions and we kept in constant touch with them. All the members of the committee expected to have their reputations assailed, being perfectly certain that Campbell would not hesitate at any measure he might be able to take to discredit them, but they went ahead nevertheless.

When the trial came on Mr. Ramsey, of the senior counsel, expected to open the case, but he became quite seriously ill and was confined to his house for days. Through his unexpected absence, the duty of making the opening statement fell to Mr. Taft. He was taken completely by surprise, but he rose to the opportunity, which was certainly a splendid one for a man so young. He had then been at bar only four years, but having assisted throughout in the preparation of the evidence he knew the case from beginning to end and he made a speech which lasted four hours and a half. Mr. Taft thinks this was an opportunity improved which had an important influence on his career. The special part it played in his subsequent promotion I shall speak of.

The result in the Campbell case was at first disappointing because the Court which heard the disbarment charges found Campbell guilty only on minor charges and, by a vote of two to one acquitted him on those which would have required his disbarment. But the public disapproval of the Court's decision and the moral effect of the proceedings drove Campbell from the city and the State and accomplished the purpose of the bar association.

The Campbell trial was finished in December, 1884, and in January, 1885, Mr. Rufus Smith, an old and intimate friend, entered the office of County Solicitor and tendered to Mr. Taft the place of Assistant County Solicitor. The advantage of this office was that it paid $2500 a year and that, while he acted as counsel for the county, he still was able to continue the general practice of law with his partner, Major Lloyd.

Mr. Taft and I were engaged in May, 1885, and were married in June of the following year.

In the summer of 1885 my mother, moved I think by some sentimental attachment to the scenes of her childhood, decided that she would take us all up into the Adirondacks, to a little camp near Lowville. My two older sisters were married so there were only six of us left in the family, but we were still something of a handful to move in a body. However, my mother was equal to it. We packed almost a van load of trunks and set out, and one evening we arrived, over the worst corduroy road that was ever laid down, at a little cottage beside a beautiful lake in a setting of pine-clad hills. The scenery indeed was most satisfactory, but the cottage was so small that the family more than strained its capacity. Then we took our meals at a sort of boarding house called Fenton's, where the only thing on the bill of fare was fresh beef. I like what is known as "roughing it" as well as anybody, but even the superlative appetite produced by outdoor living demands some variety; and variety we did not get.

Mr. Taft had elected to remain in Cincinnati all summer and save money. It was a Spartan resolution and we all applauded it, but he probably found Lowville a long way from Pike Street; and I certainly thought Mother was sacrificing a good deal for the sake of renewing the memories of her youth. However, the days went on, while the fresh beef grew less and less tempting.

I had written Mr. Taft something about the Fenton fare and he, wanting very much to join us, but having no excuse for breaking his admirable resolution to remain in Cincinnati, hit upon the only plan for escaping comment on his lack of fortitude. He went down to Peeble's, a fancy grocer, and selecting a box as big as a Saratoga trunk, ordered it filled with every kind of delicacy he could think of or have pointed out to him and brought it with him to Lowville.

We went rowing on the lake about sundown the evening he arrived, and right in the middle of a fine long stroke he suddenly dropped his oars, reached in his pocket and drew out a letter. He laughed a little when he handed it to me, then picking up his oars he rowed on without a word. The letter was from his father.

Judge Taft was at this time Minister to St. Petersburg, having been transferred from Vienna. Will had written him about his engagement and about his plan to remain in town all summer and devote himself strictly to business and the accumulation of funds; and this was the answer.

There were a lot of nice complimentary things about me, with the warmest congratulations and good wishes; then the letter closed by saying: "I am very much pleased with your decision to remain in Cincinnati this summer. I myself have found it not at all bad if you take care of yourself, and there is no doubt that during the quiet months one can make and save considerable money by staying at home. I congratulate you on your strength of character." We really had a delightful summer at Fenton's after that.

My father had given me a very nice lot at the end of McMillan Street on the site of an old quarry, which commanded a fine view of the Ohio River and the surrounding country, and Mr. Taft and I determined to build a house on it which should be ready for us when we got back from our wedding trip. So the winter before our marriage was filled with architects' plans, contractors' estimates and all the other fascinating details of building, and we thought that we had finally settled upon a design that met with every requirement of good taste and modern comfort.

For our wedding trip, we went abroad, and I had my first taste of the foreign travel of which I had always dreamed. We crossed on the *City of Chester* which was the oldest, and therefore the cheapest ship of the Inman line. We chose her for the simple reason that her rates accorded with our means, but we found, much to our astonishment, that we were the only people on board who had deliberately selected her. Everybody else had been forced to take her because of some emergency or some mishap. One man had to miss the *Germanic* in order to give his dentist time to relieve a very troublesome tooth. Another man was called to court just as he was about to board the *Britannic*. Those were the proud ships of the Atlantic in those days and it was not at all difficult to understand why anybody should prefer them to the *City of Chester*, but it amused us greatly to hear the shamefaced excuses of our fellow passengers. My husband and I were not ashamed, nor were we so particular about our comforts that we did not thoroughly enjoy ourselves. Besides, we had the gratifying consciousness of the money which the low rates had left in our pockets to be spent much more profitably abroad.

The trip was full of interest to us both. We spent the greater part of the summer in England and saw the sights of London and the cathedral towns in great detail. Our only trip on the Continent was through Holland to Paris. I remember that in Amsterdam I bought some old and rather large Delft plates. They wouldn't go into any trunk we had, so I had them carefully packed in a wicker hamper and this article became thereafter a part of our hand luggage, and was the occasion for a decided disagreement between my husband and me as to what the true object of travel was. He used to say that he "toted that blamed thing all around Europe and after all it arrived in Cincinnati with its contents in small pieces." Which was true. He had "toted" it all around Europe, but when we arrived in New York I entrusted it to an express company with the result that when we opened it we found its contents in such a condition that only an accomplished porcelain mender could put a sufficient number of pieces together to make what my husband always afterward referred to as "the memento of our first unpleasantness."

Our trip from Cincinnati to Cincinnati took just one hundred days and cost us just one thousand dollars, or five dollars a day each. I venture to say that could not be done nowadays, even by as prudent a pair as we were.

During a subsequent trip abroad, two years later, I was able to indulge my desire to hear music. We went to Beyreuth, to the Wagner festival, and heard *Parsifal* and *The Meistersingers* gloriously rendered; after which we went to Munich and attended operas and concerts until Mr. Taft rebelled. He said that he enjoyed a certain amount music just as much as anybody, but that he did want to get something more out of European travel than a nightly opera and a daily symphony.

So—we went to Italy and saw Rome and Florence in true Baedecker [tour book] style. When we arrived in Rome we opened our Baedecker and read that there was almost no foundation for Rome's awful reputation as an unhealthy place. "Rome is a very healthy place," said Baedecker, "at all times of the year except the first two weeks in August, when a visit there is attended with risk." We had arrived for the first two weeks in August!

When we came home from our wedding trip we found that our house was not yet completed, so we went to stay with Judge and Mrs. Taft for a month at the old house in Mt. Auburn. It was a nice old place, with about three acres of ground, but the air around it was just about as sooty as if it had been located down under the factory chimneys. Mt. Auburn is on a sort of promontory which juts out into the city; it is on a level with the tops of the smoke stacks and it catches all the soot that the air can carry that far.

Judge and Mrs. Taft had come home from their European mission in time for our wedding. Judge Taft had been ill in St. Petersburg and had given his family a great deal of anxiety, but he was now settled down to the business of quiet recuperation and the enjoyment of well-earned rest.

My husband's father was "gentle" beyond anything I ever knew. He was a man of tremendous firmness of purpose and just as set in his views as any one well could be, but he was one of the most lovable men that ever lived because he had a wide tolerance and a strangely "understanding sympathy" for everybody. He had a great many friends, and to know him was to know why this was so.

Mr. Taft's mother, though more formal, was also very kindly and made my visit to her home as a bride full of pleasure. The two, the father and mother, had created a family atmosphere in which the children breathed in the highest ideals, and were stimulated to sustained and strenuous intellectual and moral effort in order to conform to the family standard. There was marked serenity in the circle of which Judge and Mrs. Taft were the heads. They had an abiding confidence in the future of their children which strongly influenced the latter to justify it. They both had strong minds, intellectual tastes, wide culture and catholic sympathies.

Not long after we arrived my husband came to me one day with an air of great seriousness, not to say of conciliation, and said:

"Nellie, Father has got himself into rather a difficulty and I hope I can rely on you to help him out—not make it too hard for him, you know,—make him feel as comfortable about it as you can. The truth is he used to have a messenger at the War Department in Washington whom he was very fond of. He was a bright man— colored, of course—and he was very devoted to Father. Now this man called on Father down town to-day. He's here on a private car and Father says he's made a great success as a porter. Father got to talking to him, and there were lots of things they wanted to talk about, and besides the man said he would like very much to see Mother,—and Father, who was just about ready to come home to lunch said—right on the spur of the moment—you understand he didn't think anything about it—he said to this man, 'Come on home and have lunch with us.' He's downstairs now. Father came to me and said he had just realised that it was something of a difficulty and that he was sorry. He said that he could take care of Mother if I could take care of you. So I hope you won't mind."

As soon as I could control my merriment caused by this halting and very careful explanation, I went down to luncheon. I didn't mind and Will's mother didn't mind, but the expression on the face of Jackson, the negro butler, was almost too much for my gravity. I will say that the porter had excellent manners and the luncheon passed off without excitement.

[The Taft tolerance, to their credit, would later lead to controversy when they lived in the Philippines.]

We made a short visit at my mother's on Pike Street before we moved into our new house on McMillan Street; but we began the year of 1887 under our own roof which, though it was mortgaged, was to us, for the time being, most satisfactory.

CINCINNATI AND WASHINGTON

ONE day, after we had been married less than a year, my husband came home looking so studiously unconcerned that I knew at once he had something to tell me.

"Nellie, what would you think," he began casually, "if I should be appointed a Judge of the Superior Court?"

"Oh, don't try to be funny," I exclaimed. "That's perfectly impossible."

But it was not impossible, as he soon convinced me. My father had just refused the same appointment and it was difficult to believe that it could now be offered to my husband who was only twenty-nine years old. It was a position made vacant by the retirement from the Bench of Judge Judson Harmon who was my husband's senior by more than a decade.

One of the most prominent and prosperous law firms in Cincinnati was that of Hoadley, Johnston and Colston, and both Mr. Hoadley and Mr. Johnston had been invited to go to New York and become partners of Mr. Edward Lauterbach who was then doing an enormous business.

They went, and the old firm in Cincinnati being broken up, Mr. Colston asked Judge Harmon, who was then on the Superior Court, to take Mr. Hoadley's place. Mr. Harmon decided to do so, but he was anxious to resign his judgeship in such a way as to leave a long enough vacancy to attract a good man. It was an elective office and the law provided that a vacancy occurring within thirty days before election could not be filled by an election until the following year. Judge Harmon resigned so as to make the appointment for a period of fourteen months. After my father declined it, the choice lay between Mr. Taft and Mr. Bellamy Storer. Mr. Taft always thought that but for his opportunity in the Campbell case Judge Harmon would not have recommended him and Governor Foraker would not have appointed him. That is why he says he traces all his success back to that occasion. Mr. Foraker was opposing counsel in the

Campbell case, but he had a lawyer's appreciation for a lawyer's effort.

After the first pleased surprise at the honour which came to us so unexpectedly I began to think; and my thinking led me to decide that my husband's appointment on the Bench was not a matter for such warm congratulation after all. I saw him in close association with men not one of whom was less than fifteen years older than he, and most of whom were much more than that. He seemed to me suddenly to take on a maturity and sedateness quite out of keeping with his actual years and I dreaded to see him settled for good in the judiciary and missing all the youthful enthusiasms and exhilarating difficulties which a more general contact with the world would have given him. In other words, I began even then to fear the narrowing effects of the Bench and to prefer for him a diverse experience which would give him an all-round professional development.

He did not share this feeling in any way. His appointment on the Superior Court was to him the welcome beginning of just the career he wanted. After serving the interim of fourteen months he became a candidate for the office and was elected for a term of five years. This was the only elective office Mr. Taft ever held until he became President.

My own time and interest during that winter was largely spent on my house. We had been very particular about the plans for it and had fully intended that it should combine outward impressiveness with inward roominess and comfort. It was a frame structure, shingled all over, and with certain bay window effects which pleased me exceedingly. In fact, with our assistance, the architect had made a special effort to produce something original and, while I don't claim the result was a conspicuous architectural success, to my mind it was anything but a failure. And our view of the Ohio River and the surrounding country was really superb.

But I was not destined to enjoy my satisfaction with my surroundings very long. The section had been at one time a stone quarry, and the man who had levelled off the land and filled in the gulches made by the quarry operations, took as a part of his compensation two building lots which happened to be just across

26

the street from ours. He forthwith proceeded to put up a sort of double house which looked more like a gigantic dry-goods box than anything else, and I felt that it quite robbed the neighbourhood of the "tone" which I had confidently hoped our house would give it. The double house had just one quality and that was size.

I think the owner, whose name was Jerry something, lived in one side of it, and he had a tenant in the other who hung clothes out of the front windows. But tastes in architecture differ, as we soon found out.

We were paying taxes on our house at an assessed value of $4000 and the undervaluation had been troubling my husband's conscience for a long time, in spite of my assuring him that tax collectors ought to know their own business. Some men from the board of equalization were to call one day to make a new appraisement and I had very much hoped that my husband would not be at home. But he was; he was there to welcome them and give them every possible assistance. Without waiting for an examination of the premises, he addressed one of them, an Irishman named Ryan.

"See here, Mr. Ryan," he said, "I understand that Jerry, my neighbour across the street, has his property assessed at $5000. Now I don't think that's fair. I'm assessed at only $4000 and I'm sure my house cost a good deal more than his. As a matter of fact it cost over $6000. Now I'm a Judge of the Superior Court; I get my income out of taxes and I certainly have no disposition to pay any less than my share."

"Well, Judge, your Honour," said Mr. Ryan, "that is a sentiment very befitting your Honour. Now I'll just be after goin' over and lookin' at those houses of Jerry's, and then I'll come back and look at yours."

I watched them as they went over to the other houses; then I saw them go up the street a way and down the street a way, looking us carefully over from every possible viewpoint. When they came in they wore a very judicial aspect and I expected to see taxes go up with one wild leap.

"Well, Judge, your Honour," began Mr. Ryan, "I think you're givin' yourself unnecessary concern. We assess houses for what they're worth and not for what they cost. While your house no doubt suits your taste, it has a peculiar architectural style that wouldn't please very many people, and certainly it ain't to compare with those houses of Jerry's. There's a modem polish about those houses that will rent, Judge, your Honour."

My son Robert was born in this house on McMillan Street in September, 1889.

[Robert Alphonso Taft, 1889–1953, became a U.S. Senator from Ohio and was campaigned for the Republican nomination for president in 1940 and 1948, losing both times.]

In the following February an interruption occurred in our peaceful existence which was welcome at least to me. President Harrison offered the appointment of Solicitor General of the United States to Mr. Taft and he, with a few regretful glances at his beloved Bench, accepted it. I think that once again it was Major Butterworth who suggested my husband's name to the appointing power. I was very glad because it gave Mr. Taft an opportunity for exactly the kind of work I wished him to do; work in which his own initiative and originality would be exercised and developed. I looked forward with interest, moreover, to a few years in Washington.

Mr. Taft made his first official arrival in Washington alone. My baby, Robert, was only six months old and I concluded to remain in Cincinnati until my husband could make arrangements for our comfortable reception. His description of his first day in Washington is, in the light of later events, rather amusing.

He arrived at six o'clock on a cold, gloomy February morning at the old dirty Pennsylvania station. He wandered out on the street with a heavy bag in his hand looking for a porter, but there were no porters. Then he stood for a few moments looking up at the Capitol and feeling dismally unimportant in the midst of what seemed to him to be very formidable surroundings. He wondered to himself why on earth he had come. He was sure he had made a fatal mistake in exchanging a good position and a pleasant circle at home, where everybody knew him, for a place in a strange and forbidding city where he knew practically nobody and where, he felt sure, nobody wanted to know him. He lugged his bag up to the old Ebbitt House and, after eating a lonesome breakfast, he went to the Department of Justice to be sworn in. After that ceremony was over and he had shaken hands with the Attorney General, he went up to inspect the Solicitor General's Office, and there he met the most dismal sight of the whole dismal day. His "quarters" consisted of a single room, three flights up, and bearing not the slightest resemblance to his mental picture of what the Solicitor General's offices would be like. The Solicitor General's stenographer, it seemed, was a telegrapher in the chief clerk's office and had to be sent for when his services were required. Altogether it must have been a very disheartening outlook.

As Mr. Taft sat looking over briefs and other papers, and trying to get some definite idea about his new work, a messenger brought in a card.

"Mr. Evarts, New York," it read.

Evarts was a well-known name, of course, but it was hard for Mr. Taft to believe that *the* William M. Evarts, leader of the American Bar and then Senator from New York, could be calling on the Solicitor General of less than a day. He knew that Wm. M. Evarts had known his father.

Mr. Evarts entered.

"Mr. Taft," he said, as he gave my husband's hand a cordial grasp, "I knew your father. I was in the class of '37 at Yale and he had graduated before I entered; but he was there as a tutor in my time and I valued his friendship very highly."

Then the visitor came straight to the point.

"Mrs. Evarts and I are giving a dinner to-night for my former partner and his wife, Mr. and Mrs. Joseph Choate. Mr. Choate is in Washington for a short time to argue a case before the Supreme Court. Now, unfortunately, one of our guests has sent word that he can't come and I thought, perhaps, considering my long-standing friendship with your father, you might consent to waive ceremony and fill the place at our table at this short notice."

My husband accepted the invitation with almost undue alacrity, and when his guest left started in on his new duties feeling that, after all, Washington might afford just as friendly an atmosphere as Cincinnati, once he became accustomed to it.

There is just one incident in connection with the dinner party which Mr. Taft adds to his account of that day. As he sat down to dinner the ladies on either side of him leaned hastily forward to see what was written on his place-card. "The Solicitor General"—that was all. Of course neither of them knew who the new Solicitor General was and it didn't occur to him to enlighten them until it was too late to do it gracefully. So he allowed them to go on addressing him as "Mr. Solicitor General" while he, having them at an advantage, addressed them by the names which he had surreptitiously read on their place-cards. They were Mrs. Henry Cabot Lodge and Mrs. John Hay.

[Senator Henry Cabot Lodge (R, Massachusetts) was an historian and foreign affairs expert. His grandson was defeated by future president, John Fitzgerald Kennedy, for senator of Massachusetts in 1952. John Hay was a close secretary to Abraham Lincoln and later a diplomat and statesman.]

When my husband had been in Washington two weeks I joined him and we took a small house on Dupont Circle where for two years we lived a life, sometimes amusing, sometimes quite exciting, but, on the whole, of quiet routine.

Washington society was much simpler then than it is now. Since that time a great many people of very large means have gone to Washington to live because of its unusual attractions and its innumerable advantages as a residential city. They have changed Washington, by their generous hospitality, into one of the most brilliant social centres in the world, where large dinner parties, balls, receptions, musicals and other entertainments are of daily and nightly occurrence throughout the season. The very character of the streets has changed. The small, red brick houses, closely grouped together and neighbouring, even in fashionable quarters, on negro shacks and cheap tenements, are being everywhere replaced by marble and granite residences of great beauty and luxury.

In 1890 Society in Washington still consisted, chiefly, of the "best families" of the old city, the Diplomatic Corps and the highest among the government officials. A dinner party of twelve was still considered large, and only a few people had weekly evenings At Home. There were occasional big receptions, but for nobody was society the mad rush that it is to-day. We ourselves lived very simply even for those simple days.

My daughter Helen was born in 1891, so for the last year in Washington I had two small babies to care for. In order that he might get a little much needed exercise Mr. Taft bought a horse and, fortunately, for us, he secured a most adaptable creature. He was supposed to be a riding horse, but he didn't mind making himself generally useful. The Attorney General lent us a carriage which he was not then using—a surrey, I think it was called—and we hitched him to that; and the whole Taft family drove out of a Sunday afternoon to the Old Soldiers' Home, which was the fashionable drive in those days, or up the aqueduct road to Cabin John's bridge. My sister Maria who visited us used always to speak of our steed as "G'up," a name suggested by Bobby's interpretation of his father's invocations to the good-natured and leisurely beast. Poor old "G'up"! I suppose with his "horse sense" he finally realised that he was leading such a double life as no respectable horse should lead; he gave up and died before we left Washington.

The Justices of the Supreme Court and the Attorney General, the men with whom Mr. Taft came most in contact, were, with their wives, very kind and attentive to us, including us in many of their delightful parties. Chief Justice Fuller was then the head of the court and I have the pleasantest memories of his and Mrs. Fuller's hospitality. Justice Grey had married a Miss Matthews, a daughter of Mr. Justice Matthews. I had known Mrs. Grey in Cincinnati before her marriage.

During the course of my first weeks in Washington Mr. Taft had taken special pains to impress on me many times the necessity for my calling on Mrs. Grey without any delay. Much importance attached to the formality of first calls and I was the newest of newcomers who had to call on the wives of all my husband's official superiors before they noticed me. Still, it was a full month before I had time to go to Mrs. Grey's and I was considerably worried about it. But when, finally, I did go and had been most kindly received, I explained at once that the settling of myself and my small baby in a new house had, until then, kept me too busy for any calls. Mrs. Grey hastened to assure me that she understood my position perfectly and had not thought of blaming me.

"Indeed, my dear," she said, "I knew that you had a small baby in the house and that you must be kept constantly occupied. As a matter of fact I should have waived ceremony and come myself to welcome you to Washington except for one thing which I could not very well overlook, and that is—that Mr. Taft has not yet called on Mr. Justice Grey."

I think I have rarely seen anything more satisfactorily amusing than the expression on my husband's face when I told him this.

But, in spite of the friendliness of the Justices and others, we really went out very little. On one occasion when my sister Maria had been visiting us for several weeks we went for a Sunday night supper to the house of a lady whom Maria had known very well in Cincinnati. She was living that winter in Washington and seemed to be rather well pleased with her social success. She talked loftily throughout supper, and during a good part of the evening, about the dinner parties she had attended and the grand people she had met. Then just as we were about to start home she turned to my sister and said:

"And have you been much entertained, my dear Maria'?" "Oh, I've been enjoying myself tremendously," was the answer.

"Well, with whom have you dined, dear'?" persisted our hostess.

"Why, we've dined with the Andersons, with the German Ambassador, with the Chief Justice, and with the Maurys, and with the French Ambassador,—and with, oh, a number of other people."

Our hostess was visibly impressed.

"Why! you really have been very gay, haven't you, dear!" she exclaimed.

When we got into our cab to go home Maria turned to my husband and said:

"I had my eye on you all the time I was talking, Will Taft. I was perfectly certain that your terrible sense of fact would overcome you and that you would blurt out that I dined with all those people on the same evening at the same dinner party!"

President Harrison, in March, 1892, appointed my husband on the Federal Circuit Bench, so once more I saw him a colleague of men almost twice his age and, I feared, fixed in a groove for the rest of his life. However, he was greatly pleased and very proud to hold such a dignified and responsible position at the age of thirty-four. I think he enjoyed the work of the following eight years more than any he has ever undertaken.

We moved back to Cincinnati. Mr. Taft's circuit included parts of Ohio, Kentucky, Tennessee, and Michigan—reached in fact, from Lookout Mountain to Marquette, and he was much away from home. My own life during those years in Cincinnati was very busy, for, in addition to my occupation with family and friends, I became interested in a number of civic movements.

My principal work was the organisation and management of the Cincinnati Orchestra Association. I found, at last, a practical method for expressing and making use of my love and knowledge of music.

We had not had a good symphony orchestra in the city since Theodore Thomas left, but with our music-loving population it was only necessary that somebody should take the initiative and arouse definite enthusiasm and keep it going, in order to establish and maintain such an institution. There were many public-spirited citizens, some of them true music-loving Germans, and I saw no reason why I should not get strong popular support for my project. I was not disappointed. From the first the response was general and generous and we did not have much difficulty in raising the necessary funds for financing the orchestra, although in addition to our box-office receipts, we had to secure $30,000 a year for six

33

consecutive years. It could not have been done had it not been for such liberal friends as my brother and sister, Mr. and Mrs. Charles P. Taft, Mr. Charles Krippendorf, Mr. M. E. Ingalls, Mr. and Mrs. L. A. Ault, Mrs. Charles Fleishmann, Mr. J. G. Schmidlapp and others.

For the first year we had three different directors, Mr. Seidl, Mr. Schradick and Mr. Van der Stucken, who came to Cincinnati and led two concerts each. Then we secured Mr. Van der Stucken as a permanent leader and he remained with the orchestra ten years.

I think I regretted the Cincinnati Orchestra Association more than anything else when we left for the Philippines, but I left it in good and well-trained hands. Mrs. C. R. Holmes, who succeeded me as President of the Association, had taken a great part in the original work of organisation and management, as had my sister-in-law, Mrs. Charles P. Taft, and others. Through their efforts the orchestra has been enlarged and improved and it is still a source of great pride and satisfaction to the city of Cincinnati. Mrs. Charles Taft is now the President and through her interest, activity and generosity it has been enabled to grow in excellence.

Except for the orchestra, our life was tranquil; quite too settled, I thought, and filled with the usual homely incidents connected with housekeeping and the entertaining development of small children. My youngest child, Charles, was born in 1897, and my family was thus complete.

I come now to the years which we gave to the Philippine Islands and I must say that I wonder yet how our lot happened to be so cast.

There had never been any unusual interest in our family as to the results of the Spanish-American War. Like most patriotic Americans we had been greatly excited while the war was in progress and had discussed its every phase and event with a warmth of approval, or disapproval, as the case might be, but it did not touch us directly, except as citizens, any more than it touched the vast majority of the people of the United States. And yet, it came to mean more to us personally, than any other event in our times. The whole course of my husband's career was destined to be changed and influenced by its results.

34

Mr. Taft was strongly opposed to taking the Philippines. He was not an anti-imperialist in the sense that he believed the Constitution required us to keep the boundaries of the United States within their continental limits, but he thought the Antipodes rather a far stretch for the controlling hand, and he thought the taking of the Philippines would only add to our problems and responsibilities without increasing, in any way, the effectiveness and usefulness of our government.

Oddly enough, he had expressed himself to that effect when he happened, during the Spanish War, to be dining with a number of judges including Justice Harlan who, although later an anti-imperialist, was at that time strongly upholding the policy of taking over Spanish territory in both oceans.

[Supreme Court Associate Justice John Marshall Harlan, best known as the sole dissenter on cases that reversed civil rights for African-Americans; the *Civil Rights Cases* (1883), and *Plessy v. Ferguson* (1896).]

Mr. Taft knew just about as much about the Filipino people as the average American knew in those days. What he definitely knew was that they had been for more than three centuries under Spanish dominion and that they now wanted political independence. He was heartily in favour of giving it to them.

It was one day in January, 1900, that he came home greatly excited and placed before me a telegram.

"What do you suppose that means?" said he.

"I would like to see you in Washington on important business within the next few days. On Thursday if possible," it read. And it was signed—William McKinley.

We didn't know and we couldn't think what possible business tilt President could have with him. I began to conjure up visions of Supreme Court appointments; though I knew well enough that Supreme Court appointments were not tendered in that fashion and besides there was no vacancy.

Mr. Taft lost no time in responding to the President's summons and I awaited his return with as much patience as I could muster. In three days he came home with an expression so grave that I thought he must be facing impeachment. But when he broke his news to me it gave me nothing but pleasure.

"The President wants me to go to the Philippine Islands," he said, in a tone he might have used in saying: "The President wants me to go out and jump off the court house dome." "Want to go?" he added.

"Yes, of course," I answered without a moment's hesitation. I wasn't sure what it meant, but I knew instantly that I didn't want to miss a big and novel experience. I have never shrunk before any obstacles when I had an opportunity to see a new country and I must say I have never regretted any adventure.

"The President and Mr. Root* want to establish a civil government in the Philippines," said Mr. Taft, "and they want me to go out at the head of a commission to do it." It was only after I had accepted the invitation to go ten thousand miles away that I asked for an explanation.

*[Elihu Root, Secretary of War.]

In answer to the President's proposal, Mr. Taft said that he didn't approve of the acquisition of the Philippines in the first place, and that in the second place he knew nothing about colonial government and had had really no experience in executive work of any kind. But Mr. McKinley did not accept these objections as final. He called in Mr. Root, who was then Secretary of War, and who would be Mr. Taft's chief in the proposed mission to the Philippines, and together they presented the case so strongly that my husband could not help but waver in his decision. Neither Mr. McKinley nor Mr. Root had rejoiced in the taking over of the Philippines for that matter, but that was beside the question; the Philippines were taken, and it behooved the

United States to govern them until such time as their people had learned the difficult art of governing themselves.

Mr. Root said:

"The work to be done in the Philippines is as great as the work Livingston had to do in Louisiana. It is an opportunity for you to do your country a great service and achieve for yourself a reputation for the finest kind of constructive work. You have had a very fortunate career. While you are only slightly over forty you have had eight years on the Federal Bench, three years on the State Bench and two years as Solicitor General. These places you have filled well, but they have been places which involved no sacrifice on your part. Here is a field which calls for risk and sacrifice. Your country is confronted with one of the greatest problems in its history, and you, Judge Taft, are asked to take immediate charge of the solution of that problem 7,000 miles away from home. You are at the parting of the ways. Will you take the easier course, the way of least resistance, with the thought that you had an opportunity to serve your country and declined it because of its possible sacrifice, or will you take the more courageous course and, risking much, achieve much? This work in the Philippines will give you an invaluable experience in building up a government and in the study of laws needed to govern a people, and such experience cannot but make you a broader, better judge should you be called upon again to serve your country in that capacity."

My husband promised to consult with me and with his brother Charles and give his answer in a few days. He didn't know whether or not I would be willing to go, but that was a question soon settled.

His resignation of his judgeship was the greatest difficulty. The President told him he did not think it would be at all necessary for him to resign since the work in the Philippines would take only about six months—nine months at the longest—and that he could absent himself from his duties for that length of time, and for such a purpose, without fear of any kind of unfortunate consequences. Mr. Taft's investigation and study of the situation immediately convinced him that Mr. McKinley was wrong in his expectation that the work could be done so quickly. Nor did Mr. Root have any such idea. Even with the meagre information which was then available, my husband at once saw that it would be years before the Philippine problem would begin to solve itself. So he resigned from the Bench; the hardest thing he ever did.

After sending in his acceptance he went immediately to Washington to discuss with Mr. McKinley and Mr. Root the whole situation and, especially, the names of four other men who were to be chosen to serve with him on the Commission. He had met Mr. Worcester, a member of the first Commission, and had got from him a great deal of valuable data. If Professor Shurman, the chairman of the first Commission, had become a member of the second, he probably would have been at its head, but he did not, and this position fell to Mr. Taft. He was thereafter known as President of the Commission, until civil government was organised in the Philippines and be became governor.

After he had gone to Washington I began at once to make hasty, and I may say, happy preparations for my adventure into a new sphere. That it was alluring to me I did not deny to anybody. I had no premonition as to what it would lead to; I did not see beyond the present attraction of a new and wholly unexplored field of work which would involve travel in far away and very interesting countries. I read with engrossing interest everything I could find on the subject of the Philippines, but a delightful vagueness with regard to them, a vagueness which was general in the United States at that time, and has not, even yet, been entirely dispelled, continued in my mind. There were few books to be found, and those I did find were not specially illuminating.

I gave up my house in Cincinnati and stored my belongings, packing for shipment to the Orient only such things as I thought would be absolutely necessary. We were to leave almost immediately and I had very little time in which to do a great many things. Mr. Taft came back to Cincinnati for a short period and we entered upon a busy season of good-bye hospitality. Everybody we knew, and we knew nearly everybody, wanted to give us a farewell dinner or entertainment of some sort. Mr. Taft, especially, was feted in a way which proved to him how much more widely he was valued in his native town than he had ever realised. In the opinions of people then we were going, sure enough, to the ends of the earth, and many of our friends were as mournful about it as if they had private foreknowledge that it was to be a fatal adventure.

When the banquets and dinners and luncheons and receptions and teas had all been given; when the speeches had all been made, and the good-byes had all been said, Mr. Taft hastened off to Washington once more to meet his colleagues and make final arrangements, and I was not to see him again until we met in San Francisco a week before the date set for sailing.

I asked my sister Maria to go with me for the first year, and she accepted with delight. So, one morning in early April, with our world waving at us from the platform of the station, we started south to join the Southern Pacific railroad at New Orleans and to make our way from there to Los Angeles and so to San Francisco.

I had with me my three children, Robert, Helen and Charlie. Robert was ten years old, Helen eight, while Charlie, my baby, was just a little over two. It did not occur to me that it was a task to take them on such a long journey, or that they would be exposed to any danger through the experience. They were normal, healthy and very self-reliant little people and I made preparations for their going without giving the matter a moment's unhappy consideration. But I was to receive a few shocks in this connection later on. One of these came when I learned that some members of the party had left their children at home for fear of the Philippine climate. Then one day, at the old Palace Hotel in San Francisco, I was sitting on guard over Charlie as he played up and down a wide corridor, and reading a book at intervals, when along came an odd-looking elderly gentleman who stopped to regard the boy with a smile of the kindliest amusement. Charlie was an attractive child. Even I couldn't help but see that, and I was used to having people stop to watch him. He had big, dark eyes, soft, brown curls, very deep dimples, and a charming smile that was always in evidence. The elderly gentleman stood watching him for some little time, his face growing gradually very grave, and I wondered what he was thinking about. He didn't keep me wondering long. After a few moments he stepped deliberately up to me and said:

"Madam, I understand you are going to the Philippine Islands. Now I want to know if you are going to take that great, big, beautiful boy out to that pest-ridden hole and expose him to certain destruction."

I grabbed my great, big, beautiful boy and rushed off to my room, and it was a relief eventually to learn that the awful Philippine climate, at least so far as children were concerned, existed, largely, in people's minds.

We found intense interest in our mission in California and San Francisco. If there were any anti-imperialists there, they successfully concealed themselves. The East was uncomfortably crowded with them in those days, but the evident interest and profit that the West coast would derive from a large Philippine trade may have been responsible for the favourable attitude of the Californians. However, we must not impeach their patriotism, and we ought to attribute some of their enthusiasm in reference to the Philip- pines, and our assuming control over them, to the natural enterprise of a people who had themselves gone so far in a land of development and hope.

Everything that could be done to make smooth the path of the new Commission was done. At their own request the powers of the Commissioners were carefully defined so that complications with the military government then in force in the islands, might be avoided. They were given equal rank with ministers plenipotentiary in the matter of naval courtesies and precedence; and Mr. Root drafted a letter of instructions, which the President signed, outlining their duties in such precise and correct detail that it was afterward adopted and ratified in its entirety in the act of Congress by which the Philippine government was established.

So—I believed we were going to have "smooth sailing" in every sense, when we started on the long voyage with which began this interesting experience.

TO THE PHILIPPINES

THE United States Army Transport *Hancock* had been assigned to the Commission for the trip from San Francisco to Manila and it was at noon on a pleasant day in mid-April —the seventeenth—that she pulled away from the crowded dock and headed straight for the Golden Gate and the long path across the Pacific that leads to the other side of the world. There were forty-five people in our party and, although most of us had met for the first time in San Francisco, we soon became well acquainted, as people do on shipboard, and proceeded at once to prove ourselves to be a most harmonious company.

The *Hancock* was the old *Arizona,* a one-time greyhound of the Atlantic, which the Government had purchased and remodelled for service as an army transport. A considerable fleet of such vessels plied the Pacific at that time, carrying large consignments of troops to and from the Philippines and, though there are not so many now, I still read with interest of the comings and goings of ships whose old, friendly sounding names became so familiar to us in the course of our residence in the East. The *Grant,* the *Sherman,* the *Sheridan,* the *Thomas,* and others, all named for great American generals [Ulysses S. Grant, William Tecumseh Sherman, George Thomas all served in the Civil War], awaken memories of interesting days. The *Hancock* was later given up by the Army and turned over to the Navy on account of her heavy consumption of coal. She is now used as a recruiting ship at the Brooklyn Navy Yard.

We found her very comfortable. There were few people aboard besides the members of our party, and, as she was equipped to carry the officers and men of an entire regiment, we found ourselves commodiously quartered. Moreover, the commissary of the transport service had received instructions to give us excellent fare; this, I believe, through the thoughtful kindness of Mr. McKinley himself.

Mr. McKinley never failed to take a personal interest in the everyday welfare of all those in his administration who came under his own observation and we were made to feel this throughout our experience on the Philippine Commission, while he lived. On every appropriate occasion we were certain to receive from him some kindly compliment, a cablegram or other communication, and it made everybody who came within range of his influence anxious to serve him well and to make the work which was being done satisfactory and pleasing to him. I owe to our connection with President McKinley's administration some of my happiest recollections.

The men who made up the second Philippine Commission were Mr. Taft, General Luke E. Wright of Memphis, Tennessee; Judge Henry C. Ide of Vermont, Professor Dean C. Worcester of the University of Michigan, and Professor Bernard Moses of the University of California. A short introduction of my husband's colleagues and the members of their families who went with them to the Philippines will be necessary at this point, because I was destined to be constantly associated with them during four of the most interesting years of my life. Our co-operation, social and governmental, was based upon a common purpose, and our attachment to this purpose, as well as the bonds of friendship which united us, were greatly strengthened by the opposition we had to meet for some months after we reached Manila, not only from the Filipinos, but also from the military government which the Commission was sent out gradually to replace.

The men of the Commission, coming, as they did, from different parts of the United States, were widely contrasted, no less in associations than in their varied accents and family traditions.

General Wright was, and is, one of the ablest lawyers in Tennessee, and enjoyed, at the time of his appointment on the Commission, the finest practice in Memphis. He is a Democrat; and old enough to have been a lieutenant in the Civil War on the Confederate side. But perhaps his finest laurels for bravery and devotion to duty were won at the time when he exerted himself to save Memphis in the days when she was in the grip of a terrible epidemic of yellow fever. I don't know the exact year, but the epidemic was so out of control that all who could, left the city, while General Wright remained to organise such resistance as could be made to the spread of the dread disease.

Mrs. Wright was a daughter of the famous Admiral Semmes* of the Confederate Navy and for some time after the war she travelled with her father in Mexico and abroad, thereby acquiring at an early age a very cosmopolitan outlook. Admiral Semmes was a great linguist and Mrs. Wright inherited his gift. She had learned to speak Spanish in her girlhood, so when she arrived in Manila she had only to renew her knowledge of the language. General and Mrs. Wright had with them their daughter Katrina, who was then about fourteen years old, but their two sons, one a naval officer, did not join them in the Philippines until later.

*[Raphael Semmes was captain of the notorious Confederate raider, the CSS *Alabama*, famously sunk off France by the USS *Kearsarge* during the Civil War.]

General Wright had, on the whole, the most delightful social qualities of anybody on the Commission. He had a keen sense of humour and could recount a great number of interesting personal experiences with a manner and wit which made him, always, a delightful companion. He was a devotee of pinochle and he instructed the entire party in the game until it was played from one end of the ship to the other. He was slow to anger, very deliberate and kindly in his judgments, and offered at times a decided contrast to his wife who was a little more hasty and not infrequently founded judgments on what he would jocosely criticise as "a woman's reason."

Judge Ide was born and bred a Vermonter and had many of the rugged characteristics of the Green Mountain State, not the least among which is a certain indefinable, but peculiarly New England caution. In addition to a large and active law practice in both New Hampshire and Vermont, he had banking connections through which he had gained a better knowledge of business and finance than is possessed by the average lawyer. Moreover, a long term as Chief Justice of Samoa had given him diplomatic experience and a knowledge of the Polynesian races which were to serve him well in his work in the Philippines. As Chief Justice he exercised diplomatic and consular as well as judicial functions, and his position brought him in close relations with the English and German officials of the joint protectorate of the Samoan islands and in constant social contact with the naval officers of many countries whose ships very frequently called at Apia. He was a widower with two young daughters.

These daughters, Anne and Marjorie, or "the two Ide girls" as they were then popularly known, displayed no sign of Puritan ancestry or upbringing. They were just remarkably beautiful and altogether charming and delightful. A large part of their girlhood had been spent in Samoa; they were the product of an intermittent, but very picturesque education, and there was ingrained in them some of that happy-go-lucky attitude toward life, and that freedom from useless convention which the Occidental is not unlikely to acquire in the Orient.

These girls had, in Samoa, been great friends of Robert Louis Stevenson [author of *Treasure Island*, *Strange Case of Dr Jekyll and Mr. Hyde*, *Kidnapped*, etc.]. Anne, the elder, was the especial favourite of the beauty-loving invalid and he willed to her his birthday, as can be learned from his Samoan letters. She was born near Christmas time and had never known what it was to have her birthday celebrated, a great deprivation in childhood. But she now celebrates as her own the birthday of Robert Louis Stevenson and it is, I believe, her most cherished possession.

Marjorie, whose career, ever since our first trip together, I have followed with the greatest affection and interest, had even more of the care-free attitude than Anne. She used to convulse us with cruelly funny accounts of her adventures with admirers, of whom there were many, and with descriptions of some of the strange acquaintances she made during her travels with her father.

Among the passengers on the *Hancock* was Dr. Kneedler, an army surgeon, with his wife and two little girls. These little girls were exceedingly bright and inquisitive. Young ladies and gentlemen had particular and irresistible attractions for them and the Ide young ladies kept them very much occupied. The Ide young ladies didn't encourage their attentions and this fact engendered their hostility.

They therefore referred to the Misses Ide as "them there Ides." With their delightful sense of humour the Ides, of course, rejoiced in the designation and in all the thirteen years since then they have never met Mr. Taft or me without presenting themselves as "them there Ides."

The Misses Ide were destined to be the unrivalled belles of Manila society for six years and then to move on to broader social spheres. Anne was married to Mr. Bourke Cochran shortly after her father left the Philippines, but Marjorie continued to be her father's companion for several years, going with him to Madrid when he was appointed Minister to Spain and presiding over the American Legation there until she married Mr. Shane Leslie and went to London to live.

General Wright, Judge Ide and Mr. Taft were the lawyers on the Commission and it was felt that their familiarity with law and governmental matters greatly enhanced strength and preparedness of the Commission for the work they had to do.

Mr. Worcester was an assistant professor at the University of Michigan. He too was a Vermonter, with quite as much *fortiter in* re, but with somewhat less of the *suaviter in modo* than Judge Ide inherently had, or had acquired in his Samoan experience.

Mr. Worcester was the only member of the party who had ever been to the Philippines before. I think he had been there twice with scientific expeditions before the Battle of Manila Bay had thrust the guardianship of the Filipinos upon our country, and in the course of his trips, with his fluency in Spanish as it is spoken in the Philippines, he had acquired a very intimate knowledge of the people and their customs, as well as of the flora and fauna of the islands. He had written a book on the Philippines which came out at a most fortunate time, just when [Admiral George] Dewey's victory had turned the eyes of the country upon that never-before-thought-of corner of the world. This book led to his appointment on the first Commission and his useful, loyal, courageous and effective labours with that body led Mr. McKinley to appoint him on the second.

He is a large, forceful man with rather abrupt manners and very decided opinions and perhaps no greater contrast could be imagined than exists between him and Mrs. Worcester, who, in outward seeming, is the frailest kind of little woman, with a sweet face and engagingly gentle manners which suggest timidity. Mrs. Worcester has proved herself to possess the frailty of flexible steel. At that time we were quite concerned about her, I remember, thinking she would not be able to endure the Philippine climate even for a short period. But she has lived there from that day to this. She has been with her husband through many experiences from which the strongest woman would shrink, toiling with him over hundreds of miles of mountain and jungle trail on his frequent expeditions into the countries of the wild tribes and, meeting every difficulty without comment. She is in excellent health and is a living refutation of the familiar exaggerations as to the effect of the climate. They had with them two little white haired children, one of them quite delicate, who have grown up in the Philippines strong and healthy and have received most of their education in the schools established there under American government.

The last member of the Commission was Professor Bernard Moses of the political and historical department of the University of California. He was a man of profound learning, a Connecticut Yankee, combining a very excellent knowledge of business with his unusual qualifications as an historian, economist and student of politics. He was especially familiar with all Spanish-American countries, had travelled extensively in the South American republics and had written a learned book on the constitution of Colombia. My husband always says that he thinks Mr. McKinley exercised the wisest discretion in the selection of all the members of this Commission since they possessed, among them, qualifications for every line of work in practical government and original research.

Mrs. Moses, a graduate from the University of California, was a very attractive woman. She had a gift for vivid description and for seeing the funny side of every situation. Her book, "Unofficial Letters of an Official's Wife," gives an interesting and accurate picture of social life in the early days of military rule, which are known in Manila history as "the days of the Empire" and of that period when American civil government was in the process of organisation. Her wit sometimes had a suggestion of the caustic in it, but she never failed to contribute her quota to the day's amusement.

There were many other interesting members of the party, including Mr. Arthur Fergusson, the Spanish secretary, and Mrs. Fergusson, Mr. Frank A. Branagan, the disbursing officer, and Mrs. Branagan, and several private secretaries with their families.

The voyage from San Francisco to Honolulu was quite perfect. As we sailed toward the tropics the weather gradually grew warmer and the sheltered decks became the most attractive part of the ship. The promenade deck of the *Hancock* reaches from bow to stem. I believe there is a regular term to describe such ship construction,—"decked over all" is it?—but to me it was just a very long deck which served unusually well for exercise. The Commission held regular business sessions in a cabin which had been fitted up for the purpose, but when work was over they would start on a long march around and around the deck, covering many miles each day. My husband was especially industrious and walked one man after another "off his feet" until, finally, he was obliged to finish his long tramp alone. He set himself the task of so many miles a day, so many times around the deck being a mile, and to keep count of laps requires some concentration. His quiet persistence in this kind of exercise was calculated to make the lazy onlooker intensely nervous, and when I had done my modest little turn I was always glad to indulge in a sort of counter-concentration at a whist table, or at General Wright's ever constant pinochle.

Altogether the days passed very pleasantly and we were a very merry and friendly party by the time we reached Honolulu.

At Honolulu I got my first glimpse of real tropics, and I was enchanted. It was a glorious sensation for me that April morning when I saw these mid-Pacific islands, for the first time, rise before me out of a white-capped sea; clear-cut in an atmosphere which seems never to be blurred by mist.

American energy, ambition and initiative have wrought great material changes in the islands and these, which were even then important, were brought to our admiring attention later on. I shall always think of Hawaii,—of the island of Oahu, rather,—as it appeared to me then when our ship steamed past Diamond Head, skirted the high breakers of Waikiki and made its way up through the bright waters of the bay into the harbour of Honolulu. Honolulu is a little, modern city lying, all in sight, against the green of a narrow, gently-sloping, peak-encircled valley.

The Punchbowl, a spent and emptied volcano, outlined in perfect form against the higher hills behind it, plainly tells the story of the spectacular construction of the islands and makes it almost possible to visualise their sudden rise from the sea. They are not very old, according to scientific measurements of time, but they are old enough, at any rate, to have clothed themselves in the most brilliant luxuriance, which is the first thing to impress the traveller as his ship sails into the harbour.

The brilliance from the ship's deck is the brilliance of every imaginable shade of green, massed against the towering, pointed hills and picked into contrasts of high-light and shadow by a sun and atmosphere peculiar to the tropics. Once ashore, the green foliage becomes the background for a wealth of blooming flowers, flowers everywhere, of unnumbered different varieties, with the flaming hibiscus in every garden, striking the high note of colour. Until we left Honolulu laden with "leis"—long festoons of flower petals which are thrown upon the shoulders of departing friends and visitors—there were always flowers.

And with the flowers and the foliage and the tall palm trees and the warm tropic sunlight, there is music, the music of the native which greets one in welcome at the dock and contributes constantly to the spirit of festivity until the departing ship gets too far from shore to catch the strains of the farewell song "Aloha" whose closing words: "Until we meet, until we meet again," linger long in the mind of the grateful recipient of Hawaiian hospitality.

The first thing we were to learn when our ship came up into the harbour was that the bubonic plague had been epidemic in

Honolulu for a long time. It was our first encounter with this terror of the East. There had been seventy-one cases in all, and sixty-one deaths. Six Europeans had contracted the disease and of these four had died. When we dropped anchor we were at once boarded by the local health officer, Dr. Carmichael of the Marine Hospital Service, who was accompanied by United States Minister Sewell and Consul General Hayward. They wanted us to land, of course, and we were very anxious to do so, but as the quarantine was not yet raised they could not answer for the attitude of the Japanese health officers when we got to Yokohama. Our going ashore might result in a long detention in quarantine for ourselves and, aside from the discomfort of this, we could not afford the delay. There was no particular danger for us personally, since no new cases had been reported for twenty-four days, but it was all a question of being able to land later in Japan. It was really too much of a disappointment; there was not a dissenting voice on that score, and Honolulu kept getting more and more attractive as the possibility dawned on us that we might not see it at all. But it was arranged. We sent for the Japanese vice-Consul and explained matters to him and he finally agreed to hold himself responsible for our breaking the quarantine, in so far as it concerned Japan, if we would keep our ship out in the stream instead of tying up at the dock, and permit no member of the crew to go ashore during our stay. This we readily agreed to do and made our plans accordingly. We, too, were to live on board the *Hancock*, but there were any number of harbour launches put at our disposal.

We were received by the Americans in Honolulu with the utmost cordiality and immediately found ourselves sharing the exhilarating suspense with which the people were then awaiting the passage of the bill in Congress which was to make the Hawaiian Islands a part of the United States. The first thing the Commission did was to call on President Dole, of the provisional republican government, and with him they met the Ministers of the Treasury and the Interior, Mr. Damon and Mr. Young. Indeed, we met all the people who had the affairs of the islands in hand and were most delightfully entertained by them. We found them of one mind, just anxiously waiting to be annexed to the United States. The men, who realised the importance of our mission to the Philippines, were eager to foregather with the Commission and discuss with them, long and earnestly, this broad American venture and its possible effect upon the future prosperity of the Hawaiian Islands, but in so far as I was concerned, nothing in the way of state problems was allowed to intrude itself upon their purely social hospitality. There were dinners and luncheons and teas and receptions, and, in the intervals, sight-seeing.

There are a number of entertaining things to do in Honolulu and while I do not wish to make this, in any way, a book of travel, I must record my impressions of the world as they came to me.

The Hawaiian Islands have a background of romantic history which makes the museums, the public buildings and even the cemeteries of the capital extremely interesting. Besides all of which there are some wonderful views which every one must see.

The trip to Nuuani Pali is the first thing to be undertaken in Honolulu, perhaps because it is the greatest thing on the island of Oahu. We didn't know what the Pali was,—had no idea. It was just *the* place to go, so we went,—the very first day. We drove up the valley over a perfect road which wound in and out past beautiful, palm-shaded country homes, and along the bank of a noisy, crystal-clear little mountain stream, until we came to a point which looked to me like the "jumping off place." And it is; the "jumping off place" is the Pali. The road turns sharp around the solid rock wall of the cliff and winds its way on down into the valley on the other side, but it is a distinct surprise to find that it doesn't end right there. The Pali is the Pass of the Winds; the meeting place of all the young hurricanes of the Pacific. They say the winds in the Pali are never still. We were flattened out against the wall of the cliff, our hats were torn from our heads and we had to hold onto our coats for dear life, but before us lay one of the grandest spectacles in the whole world. Coral-tinted, purple, rose and bright-blue sea; beetling, pointed, terrible cliffs, and a broad, green plain running down to a surf-washed ribbon of beach; a panorama as wide as the compass of vision. I have been back since then thinking that, on first sight, I might have overestimated the grandeur of the Pali. But I didn't. It is one of the world's great views. And it has its touch of savage history

50

too. It was up these hills and over the cliffs of the Pali that King Kamehameha drove to certain death the offending hordes in arms against his sovereignty. There was no escape for them. Once in this pass they had either to go over the precipice or back against the spears of the enemy. This being history, and not myth, it adds much to the thrill of the spectacle.

After a visit to the indescribable "aquarium of the painted fishes"— painted, I suppose, by the bright sun-rays in the coral shallows of the tropic seas—we went, as guests of Mr. Carter, a prominent member of the American colony, who afterward became governor of the islands, out to Waikiki Beach for surf-bathing,—or, surf-riding, as it is more aptly called.

Surf-riding at Waikiki Beach is a great game. In the first place the surf there doesn't look as if any human being would dare venture into it; but when you see a beautiful, slim, brown native, naked save for short swimming trunks, come gliding down a high white breaker, poised like a Mercury, erect on a single narrow plank—it looks delightfully exhilarating. It took me some time to make up my mind, but after sufficient persuasion I finally decided to risk my life with the others. Dressed in bathing suits, we were taken out beyond the line of breakers in long canoes with outriggers and, with a native at prow and stern armed with broad paddles to guide the craft, we rode in on the crest of the waves. Even this modified version of the natives' foolhardy performance is dangerous enough. There is every likelihood of an upset and not any of us could be said to swim expertly, so there was great excitement when one member of the party after another was plunged, out of depth, into the foaming and seething water. Two members of our party, indeed, had a narrow escape, though we didn't know it at the time. General Wright and Judge Ide were capsized in a particularly vicious breaker and Judge Ide at once began to make frantic efforts to attract attention and secure aid, but in the confusion his signs of distress were taken for indications of vast enjoyment and he would have been left to drown if he hadn't been washed ashore by the force of the surf. General Wright, though much the better swimmer, had no less difficulty, and they were both quite white and shaken when they crawled up on the beach.

We stayed four days in this "Paradise of the Pacific," during which we made many interesting trips, were introduced to many strange Hawaiian customs and were regaled with many feasts, not always, I may say, particularly appetizing. I have had in my time, for politeness' sake, to eat various queer messes in all sorts of odd corners of the earth, but to me "poi" will always be "poi"—in a class by itself. It is the true Hawaiian dish and is offered to guests by the natives in the same spirit of compliment with which we offer to "break bread" with our friends. It is the custom for Americans residing in Honolulu to introduce visitors to this dish, and the native viands which go with it, in entertainments which are called "poi dinners," and we were treated to as many of these as our time would permit. "Poi" bears an unpleasant outward resemblance to cockroach paste and, try as I would, I was never able to cultivate a taste for it. But foreigners do learn to like it, for I found Americans in Honolulu eating it with the greatest relish and dipping it up with their fingers in true Hawaiian style.

On our last evening in Honolulu, after a morning of sightseeing, a luncheon, an hour in the buffeting surf, and a large tea-party, we were given a particularly elaborate "poi dinner" where we all sat on the floor and at which all the guests appeared in native costume with "leis" around their necks and in their hair. The Minister of Foreign Affairs, Mr. Mott Smith, sent the Hawaiian Band, whose leader came out from old Emperor William to King Kalakaua, and they serenaded us with most wonderful Hawaiian music, interspersed, for their own pride's sake, with well rendered selections from the finest operas. The girls came in flaming bright "Mother-Hubbard" dresses, crowned and covered with "leis," to dance for us the curious folk-lore dances of the old-time. It was a delightful whirl of music and lights and colour—added to fish and poi and a cramped position—but I was tired enough not to be sorry when the time came for the singing of "Aloha Oe" and our departure for the ship which lay out in the harbour ready to up-anchor at daybreak and start on its way to Japan.

On the evening of the tenth of May we reached the estuary near the head of which is Yokohama and further on is Tokio [the old spelling for Tokyo, previously Edo]. For at least two hours we steamed past a low-lying shore line before we came in sight of the sweep of steep cliff to the southward which forms the great outer harbour.

There was just one thing that we could really look at; one insistent, dominant point in the landscape which caught us and held us fascinated,—Fujiyama. I had seen Fujiyama on screens and fans and porcelains all my life, but I had no conception of it. For one half hour this "Queen of Mountains"—rightly called—rising thirteen thousand feet out of sheer sea-level, perfect in form, snow-capped, majestic, blazed for us against the western sky. Then a cloud curtain fell,—and the sun went down.

As we steamed up close to the breakwater in the grey light of late evening we could see nothing but the dark outlines of many ships and a long row of substantial looking buildings, under high arc lights, stretching along a wide, water-front street which I was afterward to know as The Bund.

We wanted to go ashore, but it was not possible. We had to lie outside the breakwater and wait for the doctors to come aboard. "Wait for the doctors to come aboard;" how familiar that proceeding becomes to the traveller among the ports of the East, and especially, of Japan. You arrive at Yokohama and are examined there; you go just around the bend of the coast line and arrive at Kobe and you are examined there; you go on through the Inland Sea to Nagasaki and again you are examined. Wherever you arrive in this land of much caution you must "wait for the doctors to come aboard."

But our doctors didn't keep us waiting long. About eight o'clock half a dozen of them, important little men with much gold-lace, came smiling up the gangway. We worried, rather, about the plague we had braved,—and we did hope none of our crew would develop symptoms,—but, having faith in the Japanese Vice-Consul in Honolulu, we hoped for special leniency. We were not disappointed. They examined the ship's company with great care, but our examination was a mere formality, a sort of apologetic enumeration as a matter of fact, and after giving us a clean bill of health the doctors bowed themselves most courteously away. But we had a narrow escape. Charlie's nurse developed a suspicious sore throat the very next afternoon and gave us many days of anxiety for the baby and the other children. And, as I shall make plain further on, our anxiety was not without cause.

In reading over my own and my husband's letters, written on that trip to various members of the family, I find that Charlie was very much in evidence at all times. I suppose he was spoiled because, certainly, everybody took a hand in his misguidance, but the spoiling process at least kept him in high good humour, unless it happened to take the form of secret indulgence in prohibited sweets; then I had to meet the consequences. I find my husband writing to his brother Charles: "Charlie continues to be as full of spirits and as determined to have his own way as ever. We call him `the tornado'; he creates such a sensation when he lands in the midst of the children on board the ship. He is very badly in need of discipline and I long for the time to come when he will be better able to appreciate it. Maria has become quite as much a slave to him as Nellie and you may tell his Aunt Annie that I am still the only hope the boy has of moral training." This sounds so much like the average father that I thought I ought to quote it.

When Bessie, Charlie's nurse, was taken away from him and quarantined we got for him a Japanese "amah" who filled him at first with indignation, not unmixed with fear. But she was so patient, and followed him around so much like a faithful watchdog, that he grew to be exceedingly fond of her and straightway proceeded to exchange his small English vocabulary for, to him, more useful Japanese words.

The first thing to claim our attention in Yokohama Harbour was the American cruiser *Newark,* the Admiral's flagship of the Asiatic fleet, with Admiral Kempff aboard. As soon as we came inside the breakwater she fired a salute of seventeen guns, and we wondered what it was all about, until suddenly we remembered that the Commissioners had the rank of ministers plenipotentiary and decided that it was meant for us. It was the first time in my husband's life that he had ever been saluted. In his later career he reached a point where he would have been almost willing to assume a disguise in order to escape the thunder of the twenty-one guns that roared at him whenever he approached a naval vessel of any kind, but I think he was rather elated by this first tribute to his official standing.

We found later that an old friend, Captain McCalla, was in command of the *Newark*. We had known Captain McCalla in Washington when my husband was Solicitor General. He had been court-martialed and suspended from the Navy for a year for striking an unruly and insubordinate sailor and at his request Mr. Taft read the record of the court-martial. Mr. Choate had been his counsel, but the case was given a great deal of unpleasant publicity. He displayed such bravery at the Battle of Guantanamo, in Cuba, that the files he had lost were restored to him. He also rendered distinguished service in the Philippines, taking over the surrender of one of Aguinaldo's generals at Caygayan; and later on, in China, he was in the van of the allied troops that relieved Peking and was severely wounded. Being a man of broad intelligence and great enterprise he appreciated the importance of the Philippine Commission and lost no time in extending to them all the courtesies at his command.

Shortly after we landed and got ourselves comfortably settled at the Grand Hotel, an ensign from the *Newark* came to ask when the Commission would receive the Admiral. The hour was set for this formality and when it had been duly disposed of, Captain McCalla called on us unofficially, with much news for our hungry ears from the big world that we had known nothing about for eleven long days. That was before the wireless era when going to sea was really going to sea, and seldom has the world known a more exciting year than 1900. Grim talk about the terrible Boxer insurrection [a violent anti-foreign and anti-Christian movement which took place between 1898-1900] was on every tongue and Captain McCalla told us that the *Newark* was lying in readiness to proceed to China at an instant's notice. The British were just then pressing the Boers northward in South Africa, and our own troubles in the Philippines were by no means over. We had nearly seventy thousand troops in the field, and we heard of decisive engagements between the division under General Young and some religious fanatic *insurrectos* in northern Luzon. We found ourselves feeling very much in touch with big events.

The Commission went out to the *Newark* to return the Admiral's call and when they got back to the hotel they were full of valuable information and advice about sightseeing in Japan, housekeeping in the Orient and other important things. Among other bits of news they had to tell their wives was that we would all probably be received at the Japanese Court,—which was quite exciting.

My experience is that the most formal branch of the government service is the naval branch. The state department may be as formal, but I doubt it. The ceremony on board naval vessels is constant, and the severity of the penalties for any failure to follow the regulations impresses itself upon every naval officer. Therefore, every naval officer must have diplomatic training and must be alert in finding out and in carrying out the duties of polite intercourse which prevail in every country.

Captain McCalla regarded the Commissioners as pro-consuls going to an important province, quite equal to the foremost diplomatic representatives of the United States anywhere, and he thought it was incumbent upon them to make the fact of their presence in Japan known at the Imperial Court and to apply for an audience with the Emperor. It hadn't occurred to them. Their minds were so full of the weighty problems confronting them at Manila that they had given no consideration to any possible intervening formalities, and, anyhow, Mr. Taft said he thought the Emperor wouldn't lose much sleep if he did miss seeing them. But this was not the proper attitude at all, and Captain McCalla, expostulating with them for their too casual conduct, finally prevailed upon them to communicate with the American Minister in Tokyo and ask to have application made for the audience. They were immediately informed that their arrival had been expected and that the matter had already been attended to.

The Commission had only a week in Japan and, although their purpose in stopping had been to coal ship and get some clothing suitable for the tropic heat they were going into, they naturally were anxious to see something of the country during their stay, so the days were filled with expeditions around Yokohama and Tokyo and to points of interest nearby. My sister Maria and I did not accompany them on many of these trips because we were planning to remain in Japan for the summer and wanted to view its attractions at our leisure.

The trip to Nikko was made memorable by Mr. Taft's most triumphal progress. On account of his unusual proportions he had already been an object of tremendous interest to the Japanese.

Nikko is nearly a day's ride from Tokyo, up in the hills to the north, and when you get there you find that the railway station is a long way from the hotel and that much of the distance is a steep incline. The only kind of conveyance available is a jinricksha, and when my husband climbed into one of these little perambulators the unfortunate coolie to whom it belonged began to utter strange sounds. He rolled his eyes and gesticulated frantically until he prevailed upon a second man to help him in propelling his unaccustomed burden. But even then his excitement did not abate. As they approached the first rise in the road some of the villagers along the way, attracted, no doubt, by the coolie's weird cries, came out to stare and, as usual, remained to laugh. The little ricksha man began chattering and grimacing at all of them and kept it up until he had enlisted the services of at least half the population of the village to help him in attaining the crest of the hill.

Two days before the *Hancock* was to start on her way toward Manila the great event of our visit to Japan transpired. We had our audience with the Emperor and Empress.

The first thing the ladies all asked, of course, was, "What shall we wear?" It was a most important question. I supposed we should have to wear evening gowns and was congratulating myself that I had a very nice new one that would do beautifully. But only on the afternoon before the day appointed, it was decreed that we should appear in high-necked frocks with trains. That was more difficult,— especially the trains. I didn't own an afternoon frock that I considered good enough. I was going to the tropics and had got a supply of thin white muslins and linens, but I had nothing that would do for a cold May day in Japan. Mrs. Wright, Mrs. Worcester and Mrs. Moses were as greatly concerned as I, but we finally managed. I solved the problem by having a Chinese dressmaker in Yokohama make me, overnight, a lace guimpe [a high-necked blouse or undergarment worn showing beneath a low-necked dress] which I wore with my perfectly acceptable evening gown.

Judge Ide had been particularly interested in the audience and in the fact that the ladies would also be received and he was very much chagrined when he found that "the ladies" meant only the wives of the Commissioners and that he could not take with him his two beautiful daughters. He quite lost interest in the whole proceeding, and we didn't blame him in the least.

The Palace in Tokyo is not a "Forbidden City" literally, as the old palace in Peking used to be, but it looks from the outside just as "forbidden," or more so. It is surrounded by a wide, deep moat which is crossed at intervals by curved and gracefully balustraded bridges. On the other side of the moat is a high stone wall. There is nothing of the palace to be seen except a few low, tiled roofs which peep out from the midst of many trees. The Imperial gardens are vastly more impressive than the palaces,—there are several within the walled enclosure,—and I would have wanted to linger and really look at things if I had not been so keenly interested in the experience which awaited us. Our carriage hurried on over the beautiful drives, through the most entrancing little artificial landscapes, past lakes full of little rock islands on which were perched tiny pavilions with up-tilted roofs and the most beautiful polished wood and snow-white paper windows. It was all most fascinating and much too wonderful to, be merely glanced at, but it was only a few moments before we approached a low, grey building and drew up before the door. It didn't look at all like a palace, but it seemed that we had arrived.

We were ushered into a large reception room which was neither Japanese nor European, but a curious mixture of both. The walls were of gold leaf and were decorated with beautiful Japanese paintings in exquisitely soft colourings, but the furniture was mostly of the heavy foreign type. It was unexpected to say the least and I thought what a pity it was that the Japanese had not met the European invasion in their own original and picturesquely beautiful style, instead of trying to conform to western customs, or rather, to engraft western customs upon their own unique orientalism. But so it is. They either like our ugly heaviness, or think they confer a polite compliment on us by adopting it.

We were not kept waiting long. We were separated from the men of our party and were led into another room, much like the first, where the Empress awaited us attended by three or four ladies of her court. We curtseyed very low, not without difficulty on the part of most of us in spite of much practice, and after receiving a gracious smile and bow from Her Majesty, we were able to stand erect and observe her at our leisure. Both she and her ladies-in-waiting were dressed in European costume which made them look much smaller than they would have looked in their own beautiful *kimonos*. Her Majesty's face was sweet and almost timid looking, and her voice was peculiarly gentle. Our conversation, carried on through an interpreter, was commonplace in the extreme, but her manner was pleasant and cordial. I was tremendously interested because I had been reading Japanese history and was duly impressed with the hoary antiquity of this court of the Son of Heaven. The Empress addressed a few remarks to each of us, after which we curtseyed again and retired. That was all.

Our husbands were received in a similar manner by the Emperor, though His Majesty granted a separate interview to each of them. Mr. Taft entered first with the Minister of the Household in charge of the ceremony. He bowed when he entered the door, bowed again half way up the long room, and yet again when he arrived before the Emperor. The others, also bowing, followed close behind but remained just outside of the audience chamber while my husband's audience was in progress. Mr. Nagasaki, who acted as interpreter, said that His Majesty was very much pleased to see the Commission in Japan. Mr. Taft expressed his appreciation of the audience. The Emperor asked if he had ever been in Japan before. He said he had not. The Emperor asked when he was going to leave Japan. He replied, "In two days, Your Majesty." After which this, his first audience with the Mikado, was at an end and he left the chamber while the rest of the Commissioners, each in his turn, went through the same ceremony.

After our husbands had been received by the Empress also, they rejoined us and we were conducted through some other rooms in the palace which interested us greatly. They all showed a curious mingling of Japanese and European objects of art and nobody could see them without deciding that, in that particular setting at least, the Japanese objects were far the more beautiful.

The Japanese Court is much inclined to imitate things European and the results are sometimes astonishing. Years later, when my husband was in Japan without me, the Empress presented him with a tapestry for me which had been copied from a Gobelin piece. It represented the meeting of Columbus and Isabella, and, it shows the most exquisite workmanship, but the faces have a curiously Oriental cast.

There is a story in connection with this tapestry which I think I must tell. My husband was Secretary of War when it was presented to me; and I say me with emphasis, because thereby hangs the story. He brought it home and displayed it with great pride and satisfaction, but it was so enormous and, from my standpoint, so useless, that I rather protested and wondered why, as long as he was getting such a gorgeous present he couldn't have managed in some way to make its size correspond with my circumstances.

"Oh, well," said he, "never mind. I'm going to present it to the Smithsonian Institute anyway, because you know, my dear, it is against the Constitution for an official in the United States government to accept any kind of favours from foreign courts."

This was not the first time in my life that I had met the Constitution face to face, but theretofore I had been able to accept its decrees with what I had hoped was patriotic resignation. But now that tapestry suddenly became to me a most desirable thing. It had been sent to me by the Empress of Japan and I wanted to enjoy the mere possession of it,—at least for awhile. So, as my husband would say, I took the question up with him. I tried to convince him that I was not an official of the United States government and that he, as an official, had nothing whatever to do with my present from the Empress of Japan. He stood firmly by the Constitution, as usual, and eventually I had to submit the question for arbitration to President Roosevelt, who agreed with me that I was a private citizen and had a perfect right to accept the gift. I afterward hung it in one of the big wall spaces in the state dining-room of the White House and had the pleasure of watching many a guest vainly endeavouring to locate its origin and figure out its meaning.

We concluded our first audience at the court of Japan by signing our names in the Imperial album, after which we went to the American Legation to a beautiful luncheon which the Minister had arranged in our honour. Our Minister in Tokyo then—it was some years before the Legation was raised to an Embassy—was Mr. Buck of Georgia, a most affable and agreeable gentleman. He had invited a number of his diplomatic collegues to meet us and, among others, we met for the first time Baron and Baroness Rosen, of the Russian Legation, who were afterward with us in Washington.

I sat on the right of the Minister and next to Baron Sanomiya, the Court Chamberlain, who had conducted our audience. I was greatly interested in Baron Sanomiya's wife. She was an Englishwoman at least twice his size.

At Mr. Taft's request the Minister had invited an old classmate of his, Baron Tajiri Inajiro. At Yale he was known as Tajiri, and the first two letters of both their names being "Ta" he and my husband had been brought together in the classroom, seated alphabetically, and had enjoyed a pleasant association. So Mr. Taft looked forward with great pleasure to renewing the acquaintance in Japan. Baron Tajiri, like most Japanese, was a little man, and his teeth were so formed that he was never able to master the pronunciation of English in such a way as to enable one to understand him easily. But he seems to have acquired at Yale a sound knowledge of business and finance since he became Assistant Minister of Finance under Yamagata and had taken an active part in the of the Japanese currency from- the silver to the gold standard, which was a great step in Japan's progress toward a place among the world's powers.

He had been made a life peer and sat in the Upper House. At the luncheon he wore a frock coat which Mr. Taft felt confident he recognised as an old college friend of the 'seventies. In those days the Japanese wore their "foreign clothes" only on "foreign occasions" or at court. They kept them carefully folded up and put away, and they had not yet come to recognise the desirability of pressing them when they took them out for use. Also a silk hat once was a silk hat always; vintages didn't trouble them, and they didn't mind in the least which way the nap was brushed.

Baron Tajiri wanted to be appointed Minister of Finance when Yamagata retired, but he was put, instead, at the head of the Board of Audits, a life position. Marchioness, now Princess Oyama, wife of the Field Marshal, told my husband this on the occasion of his second visit to Japan, and said that the disappointment had made Tajiri very much of a recluse. In any case, Mr. Taft has never seen him again, although he has tried to seek him out and has made inquiry about him every time he has been in Japan.

We were very much interested in our Legation at Tokyo. It was the first one we had ever seen that the American government owned. The house was not what it ought to have been, but it was surrounded by spacious and beautifully kept grounds and was so much better than the nothing that we have in other countries that we liked to dwell upon it as an honourable exception to the disgraceful and miserly policy pursued by Congress in dealing with our representatives to foreign capitals.

Mrs. Wright, with her daughter Katrina, had decided to remain with us in Yokohama for the summer, so we took a cottage together on The Bluff, a high foreign residence section of the city, and prepared to make ourselves most comfortable.

Two days later the Commissioners and the rest of the party went aboard the *Hancock* and we waved them goodbye from a harbour launch as they steamed away toward Manila.

IN JAPAN

To be quarantined in a house too small for the number of its occupants, behind closed doors, each one of which bears aloft a sinister yellow placard across which is printed in large, black letters: "Diphtheria," is no way to begin a visit to a strange and interesting country.

No sooner had Bessie, Charlie's nurse, been released from quarantine by the doctors in Yokohama than our older boy, Robert, developed suspicious symptoms which, upon diagnosis, were pronounced to be diphtheritic. The sore throat began before Mr. Taft left for Manila, and he was loathe to go, but as the new serum treatment for diphtheria had robbed the disease of much of its terror, and as we were in the hands of an excellent American physician, Dr. Eldridge, I felt confident there was no cause for serious apprehension.

We sent Helen and the baby to be taken care of at the Grand Hotel, while Mrs. Wright, Maria and I resigned ourselves to a long and tedious period of isolation. Robert's diphtheria did not develop to a dangerous stage, but the sore throat persisted and it was three weeks before we were released upon a none-too-welcoming world. Our long quarantine had marked us as objects to be avoided—in a social sense—even after the doctors had pronounced us safe.

Mrs. Wright and my sister and I spent that entire three weeks only wishing that we were in our own land where some friendly voice might at least shout an inquiry about us from a distance, and not in this far-away place where only strange and very foreign sounds came floating in to us from curious and crowded streets whose every nook and corner we were aching to explore.

Our house was charming. All the "foreign" houses in Japan seem to me to be charming. The solidity of Occidental construction, with the light touch of Japanese interior decoration, make a fascinating combination, especially in that environment. The Japanese landscape is—well, peculiarly Japanese, and the gardens, however "foreign" they may be, have an air quite unique and unmistakably oriental.

The Foreign Settlement in Yokohama consists of a broad business section, solidly built, on the low lands fronting the harbour, and The Bluff. The Bluff is a garden of beautiful homes. At one end it rises high above the bay and commands a wide view of harbour, town and Pacific Ocean, while the other end runs inland to meet the higher hills beyond and forms a deep valley in which has been built up a teeming native quarter full of colour, of picturesque outline and of never-ending oriental clamour. Around this village are terraced, bright-green rice paddies and high hills covered with dark, Japanese pines which grow at curious angles.

Our house, a spreading bungalow in a large and well-kept garden, was on the inland side and overlooked this valley. From a Buddhist temple on the opposite hill, a quaint structure with uptilted roof and great stone *lord* gateway, came the ceaseless drone of a priest repeating over and over an endless invocation to the constant, measured turn-turn accompaniment of little wooden drums, while from the narrow streets below rose the strange cries of itinerant food venders. Throughout the whole long evening sounded the long wail of the blind *masseurs* who, with their thumping bamboo sticks, tramp from door to door seeking patronage. At intervals the single low tong of a great temple bell set the hills to vibrating.

We rented the house from an Englishman who was "going home" on vacation, and with it we rented a complete *menage,* including a most efficient little Japanese woman named Matsu who served us both as waitress and housekeeper and answered to the call of "Amah!"—meaning either nurse or maid. Besides the Amah, there was only a cook, an excellent one, but the two contrived to run the house with a smoothness and an economy which I have never seen equalled. They were so economical, in fact, that we had difficulty in getting them to serve to us enough of their well-prepared food. There were six of us in family, not including Charlie, or Baby San as he was called, and at each meal Matsu would bring in just six portions of whatever there was, six chops, six croquettes, six little fishes, always six—no more. We resorted to strategy sometimes and announced, well in advance, that there would be guests.

"How many, o Ku San'?" says Matsu cautiously.

"Well, maybe two," says we.

Whereupon we would get eight little chops, or eight little croquettes, or whatever it might be. But we couldn't play this game very often because we were afraid that if too many guests failed to materialise the time would come when we really would be giving a party and be forced to act out the "Wolf! Wolf!" story to our own very great embarrassment. I'm glad to say this never occurred; Matsu always obeyed orders; but when an unexpected guest dropped in we had to exercise the principle of "family hold back" in real earnest.

However, while Matsu was in command none of us had any cause for complaint. She had plenty of native shrewdness and didn't neglect her own interests to any appreciable extent, but she displayed none of the traditional oriental duplicity which we had been warned to look out for in all Japanese servants. She relieved us of all the responsibilities of housekeeping and left us free to wander around among the fascinating shops and to go off on long sightseeing expeditions at our pleasure.

While we were still in the midst of the miseries of quarantine I got my first letter from my husband, and as he had sailed away into what to me then was a very far distant and somewhat unreal world, I was exceedingly glad to hear from him.

The *Hancock* had stopped at Kobe and had then gone on to Nagasaki where it had to lie for two days taking on coal. The Commissioners seem to have begun by that time to chafe at delays and to long for their settled, definite employment. But they had to go to Hongkong on some business matters and it was from Hongkong that my first long letter came. They were received by the British authorities with the usual formality; pompous calls to be returned as pompously; dinners, luncheons, club privileges, launch parties and much entertaining gossip; but they were interested, principally, in meeting for the first time the genus Filipino irreconcilable.

The Filipinos, after three centuries of Christian education, which had taken the form of religious instruction only, had, with reason, risen in revolt against the Spanish system of friar domination and had demanded some measure of freedom and a voice in the control of their own affairs. This is a long and complicated story which can only be touched upon here.

They were engaged in a hopeless struggle with Spanish authority when the Spanish-American War, unexpected, undreamed of, suddenly turned the tables and placed them in an entirely new situation. They saw Spain defeated and turned from the islands she had held since Magellan's first voyage, while another flag quickly rose above their ancient forts and strongholds. Then it was that the handful of ambitious "illustrados," or well-to-do and educated ones, began freely to preach independence and were encouraged by not a few Americans, including some in official relation to the situation, who, in complete ignorance of real conditions, approved the so-called aspiration and gave hope of its early fulfilment.

The idea of these Americans was that our forefathers had fought for independence and that it was against our most cherished principles to hold any people against their will. But they didn't take into consideration the fact that the Filipinos were Malays, not ten per cent of them with even a primary education, used only to a theocratic and absolute government and without any experience in the rule of the people. Nor did they consider that our forefathers had, for a century and a half before the revolution, been carrying on what was really self-government and were better fitted by training and tradition to make self-government work than any people in the world. They indulged in sentiment to the exclusion of thought; and so the situation was created.

The idea of complete independence was never shouted from the housetops in Spanish times, but the new flag represented free speech, a free press, and such freedom generally as the Filipinos had never dreamed of in their wildest aspirations and the "illustrados" and the men who had tasted power in the insurrection against Spain were not slow to take advantage of it. An alluring conception of independence, freedom from all restraint and the enjoyment of luxurious ease, really, was sent abroad among the densely ignorant masses by the handful who had education, with the result that by the time the American government was free really to face the issue, the demand for our immediate withdrawal was unanimous, or nearly so.

But it couldn't be done. Aguinaldo tried his hand at a government for six months and failed miserably. Corruption was rife. Chaos reigned; the country was impoverished and absolutely unprotected; and it didn't take the Americans long to recognise the fact that "independence" meant nothing more nor less than the merciless exploitation of the many by the few and the establishment of worse conditions than any the people had ever known.

So we stayed; there was nothing else to do; and the insurrection against constituted authority was taken up where left off when Admiral Dewey steamed up Manila Bay. It was hopeless from the start, and one after another of the leading *insurrectos,* as the months went by, abandoned the struggle in favour of prosperous peace and came in to Manila to take the oath of allegiance to the United States. But as pacification progressed a few of the leaders declared themselves to be "irreconcilable" and either took to the hills with marauding bands of *ladrones,* or went over to Hongkong and joined the little Filipino colony there. This colony in Hongkong—which still exists, by the way—was known as the "junta" and its business in life was to hatch schemes for murderous uprisings, smuggle arms and incendiary literature into the islands, raise money for carrying on hostilities and make itself useful generally.

The methods employed by these "irreconcilables" were peculiarly their own. They consisted, mainly, of coercion and threats of assassination among Filipino people who were staying at home and endeavouring to keep out of trouble. Then, too, they were reported to have made a great deal of money by compelling Filipino hemp and tobacco planters to sell to them these valuable products at prices fixed by themselves, and later disposing of them in Hongkong at the regular market price which gave them a tremendous margin of profit.

These were the conditions—merely sketched—which existed in the Philippine Islands when the second Commission was sent out, and the first Filipinos Mr. Taft ever met, he met in Hongkong. They were not members of the "junta" but were high-class, wealthy, non-combatant refugees named Cortez, who lived under a threat of assassination, who had had all their property confiscated because of their sympathy with the insurrection against Spain, had secured restitution through the government at Washington, and who came now to beg the Commission for protection against their own people and for the speedy establishment of peaceful American rule in the islands.

Then came Artacho. Artacho had been Aguinaldo's rival in the insurrection against Spain and he very much resented the selection, by the Americans in command, of Aguinaldo as the leader of the Filipino forces when Dewey went into Manila. He was sufficiently annoyed to leave the country and take refuge in Hongkong. He professed entire ignorance of the activities of the "junta" and unqualified loyalty to the government of the United States, but, as he had with him a "secretary" who very carefully listened to all he had to say, and as he seemed to be very cautious in all his expressions, Mr. Taft decided that he was being watched and was, if not actively connected with the "junta," at least "on the fence" and in his call only "casting an anchor to windward" in case the Americans should succeed in pacifying the Islands and establishing a government there with which it would be very nice indeed to be connected. It must have been a very diplomatic, a very soft-spoken and a most amusing meeting.

Among other things the Commission had to do in Hongkong was to secure Chinese servants. They had been told that this was absolutely necessary because the unsettled state of affairs in Manila made Filipino servants entirely undependable.

Captain McCalla, of the *Newark,* had given to my husband in Yokohama, a letter to one L. Charles, a Chinese who ran a sort of employment agency in Hongkong, but when L. Charles came out to the *Hancock,* in response to a message from Mr. Taft, he brought with him the surprising news that the servants had already arrived from Shanghai and had been waiting for several days. Mr. Taft was greatly astonished, as he was unconscious of having made any arrangements at all, but L. Charles smilingly explained to him that Admiral Dewey had attended to it. Then Mr. Taft remembered that, sure enough, Admiral Dewey had, several months before in Washington, offered to secure servants through his own Chinaman, Ah Man, but he, himself, had forgotten all about it.

However, he sent for the men and when they came aboard one of them proudly produced a note from the flag officer of the *Brooklyn,* enclosing a note to Ah Sing, the steward of the *Brooklyn,* from Ah Man, Admiral Dewey's servant. It read:

My dear Ah Sing:

It is *a* new Governor General coming up to Manila City. His name is Mr. Wm. H. Taft and he is going to sail from here first of April. The Admiral asked me to write to you and ask if you please find him some good Chinese servants for Mr. Taft. He like to have a very good cook just like myself the Admiral said and two men to wait on table a butler and second man just like you. Now would you be so kind as to try to find some very nice people that will take good care and will understand their business. The Admiral will be very much oblige to you I am

Your truly friend,

AH MAN.

This is an example of what is known in the East as "flen-pidgin," which may be literally translated as "friend-work." It is a Chinese system, but it has been adopted by the representatives of every country in the world to be met out there and it is by no means the least of the elements which enter into the charm of the Orient.

One of the objects for stopping in Japan was to enable the Commissioners to get white duck and linen clothes for the tropics and Mr. Taft had the worst of luck in getting anything to fit him. In the beginning we had some rather heated discussions as to the style of dress that he should adopt. He had been assured that the most comfortably dressed men were those who wore "straight button ups" as they are called. These are coats which have a high, round collar and button straight down from the chin—plain military jackets, in fact. They are worn without shirts, collars, ties or anything except underwear and trousers and are, no doubt, very nice for the tropic heat. But I did not consider that such a severe style would bring out the lines of my husband's figure to the best advantage, so I prevailed upon him to have all his clothes made with sack coats which should be worn with the usual accessories. It was a sad experience in Yokohama, but he left for Hongkong full of hope, having been told that the tailors there were much better. He wrote in utter disgust. The tailors were not good; he had been to every shop in town looking for wearing apparel of all kinds and could find nothing large enough for him. He said he had imagined that Englishmen were, as a rule, large enough to demand men's sizes,—but evidently not. He had to have everything, shoes, stockings, underwear, shirts, collars and hats made to order—and then they didn't fit.

My husband's letter, full of strange names, of assassination, of smuggled arms, of dark intrigue and unrest generally, left a vague impression in my mind that he was going into a country where he would be subjected to murderous attacks every few minutes. Then I reflected that he was not quite alone; that General MacArthur [not the famous World War II general, who also later served in the Philippines] and about seventy thousand American troops were down there too, and that they could probably be depended upon to do everything in their power to protect him.

Our life in Yokohama was very placid. It was some time after our yellow placards were removed before our neighbours began to call on us, and we didn't blame them. No doubt they felt that it would be foolish to risk getting diphtheria just for the sake of being formally polite. We were delightfully entertained, both before and after the Commission sailed, by Mr. and Mrs. T. Williams McIvor, who are among the old American residents of Yokohama. Mr. McIvor had been American Consul General, but when we met him he was engaged in a private law practice, representing the American Tobacco Company and other large foreign concerns. As Consul General he had taken care of the Chinese during the Japan-China

War and had sent about eight thousand of them out of the country. He was now representing the foreign business community in its dispute with the Japanese government as to whether or not the property known as the Foreign Concession, or The Settlement, was taxable. This area had been granted by the Japanese government on perpetual lease at the time the first treaties with Japan were made, and the holding of it by foreigners was conditioned on the payment of a ground rent to the government which, it was provided, should never be increased beyond a certain amount. But now Japan was greatly in need of money, was taxing its own people in every way possible, and eventually decided to levy a tax on the houses and improvements upon this land, on the theory that improvements on land are not a part of the land itself. But by the Civil Law and the Common Law the provision in the treaties that no tax should be paid on the property greater than that fixed in ground rent would have prevented the levying of any tax on the buildings because, by such laws, improvements are considered to be a part of the land. But in Japanese law it was said they were not so regarded and the question was whether the treaties were to be construed according to Japanese law or according to the laws of foreign governments. The subject was one of endless discussion while we were there, and Minister Buck had already referred the question to the State Department at Washington.

We also dined with Mrs. Scidmore, whom I was to meet many times in after years. Mrs. Scidmore is the mother of Eliza Ramaha Scidmore, the well known writer about Far Eastern countries, and is, I suppose, the most notable foreign figure in the Orient. She had lived in Japan since the early days, not so long after the country's doors were opened to the world. Her son was in the Legation service when I met her and she had a charming house on the Bund, in which was gathered a remarkable collection of Japanese curios and objects of art. Mrs. Scidmore was then nearly eighty years of age I think, but she was as bright and young as a woman of fifty. The last time I saw her she was nearly ninety and she entertained us at luncheon in Nagasaki, where her son was American Consul. She dresses with as much care and is as interested in fashions and fabrics as any girl, and it is a rare pleasure to see her, with her snowy hair piled up on her head and a white silk gown spread out about her, sitting in the centre of a group of people discussing, with great animation and entire comprehension, general topics of current interest. She afterward went to "keep house" for her son in Seoul, Korea, where he became Consul General, and she continues to be a sort of uncrowned queen of foreign society.

Leaving our children at the bungalow with their nurses, Mrs. Wright, Maria and I went about, to Nikko, to Kama-kura, to Kyoto and other interesting places, and we spent the intervals, indeed all our time, in restraining our intense desire to purchase everything we saw in the extraordinarily attractive little shops.

About the last of July, when the heat began to be rather more than we could stand, we left Yokohama and went up into the Hakone Mountains to Miyanoshita. The trip to Miyanoshita includes a two hours' climb in rickshas up a steep incline from a village on the railway, where there was then no sort of accommodation for "Europeans,"—only Japanese inns which, though they may have been excellent from a Japanese standpoint, did not seem to us to have been built for inn purposes. When we got out of the train it was seven o'clock in the evening. There were Mrs. Wright and her maid, her daughter Katrina, my sister Maria, the three children, Bessie the nurse, and I. We wanted dinner above all things else and we decided to get it. It all had to be prepared "European style" at one of the little inns, so by the time it was served and disposed of the night was upon us, and, I may say, the blackest night I ever remember seeing. We debated at length the possibility of taking the two hours' ricksha ride in such darkness, but the chattering coolies, mainly by gesture and facial expression, succeeded in convincing us that it was the most desirable thing in the world to do. Incidentally, and aside from our objection to the bedless inns, we were most anxious to reach our journey's end. So—we set out, in eight rickshas, six for us and two piled high with hand luggage. I put Helen and Robert together in one and took Charlie in with me, and each of us had an extra man behind to push, also two men each for the baggage rickshas, which made sixteen men in all. We made quite a cavalcade and I felt fairly satisfied, not to say mildly festive, until we got away from the lights of the town and discovered, to our amazement, that for some reason or other, the ricksha men had failed to bring lights. I believe the idea was that they could keep the road better without them. We went along for a short distance in the Stygian darkness, then Maria decided that she wouldn't have it. Whatever we might do, she was going back for a lantern. We were not in an argumentative mood, so we let her go without a word, while we plunged on.

By that time the wind was tearing down through what seemed to be a very deep, and what certainly was a very dark, canyon, and it was raining steadily. My coolies lagged behind and the first thing I knew I found myself entirely alone. The others had gone so far ahead that I couldn't even hear the sound of their ricksha wheels, though the ricksha of those days was a very noisy little vehicle. I had been nearly two months in Japan, had had plenty experience with ricksha coolies and I knew them to be the most inoffensive little men in the world, but the darkness and the wind-driven rain and the discomfort generally, must have got on my nerves because I began to be perfectly sure ,that my two men were nothing less than brigands and that the separation from my party was a prearranged plan for murder and robbery. I didn't know how wide the road was, but I knew that on one side there was a very deep chasm because I could hear the roar of a mountain torrent far down and directly below me. Then the coolies chattered and grunted incessantly, as Japanese coolies always do, and I was convinced that they were arguing about which should take the initiative in violence. But I sat tight and said nothing, which was the only thing I could do, of course—except to soothe Charlie who was crying with discomfort and fright—and after awhile—ages it seemed to me—I came upon the rest of my party where they had halted in the road to give their men a breathing spell. I couldn't see them; I couldn't even make out the outlines of a ricksha, but I could hear Helen sobbing and stammering something about having lost her mother for good and all.

The coolies were chattering at each other at a terrific rate and I judged, from their tones, that they liked the night no better than we. While we were standing close together in the road, all talking at once and trying to tell each other what horrible experiences we had had, we saw a faint glimmer away in the distance, growing more and more distinct as it came up the long hill. It was the dauntless Maria with a light. We fell upon her with the warmest welcome she probably ever received in her life, and everybody at once cheered up. Even the coolies got happier and seemed to chatter less angrily in the lantern's dim but comforting yellow glow. Nor did we separate again. Everybody wanted to keep close to that light. It revealed to us the reassuring fact that the road was, at least, wide enough for safety, and so we rolled soggily along, with no other sound but the rattle of many wheels and the splash of mud, until we arrived at the Fujiya Hotel, sometime after ten o'clock, in a state of utter exhaustion.

I am not going to describe Miyanoshita because it has been very well done by scores of writers, but I will say that the Fujiya Hotel, away up in the mountains, at the head of a glorious canyon, is one of the most splendidly situated, finely managed and wholly delightful places I ever saw.

And there are plenty of things to do. We were carried in chairs over a high mountain pass to Lake Hakone, which, still and bright as a plate-glass mirror, lies right at the base of Fujiyama and reflects that startlingly beautiful mountain in perfect colour and form.

Then there are temples and wayside shrines, and tea-houses—tea-houses everywhere. We were coming back from a tramp one day and stopped at a tea-house not far from our hotel where we encountered an Englishwoman who gave us our first conception of what the terrible Boxer Insurrection was like. She entered into talk with us at once and told us a most tragic story. She was a missionary from the interior of China and had been forced to flee before the Boxers and make her way out of the country in hourly peril and through scenes of the utmost horror. Her husband had elected to remain at his post and she didn't then know but that he might already have died under the worst imaginable torture. She made our blood run cold and we were tremendously sorry for her, though she did tell her harrowing story calmly enough. It seems she had with her a young Chinese refugee who was a convert to Christianity and, because of that fact, in even more danger in China than she.

We expressed our sympathy and good wishes and continued on our way. But we hadn't gone far when we heard a frantic shouting behind us:

"IIave you seen my Chinaman! Have you seen my Chinaman anywhere on the way!"

It was the missionary, distracted and running violently after us; and, we had not seen her Chinaman. She rushed past and up into the woods faster than one would have thought she could run, and all the time she kept calling, "Joseph! Joseph!" at the top of her voice. We decided that Joseph was the Chinaman's new Christian name since we had heard that they all get Biblical names at baptism. We hastened along, thinking she might have gone suddenly mad and we wondered what in the world we should do. But as we came around a bend in the road we saw her coming toward us with a grinning little queued heathen marching meekly before her. She was looking very much relieved and stopped to explain her rather extraordinary conduct.

"I was perfectly certain that boy had committed suicide," she began.

"Why, what made you think that?" I asked.

"Well, he wrote that, and I found it!" And she thrust into my hand a piece of paper on which was scrawled in printed characters:

Just as I am, without one plea, Save that Thy blood was shed for me, And that Thou bid'st me come to Thee, o Lamb of God, I come, I come.

She explained that Joseph had had a great deal of trouble; was away from his people; that Chinamen didn't care anything about their lives anyhow; and that she had been afraid for some time that he would grow despondent and do something desperate.

But there stood Joseph, broadly smiling and looking for all the world like an oriental cherub who would have liked very much to know what all the commotion was about. Poor chap, he didn't understand a word of English and had been merely trying to learn the words of an English hymn by copying them, in carefully imitated letters, on bits of paper.

In the meantime my husband had arrived in Manila and had already sent me several letters through which I came gradually to know something of the situation he was facing.

The principal impression I received was that between the Commission and the military government, in the person of General Arthur MacArthur, there did not exist that harmony and agreement which was considered to be essential to the amicable adjustment of Philippine affairs. In other words, General MacArthur seemed to resent the advent of the Commission and to be determined to place himself in opposition to every step which was taken by them or contemplated. It was not very easy for the Commissioners, but as far as I can see now, after a careful reading of all the records, they exercised the most rigid diplomacy at times when it would have been only human to have risen up and exercised whatever may be diplomacy's antithesis.

The description of the arrival of the Commission made me rather wish I had accompanied them;—except for the heat. It was June and my husband said the sun beat down upon and came right through the heavy canvas awnings on the decks of the *Hancock*. The men had, by this time, become accustomed to their ill-fitting white linens, but they had not yet mastered the art of keeping them from looking messy, and they must have been a wilted company during their first few days in Manila.

They came up into the harbour on Sunday and during the course of the day received many interesting visitors. General MacArthur was not among them, but he sent a member of his staff, Colonel Crowder, to present his compliments and make arrangements for the going ashore ceremony the next day. Then came the *Americanistas*, as the Filipinos who sympathised with American control were called. These had been recognised by General Otis before General MacArthur had arrived and many of them have always been prominently associated with the American government in the Islands. Among others were Chief Justice Arellano, Mr.

Benito Legarda and Mr. Pardo de Tavera. The Commissioners talked about the situation with these gentlemen, through Mr. Arthur Fergusson, the Spanish Secretary of the Commission, and found them not altogether despondent, but certainly not optimistic about the outcome. They thought the Commissioners were facing very grave problems indeed, if not insurmountable difficulties.

The next day—"just when the sun got the hottest," wrote Mr. Taft— all the launches in the harbour gathered around the *Hancock,* many whistles blew, many flags and pennants fluttered, and the Commission was escorted to the shore. They entered the city with great pomp and circumstance, through files of artillerymen reaching all the way from the landing at the mouth of the Pasig River, up a long driveway, across a wide moat, through an old gateway in the city wall and up to the Palace of the Ayuntamiento where General MacArthur, the Military Governor, had his offices. But it was not a joyous welcome for all that. All the show was merely perfunctory; a sort of system that had to be observed. Their reception was so cool that Mr. Taft said he almost stopped perspiring. There were few Filipinos to be seen, and as General MacArthur's reception to the Commission was anything but cordial or enthusiastic they began to feel a discomforting sense of being decidedly not wanted.

If they had any doubts on this point General MacArthur soon cleared them up. He frankly assured them that he regarded nothing that had ever happened in his whole career as casting so much reflection on his position and his ability as their appointment under the direction of the President. They suggested that he could still rejoice in considerable honour and prestige as a man at the head of a division of more troops than any general had commanded since the Civil War and that he was, moreover, still enjoying the great power of Chief Executive of the Islands.

"Yes," said he, "that would be all right if I hadn't been exercising so much more power than that before you came."

Whereupon Mr. Taft gently reminded him that he had been exercising that power for about three weeks only and said he hoped he had not become, in that time, so habituated to the situation as to prevent his appreciating the rather exalted position in which he would still be left. They afterward exchanged some correspondence as to what powers each did have, but they seemed to have disagreed from the first.

General MacArthur succeeded General Otis in command of the United States Army in the Philippines and he had fallen heir to a policy with which he was entirely out of sympathy. General Otis had scattered the troops in small divisions and detachments all over the Islands, and General MacArthur found himself in command of about seventy thousand men, but with only a few regiments where he could lay his hands on them for action in his own immediate vicinity. He believed that the only way to get rid of the predatory bands and bring order out of a chaotic state, was to concentrate the army on the island of Luzon where most of the active *insurrectos* operated. And he thought it would be many years before the Filipinos would be ready for anything but the strictest military government. But the trouble was that thousands of Filipinos all over the Islands had already sworn fealty to the United States, or had gone quietly back to work, and it was known that the lives of many of these would not be worth a moment's purchase if the protection of the American troops was withdrawn from them. That was the situation.

The last engagement between real insurgents and American troops had taken place in February before the Commission arrived. There had been men of some ability and real patriotism in Aguinaldo's cabinet and among his followers at Malolos, but by this time the best of them had come in and taken the oath of allegiance to the United States, others were in prison slowly making up their minds as to whether they would or would not follow this course, while still others had gone over to Hongkong to join in the activities of the "junta." Aguinaldo was still roaming around the mountain fastnesses of Luzon, posing as a dictator and issuing regular instructions to his lieutenants for the annihilation of American regiments; but the insurrection had degenerated.

The companies of men who still kept the field did so, for the most part, because they found that the easiest way to make a living. Money was getting scarce and the people were steadily refusing to contribute to the cause. A letter from one of Aguinaldo's lieutenants was intercepted in which he said that he had found a certain town obdurate and that he thought it would be necessary to take four or five lives before the people could be induced to give money. Murder and rapine, torture and robbery; these were the methods employed, and very little of the money realised ever found its way into the general revolutionary coffers. Most of the remaining "patriots" had become *ladrones* and were harrying their own people much more than they were opposing the American forces.

These conditions led the Commission to think the time had come to organise a native constabulary, under American officers, with which thoroughly to police the Islands. But General MacArthur did not agree with them; thought it would be folly to trust any Filipino with arms and cited instances of where those who had been armed as scouts had proved entirely untrustworthy. But the suggestion was received by many of his own officers with the utmost approval and one man, in the Ilocos country in northern Luzon, said he had only to issue a call and he could have five thousand as loyal men as ever wore uniform enlisted in twenty-four hours. I may say here that the Filipino people are divided into a number of distinct tribes and that some of these never did take much, if any, part in the insurrection. The insurrection is to-day referred to as the Tagalog rebellion, the Tagalogs being one of the principal tribes, though not the largest.

There had always been a great number, a majority in fact, of Filipinos who did not like the awful conditions created by the insurrection and who easily could be persuaded to an attitude of loyalty toward any decent and peaceful government; and it was from this number that the Commission wanted to recruit a native constabulary. But no. The Commission would not begin to exercise such powers as it had until September and in the meantime General MacArthur was absolute and in answer to this proposition he merely reiterated his belief that the only way to meet the situation was with additional American troops.

In my husband's earliest letters he characterised the Filipino people much as he did after years of experience with them. He wrote me that of the six or seven millions of Christian Filipinos about two per cent were fairly well educated, while all the rest were ignorant, quiet, polite people, ordinarily inoffensive and light-hearted, of an artistic temperament, easily subject to immoral influences, quite superstitious and inclined, under the direction of others, to great cruelty. He thought them quite capable of becoming educated and that they could be trained to self-government. He was inclined to think that they had, because of their environment and experience under Spanish rule, capacity for duplicity, but he did not think they had the Machiavellian natures which people attributed to them. Some of those who call themselves *"illustrados"—the* higher class— took to political intrigue with great gusto.

Almost the first experience which the Commission had with Filipino Machiavellian methods involved them in a complication which might have proved quite serious. If there is one thing in the world that the Filipino people, as one man, love, it is a *fiesta*. A *fiesta* is a holiday, a celebration with music, marching, many flags, best clothes and plenty of high-flown speechmaking. Now there was one Pedro A. Paterno, an unctuous gentleman, who, while he had taken the oath of allegiance and had fairly put himself in the pocket of American authority, was still supposed to be more or less in sympathy with Aguinaldo. He made himself the mediator between General MacArthur and Aguinaldo and occasionally promised Aguinaldo's surrender. Nobody ever knew what he promised Aguinaldo, but it was known to a certainty that he was "carrying water on both shoulders" and doing his best to keep in well with both sides. He had played the same role in Spanish times. He made what is known in history as "The Peace of Biacnabato," between the *insurrectos* and the Spanish government, by the simple means of "interpreting" to each the demands of the other in perfectly satisfactory terms. He did all the translating, on both sides, himself and the "Peace" was signed. Then before its irregularities were made clear he asked of the Spanish government, as his reward, a dukedom and a million dollars upon which to live up to the title. His letter to the Spanish governor is still extant.

This gentleman one day, out of a clear sky, proposed what he called an Amnesty Fiesta; a grand banquet in honour of General

MacArthur to follow a day of celebration and all-round relaxation from the strain of hostilities. General MacArthur didn't see that it would do any harm, but said he would not attend the banquet in his honour and that all the speeches that were to be made would have to be carefully censored. To this Pedro readily agreed and went immediately to work to make elaborate preparations for the occasion. He got a committee together and sent them to wait on the Commission with an invitation to the banquet. Only three of the Commissioners were in town, but these, after making careful inquiry as to the nature of the entertainment and discovering that no incendiary speech-making was to be allowed, decided to accept the invitation. Paterno was in high feather and nothing but the *fiesta* and the *banquete* was talked about for days. But gradually information began to reach the ears of Mr. Taft that all was not as it should be. He learned that arches were being erected across certain streets bearing inscriptions that were insulting to the American flag. One arch, in front of Malacafian Palace, where General MacArthur lived, had a picture of President McKinley on one side and a picture of Aguinaldo on the other, and it was said that General MacArthur had ridden under this arch without noticing it. That would be taken for sanction by an ignorant Filipino. But as soon as notice was called to them all the objectionable features of the arches were removed and preparations went on. But rumours kept coming in about the speeches until Mr. Taft became curious. He went to General MacArthur and asked who was doing the censoring.

"Why, Pedro Patemo," said the General; as much as to say, "What more could you ask?"

Mr. Taft went back to the office and straightway set about to get copies of those speeches. And, he got them. Some of them were already in type at a local newspaper office and were to be printed in full the next morning. This was the day of the *fiesta* and it was proving a very quiet affair. There was little enthusiasm on the streets, but there was plenty of interest in the coming *banquete*. The Commissioners looked over all the speeches and found them, without exception, seditious in the extreme. So, of course, they could not go to the banquet. They could not sit by and listen to misrepresentations without getting up immediately and making vigorous denial and protest and they could not lend the sanction of their presence to an entertainment that had been so arranged. The *banquete* was in General MacArthur's honour and the speeches glowingly promised everything short of immediate evacuation and complete independence.

The Commissioners wrote a polite little note to Senor Paterno and said they were very sorry to find that it was not possible, under the circumstances, for them to be present that evening.

Mr. Taft and General Wright were living together in the house that my husband had secured for us, and they went home and had a comfortable dinner in their everyday white linens and were enjoying post-prandial talk on the cool verandah when Pedro Paterno came rushing in and, figuratively, threw himself on his knees before them. He begged them to come with him to the *banquete;* the crowd had assembled; it was past nine o'clock; and he would be placed in a terrible situation if the gentlemen of the Commission did not reconsider their cruel decision. The gentlemen of the Commission asked how about the carefully censored speeches. Paterno vowed that no speeches at all should be delivered, that no word of any kind should be said, but that they must show themselves to the people, if only for a little while. All right. They quickly got into their hot evening clothes and went down to the banquet hall. They sat through a couple of silent, weary hours, took a few sips of wine, smiled a few smiles, shook a few hands, and then went home. That was all there was to it. But Pedro was discredited in both camps. His purpose had been to have the speeches made before the Commissioners, claim all the credit with his own people for getting the Commissioners there and then to deny to the Commissioners all responsibility for the occasion.

The forms of military government were being strictly observed; there was a nine o'clock curfew and nobody was allowed on the street after that hour without a pass. Mr. Taft wrote of several trying experiences when he went out in the evening and forgot his pass and, starting home about half past ten, was held up by one sentry after another who demanded an explanation at the point of a gun.

Mr. Bryan was running for President at this time and he was making a good deal of political capital out of the Philippine situation. He had promised to call a special session of Congress, if he were elected, to consider means for settling the Filipinos in immediate self-government, and he had a large following of mistakenly altruistic anti-imperialists supporting him. Mr. Taft was inclined to think that the whole anti-American demonstration, which was to culminate in the Amnesty Fiesta banquet, was planned by a Mr. Pratt, an American politician then visiting Manila, who wanted the "grandly patriotic" speeches to publish in American newspapers. They probably would have been perfect material for the anti-imperialists to grow sentimental over.

In the meantime Mr. Bryan's promises and the possibility of his being placed in a position to redeem them, were retarding pacification. All that was needed to discourage the last of the insurrectos was Mr. McKinley's election, and the Presidential campaign of 1900 was probably not watched anywhere with more breathless interest than it was in the Philippine Islands.

Such were the lessons in letters that I got from my husband, and my imagination was fired. He had great projects in hand. The Commission proposed to establish municipal governments wherever conditions made it possible and among the fitst things they undertook was the framing of a municipal code upon which to base such governments. They sent this to General MacArthur for his comments, but his comments consisted in a rather pointed intimation that military rule was still in force and that he thought they were several years ahead of possibilities, but that they might go on and amuse themselves since their municipal code would not deter him in any action he found it necessary to take at any point where it was in operation. All this was couched in most excellent diplomatic language, of course, but it amounted to just that. An equally diplomatic reply seems to have brought the General to a realisation that the powers of the Commission were well defined, that their object was peaceful pacification wherever it was possible and that they would probably be supported by Washington in any reasonable measures they might take to that end.

They had many plans already; a big general school system for the organisation of which they had engaged a superintendent from Massachusetts; good roads to open up the country for commerce; harbour improvements; health measures; a reliable judiciary; a mountain resort where American soldiers and civilians might recuperate from tropic disease, thereby saving many lives to say nothing of millions of dollars to the government in troop transportation charges; and they were already attacking the vexed friar question that had caused all the trouble in the first place.

The letters made me anxious to finish my visit in Japan and get down to Manila where so much of vital and engrossing interest was going on. My husband wrote rather discouragingly about the house he had taken, but he was having some improvements made and, though I did not expect to find comfort, I was sure I should manage to get along. I had purchased in Japan a number of bright and artistic objects in the way of house decorations and I thought that, with these, I should be able to make almost any place look inviting.

The Boxer rebellion was troubling us more than anything else at the moment. We wanted very much to go to Shanghai, but were told that it would be absolutely unsafe for us to go anywhere in China except to Hongkong.

I didn't know much about the East at that time and was ready to believe anything that was told me. However, I remembered that there were thousands of foreign residents in Shanghai who were going on about their daily affairs much as if there were no such thing as a Boxer. So we, too, decided to go on our usual tranquil way and we set sail for Manila, via Shanghai and Hongkong, on the Japanese steamer, *Kasuga Maru,* on the tenth day of August.

FIRST IMPRESSIONS OF MANILA

THE China Sea has an evil reputation. On its shores one hears much about the typhoon season and the changing monsoons, and bad sailors would, no doubt, like to have their sailing dates determined by the Weather Bureau; but this is not always possible.

The *Kasuga Maru,* on which we made the voyage from Yokohama to Manila, lay in Hongkong Harbour while one of the great mid-August storms tore up from the south and set skippers and seamen agog with fears of dreadful conditions we would have to meet on the trip across to Manila. In the China Sea there are cross-currents which make for bad going at the best of times, and when they are piled up by a typhoon into great, warring waves the result is likely to be extraordinary.

My husband cabled me to take a larger vessel, a United States army transport which left Hongkong about the same time we did, but I was comfortably located with my family on the little *Kasuga Manz;* the transfer of baggage was a troublesome task; and I figured that as long as the *Kasuga Maru* had been afloat in south seas for a good many years, she might be trusted to keep afloat for a few days longer.

We caught the calm between two storms. The sea had been beaten down by torrential rains; and while great, smooth waves rose under us and sent us rolling in a sickening zigzag all the way across, there was in them no threat of destruction, and I really began to feel that the China Sea had been maligned.

A feeling of intense curiosity got me out of my stateroom bright and early on the morning of our arrival in Manila.

To the northward lay a stretch of unbroken, mountainous shoreline; while we were headed for a narrow channel guarded by rock islands against which the surf broke in clouds of spray.

"Corregidor," said the skipper, pointing to a high, green hill behind the rocks. Corregidor,—it was the first time I had ever heard the name which since has become synonymous, in so many minds, with Gibraltar. On the other side of the entrance to Manila Bay stood

Meriveles, a beautiful mountain, sloping gently back from the sea and up into soft, white clouds. But Manila,—where was Manila? Cavite,—where was. Cavite? And where did the Spanish ships lie, when Dewey sailed in past Corregidor not knowing what he would find? Questions, these, which everybody asked in those days. Manila was twenty miles ahead at the far end of the Bay, while Cavite, across on the south shore, in the nearer distance, lay flat and almost invisible under low-spreading trees.

Flat; that is the word which occurs to everybody who sails for the first time into Manila Bay. The city is built on the low-lands; low, as I afterward learned, to the point of being below sea-level in certain places, and subject to sudden floods in the big typhoons. But far behind the flats are towering ranges of blue and purple hills, with here and there a softly rounded mountain standing, seemingly, alone.

The hot sun beat down on the glassy surface of the Bay and sent back a blinding glare which brought an ache into eyes and nerves, but we were all too interested to seek shelter in the darkened cabin.

While our ship was still miles from shore we could see long lines of low, red roofs and the white gleam of many domes and spires; and off to the right we had pointed out to us the eloquent wrecks of some of the Spanish fleet whose masts and battered hulks rose high out of the shallow water in which they were sunk.

But for ourselves, for me, for Mrs. Wright, for and the children, the most important thing in sight was a little fleet of harbour launches which came hurrying down the Bay to meet us. I saw my husband and General Wright standing in the bow of one of these long before they could pick us out in the crowd of passengers lining the rails of the *Kasuga Maru*.

Then came the happy welcomings which make absences worth while; excited children; everybody talking at once; explanations begun and never finished; interruptions by customs officials— American soldiers in those days; comments on the heat and the bright white light, and laughing assurances that it wasn't hot at all and that the climate was perfect; transferring baggage to the launch;

glimpsing, occasionally, strange scenes and strange peoples; asking and answering a thousand questions; busy, bustling, delightfully confusing hours of landing in the farthest orient.

Our husbands turned themselves into willing "Baedekers" and instructed us on the way. We steamed up in our little launch to the mouth of the Pasig River, wide and deep and swift, and covered with what looked to me like millions of small, green cabbages.

"Carabao lettuce; the river's full of it," explained Mr. Taft, but I was much too occupied just then to stop and ask what "carabao lettuce" might be.

We came up past a bristling fort at the corner of a great, grey, many-bastioned and mediaeval wall which stretched as far as I could see down the bay shore on one side and up the river on the other.

"The Old Walled City," said General Wright, and I knew at once that I should love the old Walled City.

"The oldest parts of the walls were built in the seventeenth century," continued our animated guide-book, "and the fort on the corner is Santiago. The big dome is the Cathedral and all the red tile roofs are convents and monasteries. The twentieth century hasn't reached here yet.

To all intents and purposes the Walled City is still in the Middle Ages." The truth is that only part of the walls are really very old—some parts have been built within seventy years.

The river was full of strange craft; long, high-prowed, cumbersome looking boats, with rounded deck-houses roofed with straw matting and painted in every conceivable colour and pattern, which, we were told, were *cascoes—cargo* boats which ply the length of the Pasig and bring down the cocoanuts and sugar-cane and other products from the middle provinces. The only visible propelling power on these *cascoes—and* the only power they have—are natives, naked to the waist, armed with long bamboo poles upon which, having fixed them firmly in the mud at the bottom of the river, they push steadily as they walk the length of the narrow running board along the outer edge of the deck. I should say they might make a mile in about two hours.

Then there were the curious little *bancas;* narrow canoes, hewn out of single logs and kept on an even keel, usually, by graceful outriggers of bamboo.

Across the river from the Walled City is the Custom House, and there, in a few moments, we drew up at a slippery, low, stone landing and climbed ashore. My feet, at last, were on Philippine soil.

If I had, for the time being, forgotten that a war was going on I was immediately reminded of it. The Custom House was in the hands of the Military Government and it was surrounded by khaki-clad guards who all stood stiffly at attention as my husband and General Wright passed. All our necessary luggage had been released and put into the hands of orderlies to be delivered, so we were free to start at once for home.

My husband had written me that the Philippine horses and the Philippine cockroaches were just about the same size, but I was hardly prepared for the diminutive turnout to which he proudly escorted me. Two little brown ponies, no higher than my shoulder, and with very shaggy manes and foretops, were hitched to a Victoria which had been built to fit them. When I stepped in and sat down, with Charlie on my lap, I felt twice my natural size and it seemed impossible to me that there was still ample room for Mr. Taft.

On the box were two stolid little men, dignified by the titles of coachman and footman. They each wore white linen trousers and thin shirts which hung outside, making them look as if they had forgotten a most important act in the process of dressing. Their bare feet were thrust into heelless red carpet-slippers, while on their heads were wide, flopping, shapeless straw hats which they did not trouble to take off at our approach.

The streets were full of such conveyances as ours, and others of varieties even more astonishing. Maria, with Robert and Helen, followed in a *quilez—a* miniature, one-horse omnibus affair into which the passengers climbed from the rear. Then there were *calesas, caromatas, carretelas* and carabao carts.

88

The carabao carts interested me particularly, and there seemed to be more of them than of anything else. The cart itself was nothing,— just a few planks nailed together and balanced upon a pair of heavy, broad, wooden wheels, —but the beast attached to it was really extraordinary. The first carabao I saw had horns at least six feet across. Indeed, they all have very long horns, and how they keep from obstructing traffic in the narrow streets I never did understand. They do obstruct traffic, as matter of fact, but not with their horns; only with their slow motions. Nobody can possibly know just what the word slow signifies until he has seen a carabao move. Great, grey, thick-skinned, hairless beast; his hide is always caked with mud, and he chews and walks at exactly the same pace while the half-naked, sleepy driver on the cart behind him gives an occasional jerk on the thin rope attached to the ring in his nose.

It was sometime before I came to know *calesas, caromatas* and *carretelas* apart, though their only likeness lies in the fact that each has two wheels and to each is attached one busy little bit of a horse. The *calesa* and *caromata* are the better class vehicles, while the *carretela* is a plebeian public carryall in which there always seems to be "room for one more." I saw dozens of these packed with Filipinos; the driver—always and inevitably smoking—sitting close up behind his horse and lashing it continually while it struggled sturdily along and looked every minute as if it would be lifted off its feet by the overbalancing weight behind it. It was something of a shock to see many women, in *carretelas* and on the street, smoking huge black cigars; while I noticed, immediately, that the men, as a rule, smoke only cigarettes.

I didn't look for speed from our little brown creatures, but I was yet to become acquainted with the Philippine pony. We started off over the rough cobblestones at a pace that was truly terrifying, and everybody else seemed to be going at about the same rate. I expected a collision every moment. Wheels passed wheels without an inch to spare, and without an instant's slackening of speed. My heart was in my mouth until we got through the maze of narrow streets in the wholesale district near the Custom House and came out into a wide plaza which my husband informed me was the end of the Escolta, the principal business street of the city. I was very glad we didn't have to drive through that; it was just about wide enough for two carriages to pass, but it had a street-car track right down the middle, and it was thronged. On the track was a jingling little horse-car which seemed to get very much tangled up with the rest of the traffic.

I got an impression of a great variety of colour in which red and yellow seemed to predominate. The soldiers were in khaki, the officers and civilians were in immaculate white linen, while the Filipino men and women of the ordinary class looked as if they had made a heavy draft on the world's supply of red and yellow muslin, to say nothing of many calicoes of extravagant hues and patterns.

We hurried on around the corner and came again to the banks of the river and the Bridge of Spain. Mr. Taft wanted me to know all about everything right away, so he kept on busily explaining things to me, but using so many unfamiliar words that I got only a hazy impression after all.

But here was the Bridge of Spain, originally built in sixteen hundred and something, the oldest monument to Spanish enterprise in the Islands. And across on the other side we came abreast of the inner wall of the city and whirled along awhile beside a wide, stagnant moat. From the inner side I got a better idea of what the Walled City was like, and I promised myself an early inspection of its mysteries. I wanted to walk across the old drawbridges and through the beautiful gateways which looked so ancient and were so suggestive of piratical and warlike history.

"Those are the Botanical Gardens," said Mr. Taft—"the man from Cook's"—making a general sort of gesture toward the other side of the street. What I saw was a small gravelled park with some avenues of fine palms, some other kinds of trees, and a few clumps of shrubbery. We were driving under the low-hanging branches of some magnificent old acacias, but everything looked neglected and run down, and there didn't seem to be a bit of grass anywhere; just scorching sand and clay. It was really a relief to rest one's eyes on the awful green scum on the surface of the moat. Manila in those days was not the beautiful, park-like, well-kept city that it has since become. There were soldiers everywhere, and it seemed to me we were being constantly saluted.

"And now we come to the far-famed Luneta," said Mr. Taft, quite proudly.

"Where?" I asked. I had heard much of the Luneta and expected it to be a beautiful spot.

"Why, here. You're on it now," he replied.

An oval drive, with a bandstand inside at either end,—not unlike a half-mile race track,—in an open space on the bay shore; glaringly open. Not a tree; not a sprig of anything except a few patches of unhappy looking grass. There were a few dusty benches around the bandstands, nothing else;—and all burning in the white glare of the noonday sun.

"Why far-famed?" I asked.

Then he explained in a way which made me understand that the Luneta is not what it is, but rather what it stands for in the life of the community. He said that in the cool of the evening there were bands in the bandstands and that everybody in the world came and drove around and around the oval, exchanging greetings and gossip, while the children with their nurses played in the sand on the narrow beach. It didn't sound exciting to me, but I was afterward to learn that the Luneta is a unique and very delightful institution.

We tore on at a terrific rate and came, at last, into a narrow residence street where the rapid clatter of our ponies' feet awoke echoes from closely set houses which looked as if all their inhabitants were asleep. And they were, of course, it being the *siesta* hour.

The houses were nearly all built in the Spanish style with high stone basements—covered with mouldy whitewash—and frame superstructures overhanging the street, and screened from the heat and glare with finely woven, green bamboo curtains. Here and there the "nipa shack" of the low class native had elbowed its way into this fashionable neighbourhood, and through open spaces I caught glimpses of wide stretches of thatch roofs in the near distance, where hundreds of these inflammable huts were huddled together in "native quarters."

When the end of the street came in sight I began to wonder. It seemed to me we had driven many miles.

"Well, where do we live?" I asked. "Have you taken a house in the country?"

"Not quite," said Mr. Taft, "but nearly."

It was the last house in the street, surrounded by a very formidable looking, high stone wall. The first thing I knew we had whirled through a gateway and were driving past a row of soldiers who stood at attention, with their guns held stiffly in front of them. I knew our house had to be guarded, but it was something of a shock for a moment, just the same, to see the guardhouse and the trim soldiers with their business-like equipment.

If I had expected anything very fine or beautiful in the way of a tropical garden, I was disappointed. I don't know whether I did or not. The wonder to me now is how Americans ever did succeed in getting parks and gardens made. It only means that the Filipino has learned, or is learning how to work. He always was willing to work, a certain amount, but he didn't know how. My husband's description of how he got a bit of grading done is typical. The first conclusion he reached in Manila was that the people knew nothing about the value of time, and it must have been a strain on his temperate-zone nervous system to watch a squad of men at work in his garden.

They deposited the material—as usual—as far as they could from the spot where it was to be used; then, one after another, barelegged, bare bodied, incessantly smoking, they would take up small shovels full of earth, carry them all the way across the garden, resting once or twice on the way, dump the material somewhere in the vicinity of the place where it belonged, then drag slowly back and repeat the operation. This was the sort of thing which made Americans, in the early days, dance with impatience; the sort of thing which made Mr. Bryan's campaign talk about "cheap" Filipino labour invading the United States seem to us so utterly ridiculous. We knew that Filipino labour was the most expensive labour in the world; since it took ten men to do one American's work.

My husband had written me about the difficulty he had had in securing a suitable house, and had also explained that he was having a number of repairs and changes made which, he hoped, would put the place in good order by the time I arrived. The garden was large, but it boasted neither lawns nor flowers of any kind. A few patches of grass struggling with the hard white gravel and clay, and looking pretty hopeless, nothing else. Around a curving drive we swung up under a porte-cochere, over which hung a magnificent rubber tree, and, stepping from the undersized Victoria onto the finest of white marble steps, I found myself at home.

Our house was really the best that my husband could secure. When he first looked at it he was certain it wouldn't do at all. It belonged to Chief Justice Arellano, and the army officer who went with him to look for quarters assured him that it was the only thing in town that he could possibly live in; but he didn't believe it. It had been occupied by army officers and had been greatly abused. Its furniture was broken and piled in heaps; its walls were ragged; and its floors were scarred and dirty.

"I'll just have a look at some others," said Mr. Taft. And he did. He went all over town, and he says every house he looked at added some new, desirable aspect to the Arellano house, until, finally, it became in his eyes a sort of palace which needed only a touch here and there to make it quite perfect.

It backed directly on the Bay, and among the first things he did was to have a sea-wall built which he thought added safety to the top-heavy structure, but which, during the typhoon season, really cost him more than it was worth. Every time a big wind came and roughed up the Bay a little, a part of his wall went out. His first complaint to me was that he had been "holding that wall down" all summer, and that part of it was always sure to try to get away every time he found himself particularly occupied with harassing governmental difficulties.

He had had sod laid down between the house and the sea-wall, and had watched it for awhile with a faith which should have been rewarded, but the salt spray came dashing over it and he had to have it carefully taken up and moved around to the sheltered side of the house. Good sod was scarce in Manila in those days.

My husband was certainly glad to see me, and I don't doubt that General Wright was just as glad to see his wife. The two of them had been "keeping house" together for three months under conditions wholly new to them, and I gathered that they found a bachelor existence rather complicated and, in certain details, annoying. In some ways, after the manner of men, they had permitted the house to run itself and I did not find it easy to break up the system which had been inaugurated.

The house was not perfect, by any means, but it was big and roomy and had what a woman knows as "great possibilities"; possibilities which I found had to be slowly developed with the assistance of a somewhat taciturn and not altogether willing *menage*.

Coming in from the grand marble steps one passed up a short, but spacious hardwood stairway into a wide central hall which opened out on a tile floored verandah, overlooking the Bay and running the entire width of the house. This verandah was enclosed by sliding windows divided into panes about six inches square, not any two of which were the same colour. All the other windows in the house were made of beautiful, translucent pearl-shell in four inch sections—more like screens than windows—which let in the light and kept out the glare, but on the verandah the architect had tried to surpass himself, with the result that royal purple, orange, pink, bright blue and green glass disclosed to one a multi-coloured and distracting stretch of otherwise beautiful bay. The hard white light was a thousand times more bearable than such a kaleidoscope, and after I got home those windows were seldom closed.

On either side of the broad central hall were two large rooms; one the dining-room, the others commodious bedrooms; while over the porte-cochere was a small drawing-room. Downstairs were the baths and three large rooms and a duplicate of the upstairs verandah. This part of the house, which was dry and well-built, I forthwith turned over to the children.

Some of the furniture was very fine; big hardwood tables and old Spanish pieces made from the beautiful woods of the Islands, but everything was greatly in need of the polisher's brush and chamois. The floors, alternating, broad, hand hewn planks of *nara* and *ipil,* were as fine as any I ever saw, though they, too, needed long and painstaking attention. In the bedrooms were high canopied and mosquito-netted beds with cane bottoms, exactly like cane-bottomed chairs, and without mattresses. Everything else was wicker.

The thing which caught my attention first, however, were the fans. My husband had written me, with great pride and satisfaction, that he had put in electric fans, and they had "saved his life." I had some sentimental attachment for them on this account—until I saw them. But when I saw them I felt at once that everything else, to be in keeping, ought surely to be swathed in fly-specked pink gauze. The electric fans were of the variety associated in one's mind with ice-cream "parlours"; two broad blades attached to the ceiling in the middle of the room. They had been installed in both the dining-room and *sala—or* sitting-room—and it was not possible in either room to see anything else. These fans were the subject of endless contention between Mr. Taft and me, but I gave in and left them to continue their mission of saving his life. He says yet that I often acknowledged on hot nights that he was right about them, but I never did.

My husband had secured his house staff in Hongkong, through the kind offices of Admiral Dewey's servant, Ah Man, as I have already written, but being new to the ways of the Oriental, he was destined very quickly to gather some unique experience. There were four of them: the cook, the number one boy, the number two boy and the laundryman. The laundryman was Mr. Taft's own inspiration. The Filipino laundryman, he had heard, takes the linen of his master's household down to some stream, preferably the shallows of the Pasig, and hammers it into ribbons on smooth rocks which he uses for washboard purposes. Then he spreads the articles on the grass to dry, and the consequences were found, not infrequently, to be a bad outbreak on the master's skin of what is known as "adobe itch," a troublesome disease. So Mr. Taft had engaged a Chinese laundryman and had sent back to San Francisco for tubs and washboards and wringers and all the necessary paraphernalia, and had installed an up-to-date laundry in his own house, where the orders were to boil the clothes and hang them on a line. It worked perfectly, though it did take the Chinaman from the wilds of Shanghai time to learn the uses of the various modern implements.

In Manila the marketing is usually done by the cook, but in our household this duty was delegated to the number one boy. One day the cook and the number two boy came to Mr. Taft with the announcement that they could not remain in the house with number one boy; that number one boy was a thief; that he smoked opium all the time he was supposed to be marketing; and that he was a bad Chinaman generally. Mr. Taft had always given number one boy the money with which to pay the other boys' salaries and the cash market charges, so he said to the cook:

"Has number one always paid your wages?"

"Yes," said the cook, with an eloquent shrug of his shoulders, "just my wages and nothing more."

This meant, of course, that number one boy was committing the unforgivable sin of not dividing the "squeeze."

There is no use going into what "squeeze" means in the Orient. It may come partly out of the master's pocket and partly out of the pockets of the tradesmen; nobody knows. But the housekeeper soon learns that she gains nothing by trying to circumvent the system in doing the marketing herself. The "squeeze" works, no matter who does the buying, and it soon comes to be recognised as a legitimate part of household expenses. The only thing that one can do is to make a complaint when it becomes too heavy.

It seems to have been very heavy in my husband's establishment, and investigation proved to him that it was necessary to let number one go, so when I arrived there were just the two upstairs servants, the cook and number two, who had been promoted to the proud position of number one.

I went immediately to work to order my household as I always had been used to doing, and there's where I began to get my experience of the Oriental character. My cook was a wrinkled old Chinaman who looked as if he had concealed behind his beady little eyes a full knowledge of all the mysteries of the East, to say nothing of its vague philosophies and opium visions. He called me "Missy" and was most polite, but in all the essentials he was a graven image. He was an unusually good cook, though he did exactly as he pleased, and seemed to look upon my feeble efforts at the direction of affairs with a tolerant sort of indifference. He would listen to my instructions most respectfully, carefully repeat after me the nice menus I devised, say, "yes, Missy," then return to his kitchen and cook whatever suited his fancy.

It took me sometime to get used to this, but I came to value him highly, especially when I learned that he had, finely developed, one glorious characteristic of his kind. He could make something out of nothing. If Mr. Taft sent word at six o'clock, or even as late as seven, that he had invited four or five of his associates to dinner to continue a discussion begun earlier in the day, or for some other reason, I had only to tell Ah Sing that there would be seven or eight instead of three at dinner, and a perfect dinner would be served. Where he got his supplies with which to meet these sudden demands I never knew. I learned to accept the gifts of the gods without comment, which is the only thing to do in the East.

Ah Sing was particularly proud of his sweets. He loved to make puddings and pies with lavish decorations upon them, though none of the family cared much for such delicacies. One evening, shortly after my arrival, I was giving quite a formal dinner party; I had, as usual, given the cook a menu well thought out and, I believed, wholly appropriate to the occasion and the climate. For a sweet I had ordered an ice with some small cakes, and I was pleasantly surprised to see them duly served. But just as the party was about to rise from the table and go out on the verandah for coffee, in came Mr. Number One Boy with a ponderous, steaming bread-pudding, all covered with coloured ornaments, which he smilingly displayed for the benefit of the astonished party. It had to be served, of course, and I felt that my explanations regarding Ah Sing's eccentricities didn't make much of an impression.

Over none of the servants did I exercise the control I thought to be necessary, but this was due to the fact that for three months they had been obeying the master; the master had paid them their wages, and to the master they looked for all orders. It took me sometime to discover this, but when I did I began to handle household accounts without assistance.

It was about the end of the typhoon season and the predictions were that there would be no more heavy, storms. But it began to rain and blow one day with rather more force than I had ever seen before, and I was told that we were in the midst of a typhoon. "Oh, well," I thought, "if this is all I don't see why there is so much talk about it." It was just a very hard and very persistent storm. When I began to think it was about time for it to have blown itself out I was awakened one night by what seemed to me to be the bombardment of heavy artillery. My bed was shaking under me, the house was swaying, and the noise was terrifying. I jumped up with an instant idea of *insurrectos,* and a feeling that I must meet the situation on my feet; then I realised, at once, that it was the typhoon. It was as if all the winds that had blown for two days had gathered themselves together and were hurling themselves in one blast upon us. I reached for the electric switch, but there were no lights; I turned the button time and again; nothing happened. I fumbled for matches all over my room and could find none. My nerves were just at the crying out point when my door was thrown open and in rushed Maria, holding aloft a glimmering candle.

She was shaking with fright.

"Nellie," she exclaimed, "I just can't stand it any longer! Do let's find everything there is to light and call Will and sit out in the *sala.* Heaven only knows what's going to happen!"

We searched around and found some more candles; then I went to call my husband. He was sleeping as soundly as if nothing at all were happening. I shook him and called him and shook him again. I thought he never would wake up, but finally he did, and just then I heard the crash of a tree blowing down in the garden, while the floor seemed to heave under my feet.

"What's the matter?" asked my sleepy husband.

"Will, there's an awful storm. Please come out in the *sala* and sit with Maria and me."

"All right," he said, and slowly got himself into an all-enveloping dressing gown.

We huddled ourselves in chairs in the big hallway and sat listening. Rain always comes with the wind in typhoons and the dash of water against the windows and the sides of the house was deafening. But the noise was suddenly punctuated by a gentle snore. Mr. Taft had settled himself back in his chair and gone quietly to sleep. Maria's nerves were on edge; without a word she jumped up and shook her tired-out brother-in-law most vigorously, crying above the roar of the storm:

"Will Taft, what do you think we waked you up for? You can't go back to sleep. We want you to stay awake and comfort us!"

"All right, Maria," said he, with the utmost good nature; whereupon he sat up, changed his position to one more comfortable, and proceeded to lapse again into peaceful slumber.

The next morning Maria and I drove down through the town to see the effects of the typhoon. Three trees were uprooted in our own garden, and across the street a house was flattened out. Groups of Filipinos stood here and there talking and gesticulating in their usual manner, but nobody seemed unduly excited. We saw many houses unroofed, and once in a while we met a native with a piece of nipa or tin roofing balanced on his head, quietly carrying it back where it belonged.

We drove down through the Escolta and into the crowded Tondo district beyond, and there we suddenly found ourselves hub-deep in a flood. The below-the-sea-level quarters were under several feet of water, and we got a sudden revelation as to why all the nipa houses are built on such high and unsightly stilts. Crowds of Filipinos were paddling through the flood, most of them carrying some part of a house, or other belonging, and nearly all of them playing and splashing like pleased children. *Bancas—long* canoes from the river—were plying from house to house as if it were an everyday affair and conditions were quite normal.

I had heard a great deal about the severity of typhoons, but as I had passed a whole season in the East and had crossed the China Sea during the typhoon season without encountering one, I began rather to scoff at the general fear of them. But I never did after that; when anybody said typhoon I knew exactly what it meant. The water subsided rapidly and in a day or two Manila showed few signs of the fury which had passed, but for several days the Commission continued to receive reports of the damage done and the lives lost throughout the surrounding country. It was the worst and the last storm of that year.

When we arrived in Manila we found the social atmosphere somewhat peculiar. Members of our own party, who had crossed the Pacific on the *Hancock,* welcomed us at once with dinners and teas and other kinds of parties; also a number of Army ladies called without delay, and our circle broadened rapidly. But General MacArthur, who was the Military Governor and lived at Malacanan Palace, did not entertain anybody except a select military circle. He sent an aide with cards, of course, and he accepted our invitations to dinner, but that was all. Not that we minded, except that it made it rather awkward and added something to the "feeling" that all was not well between the Army and the new civil government.

The Commission had been for three months busily engaged in investigating conditions, as directed by the President, before they assumed any authority, and then they acted with no haste. We were impatiently awaiting news from America with regard to the Presidential election. It was thought to be futile to take any definite steps toward the establishment of local governments and the inauguration of far-reaching reforms until the status of American control should be settled. Mr. Bryan had promised political independence, and if Mr. Bryan were elected all the Commission's plans would go for naught.

The provincial and municipal codes were completed; certain important questions between the Church and the people were being considered, and many open sessions were held for discussion, with the purpose of advising the people that they would be listened to by a civil government. In the meantime the *insurrectos* were keeping things lively in a guerilla warfare with small squads of greatly harassed and very much disgusted American soldiers. There were occasional rumours about uprisings in Manila—when the guard at our gate would be doubled—but Mr. Taft assured us that Manila was as safe as New York or Chicago and we really had few fears.

General MacArthur continued to resent the coming of the Commission and to consider himself personally humiliated by their being appointed to divide his power. He was still in command of about seventy thousand men and the general executive control of a large civil force, but this, apparently, was not enough. The tone he adopted in his correspondence with the Commission kept them in a constant state of controlled anger. They were very careful in return to observe every courtesy and to manifest an earnest desire for harmony and co-operation. They were tremendously interested in their problems and wanted much to succeed, but their efforts at conciliation did little good. The General objected to almost every suggestion put forward by them and did not hesitate to tell them in plain words that he did not welcome advice from them concerning military or any other matters. It was really a very difficult situation.

The Commission thought General MacArthur took an entirely erroneous view of the attitude of the Philippine people in general, and that in everything he did he moved with an exasperating slowness. They wanted a large native constabulary which they knew could successfully be organised and relied upon to render great assistance in the pacification of the Islands. He did not agree with them and held the matter up for many months. He was not in sympathy with any move they made, and his greatest cross was that he had no power to veto their legislation. He saw military dangers in all manner of things without being able to state just what they were, and he was always calling for more troops, while the Commission was entertaining hopes that it would not be a great length of time before a large part of the troops already there could be recalled. I find my husband writing at this time:

"General MacArthur, knowing that we differ from him as to the condition of things in the Islands, makes it a point to send me an account of each disaster as if it vindicated his view. This is not the spirit of a man who is likely to succeed in giving energy to a campaign which will bring about successful results, but the matters will solve themselves in spite of his slowness of movement and lack of enthusiasm....

"The minute the policy with respect to these Islands is settled by Bryan's defeat and the election of McKinley, the leniency which has been almost too great towards *ladrones* and these murdering generals will have to be changed. They must be given an opportunity to come in and if they do not come in in a short time, they ought to be deported from the country and sent to Guam. This will have an effect so healthy that a short time will see accomplished what we desire. There will be a great awakening for some of these men who have come to rely on the supineness of the Americans, and who do not understand that we can be severe when we choose....

"It was General Otis who inaugurated the plan of laughing at the insurrection, of capturing men and letting them go, and the result is that they have laughed at us, but with a little tightening of the reins their laugh will cease....

"They dread deportation more than anything else and I have written to Secretary Root and asked him to have a prison constructed at Guam to which we may send those whom we think worthy of a less punishment than hanging. The insurrection must be suppressed for the benefit of the United States and, still more, for the benefit of the Filipino people. The lenient methods, having been tried for two years, must be changed to those more severe....

"The insurrection, such as it is now, is nothing more than a conspiracy against the sovereignty of the United States sustained by murder and assassination of Filipinos by Filipinos....

"MacArthur is drawing the reins a little tighter, though not as tight as we think he ought to draw them, and he has now imprisoned about fifteen hundred insurgents. There have been a great many arrests made in Manila, which has been the head centre of the insurrection in way of raising money. I should think there have been fifty or sixty insurgent officers arrested in the city....

"I sent a telegram to the Secretary of War on Sunday night which was signed by Buencamino and other prominent Filipinos, about a dozen of them, in which they spoke out with emphasis about the continuation of the insurrection. They propose to organise what they call a counter-revolution; that is, they mean they will organise a military movement among the Filipinos against Filipinos. They are getting very tired and weary of this murder and assassination policy without which the insurrection could not last a week....

"You could hardly believe the closeness with which the Presidential matters are being watched by the Filipinos, and how they follow the speeches made against the Republican cause. General Smith, away down on the island of Negros, told me he had found speeches by Hoar and Bryan, and other anti-expansionists and anti-imperialists, in the most remote mountains of his district....

"Every one is waiting and it is not impossible that should Bryan be elected there might be some riotous demonstration among the natives. The Chief Justice of the Supreme Court, Senor Arellano, has made arrangements, should Bryan be elected, to leave the islands three days after the announcement. He is the ablest Filipino in the islands, by far the best lawyer and a man of the highest probity. He says that much as he is interested in the success and prosperity of his fellow-citizens, he knows that they are utterly incapable of self-government and should the guiding hand of the United States be withdrawn, chaos, conscription and corruption would follow inevitably...."

I have taken these excerpts at random from my husband's letters to his brother during the months of September and October, 1900, and they serve to show the situation which existed and will illustrate the fact that we were living interesting times. But they deal only with the insurrection, while the main body of his correspondence shows that the Commissioners were engaged upon legislative matters of the gravest import which would be rendered entirely superfluous should Mr. Bryan be elected and his announced policies be carried into effect. In that event they proposed immediately to turn matters back to the military government and withdraw, leaving Mr. Bryan to face the problems which they knew he would soon discover had to be dealt with from the standpoint of constructive statesmanship.

In the meantime the peace movement was rapidly gaining adherents among the people in spite of the still active *insurrectos,* or rather, because of them and their methods; while everybody seemed to welcome the change from a strictly military to a partially civil government.

The popularity of the Commission, as offering a change from the strictness of military rule, was becoming every day more marked. Juan de Juan, a Spaniard, and editor of the lively organ *El Progreso,* which was always in opposition to anything American, said that on the first of September when the Commission began to exercise its authority, he intended to devote the whole front page of his paper to just three words: "Gracias a Dios,"—Thanks to God! Juan de Juan was a good deal of a Bohemian and really cared little what happened so long as he got a sensation out of it. September first came and went, and I don't remember whether he made good this extravagant threat or not. I presume he didn't for, though I had been in Manila less than a week, I surely would have remembered.

After the Commission had been in power for just a month, and while the excited interest in events in the United States was at its height, Juan de Juan broke out in a characteristic Spanish editorial, a translation of which has been preserved. We had entertained Juan de Juan at dinner, and he evidently was impressed. We made it a rule from the beginning that neither politics nor race should influence our hospitality in any way, and we came thus to have a very wide and diverse acquaintance. The editorial in *El Progreso* gives such a curious picture of attitude and conditions in general, as well as of my husband, my family and my home, that I think I must quote it,—at least in part. It is headed simply:

SEÑOR TAFT

The most uncompromising jingoes; the rabid partisans of militarism, as well as the men of democratic sentiments who consider the occupation of the Philippines as an odious Cæsarism, respect and venerate the President of the Civil Commission, whose surname serves as the caption of these lines. Uprightness and *bon-hommie* always demand recognition.

Before the *Hancock,* bearing this statesman, had anchored in Manila Bay, the echo of his reputation and the radiations of the brilliant aureole which his success in the judiciary of his country had *imposed* upon him—and we underline the word imposed because the characteristic trait of Mr. Taft is his modesty—had reached the Philippines. The Filipinos awaited him with the same pleasing curiosity with which a child opens a toy with a concealed surprise, and the foreigners as the incarnation of those American patriarchal, democratic ideas with which Castelar portrayed to his followers the country of Lincoln.

Behind that spacious brow of the thinker, between his liberal tendencies and the incomparable exactions of the enormous burdens which his country undertook in Paris, fierce struggles are waging. The President of the American Civil Commission has broad shoulders, but the weight of a people whom patriotism endows with the strength of a colossus is very great.

We must concede to all the leading authorities whom America has sent to the Philippines the trait of being industrious. We know that General Otis worked more than twelve hours a day; MacArthur, that Daban of the American Army through the rapidity of his advancement, follows the same course as his predecessor, and Mr. Taft leaves his house every morning at eight and, as unostentatiously as a clerk, proceeds to become a part of his chair in the Ayuntamiento. There his first occupation is glancing the American press, and what is of interest in the Spanish papers.

Then the show begins. Paterno, Macabulos, Montenegro, some envoy from Cebu, for example, who come to sound him, as the slang saying goes, arrive. Mr. Taft has the same respectful smile for all, the same courtesy, and addresses them all in the same terms, which his athletic Secretary, Mr. Fergusson, repeats in Spanish with the gravity of a Sphinx and the fidelity of a phonograph. When the matter warrants it, Mr. Pepperman, the chief stenographer of the Commission, enters the office and proceeds to take notes of the interview.

In this way the Americans are forming a luminous record which, united to what were our archives, which they preserve through the terms of the Treaty of Paris, will guide them well in the administration of the Philippines.

Later Mr. Taft becomes engulfed in the examination of the bills which the other members of the Commission present for him to study; he discusses their text with his colleagues, listens to all their observations, and judging them by a standard most favorable to the interests of the Philippines, the most liberal within the instructions from Washington—it is proper to say that Mr. Taft is the most democratic element of the Commission—he expresses his opinion, generous, calm and noble, which assuredly, in view of his personal prestige, must carry great weight in ,the framing of the bills, whose execution is entrusted to the Military governor.

To dissipate the gloomy smoke of the conflagration, to still the groans of those who fall in this immense *expoliarium* into which fatality has converted the Philippine fields, is the mission which the men composing the American Commission desire to bring to a successful issue. To make peace. For this they came, and if fortune does not reserve for them the happy chance of accomplishing so beautiful an ideal, they will retire, and the factor they represent in the problem to be solved, with its distinguishing traits of civil moderation, will be substituted as a system that has failed, by another, wherein the martial power will prevail over political wisdom.

As General MacArthur undoubtedly spends many hours over maps of the Philippines, Mr. Taft also often rests his gaze on a map covering one of the walls of his office, tracing, *in mente,* a railroad which, crossing the island, shall drown with the cheery whistle of the locomotive the moans of the victims of war. Thus would Mr. Taft like to pacify the Philippines.

It is now one o'clock P. M. and Mr. Taft is at home, where this personage stands out more boldly before us, since the trials through which the country is passing do not permit us yet to judge him politically.

The President of the Commission, in his private life, has many points of similarity with Count de Caspe, that stainless gentleman the Filipinos still recall with veneration. Excepting the brilliancy of those splendid entertainments with which he endeavoured to blot out all racial differences by mingling in fraternal embrace Filipinos and Spaniards at the Malacalian villa, there ordinarily reigned in the governor's mansion the placid silence of the home of a well-to-do retired merchant. The Countess, who on Thursdays did the honours of her *salon* with exquisite tact, was during the other days of the week a housekeeper who did not disdain to go to a grocery store to make purchases, or to look over the laundry list.

The same thing happens in the elegant *chalet* at Malate where Mr. Taft lives. This is a quiet and peaceful home, a temple erected to the affections, under whose roof Mr. Taft rests some hours after the efforts which his political work demands.

His table reflects his modest character. Four courses, two kinds of fruit, a dessert and sauterne compose the menu of the luncheon where Mr. Taft is always accompanied by some guest, either Filipino, American or Spanish. During the meal politics are banished; if the guest is a Filipino who speaks French Mrs. Taft interrogates him on the customs of the archipelago; if he is Spanish, as to the toilettes worn in Manila by the ladies at the most brilliant receptions held here; as to the favourite musical composer of the Hispano-Filipino society; and this conversation increases in attraction when Miss Herron, sister-in-law of Mr. Taft and the incarnation of the modern woman's education, takes part therein. Miss Herron speaks French correctly, has travelled much, and journeyed through Spain like an intelligent tourist. The architectural lace-work of the Alhambra charmed her, and she went into ecstasies over the orange blossoms growing along the banks of the Guadalquivir. With what Miss Herron was not in harmony, and she berates them like an unsubsidised journalist, were the Spanish railroads. Miss Herron is right.

The children, Robert, about eleven years old; Helen, a girl of nine, and Charles, a baby of three, who is the king of the household:—the McKinley, as it were, of this patriarchal republic—do not come to the table; they eat with the governess.

After the meal, in the fine gallery overlooking the sea, sipping the coffee, Mr. Taft talks of the education of his children, of the difficulties met in the Philippines in the solution of so interesting a problem; and his wife converses of the charitable work she expects to undertake when she shall have assumed a more permanent place in the Archipelago, which Magellan discovered for Spain, and which, through a horrible fatality, is no longer ours. Politics are also eschewed on the gallery.

Needless to say this extraordinary editorial afforded us all boundless amusement; we began to caution Mr. Taft frequently about the careful preservation of his "aureole" and Maria and I decided that we would have to walk warily indeed, if we were destined to be so minutely reported.

A STRANGE ENVIRONMENT

IN the Far East one meets certain expressions the significance of which may be described as adamantine. Each represents a racial attitude against which it is useless to contend. In Japan it is the equivalent of it cannot be helped; a verbal shrug of the shoulders with which the Japanese tosses off all minor and many grave annoyances. *"Masqui,"* down the China coast, has the same import, but with the added meaning of "what difference does it make." In the Philippines the phrase which must be met and which cannot be overcome by any system of reform is *"el costumbre del pais"*—the custom of the country.

If it is *el costumbre del pais* it has to be done and there is nothing more to be said about it. The *manaiia* habit—putting everything off until to-morrow—is, perhaps, to Americans, the most annoying of all the *costumbres del pais* in the Philippines, but it yields to pressure much more readily than do many others, among which is the custom of accumulating *parientes;* that is, giving shelter on a master's premises to every kind and degree of relative who has no other place to live. This is, I suppose, a survival of an old patriarchal arrangement whereby everybody with the remotest or vaguest claim upon a master of a household gathered upon that master's doorstep, so to speak, and camped there for life.

In my first encounter with this peculiarity of my environment I thought there was a large party going on in my *cochero's* quarters; and an indiscriminate sort of party it seemed to be. There were old men and old women, young men and young women, many small children and a few babes in arms. We had only Chinese servants in the house, but the stables were in charge of Filipinos and, as I soon discovered, the "party" was made up entirely of our stablemen's *parientes.*

I had a pair of ponies and a Victoria; Mr. Taft had his two little brown horses and a Victoria; besides which there was an extra horse to be used in case of accident to one of the others, as well as a pony and *calesa* for the children. This rather formidable array was necessary because we found it impossible to take a horse out more

109

than twice a day, and usually not more than once, on account of the sun. My ponies were taken out only in the early morning or the late evening, and those of Mr. Taft had all they could do to take him to the office and bring him home twice a day. Distances were long and there were no street-cars which ran where anybody wanted to go.

This number of conveyances made a good many stablemen necessary and all of them, with their families, lived in quarters attached to the stables. These families consisted of fathers, mothers, sisters, brothers, uncles, aunts, cousins near and far removed, wives, children, grandchildren, and a few intimate and needy friends with their family ramifications. Besides our three *cocheros* and the stable boys, there was a gardener with his *parientes,* so it is no wonder that on my first inspection of the lower premises I should have thought that some sort of festivity was in progress. I might have lived in Manila twenty years without being able to straighten out the relationships in this servant colony; it was not possible to learn who had and who had not a right to live on the place; and my protest was met with the simple statement that it was *el costumbre del pais,* so I, perforce, accepted the situation.

Filipino servants never live in the master's residence; they never want to; they want the freedom of a house of their own, and these houses are, as a rule, built on the outer edges of the garden, or compound. I believe Americans now are learning to meet the *pariente* habit by having room for as many people as they need, and no more. But those who live in the old places, with their ample quarters, still gather the clans and are permitted to enjoy a most expansive and patriarchal sensation.

My horses, when I first saw them, were a source of the greatest pride. A beautifully matched pair of coal-black, stylishly-paced and glossy little stallions, hardly larger than Shetland ponies, they looked as if they had been washed in some sort of shrinking soap and had come out in perfect condition except that they were several sizes smaller than they ought to have been. These Philippine ponies are doubtless descendants of the Arabian horses brought over by the Spaniards and have been reduced to their present size by the change of climate and the difference in food and environment, but they still have the fine lines and the general characteristics of their progenitors.

Mr. Taft secured mine from Batangas, where all the best ponies come from, through the kindness of Mr. Benito Legarda, the staunchest of *Americanistas*. Batangas was a most unquiet province, the last, in fact, to become pacified, and Mr. Legarda had to pay an *insurrecto* for bringing the horses through the insurgent lines and delivering them at Calamba, near Manila. Although he did not know their exact origin when he bought them, Mr. Taft said that if the facts became known he would be accused, in certain quarters, of giving indirect aid to the revolutionists; but he wanted the ponies so he did not return them.

When they were hitched to the shining little Victoria which had been built for them, they were as pretty as a picture and, as I did not propose to have such a turn-out ruined by a couple of Filipinos on the box in untidy *camisas* hanging outside of as untidy white trousers, I had made for my *cochero* and boy, or coachman and footman, a livery of white and green in which they took such inordinate pride that they seemed to grow in stature and dignity.

Maria and I felt a sense of the utmost satisfaction the first time we stepped into this carriage for a drive down to the Luneta where we were sure to see everybody we knew and hundreds of people besides; but our vanity was destined to be brought to a sudden termination.

As we were driving along with much satisfaction, a bit of paper floated down alongside the blinkers of the little ebony steed on the right and he made one wild leap into the air. His companion gave him an angry nip, and then the fight was on. Maria and I jumped out, which was not difficult in a low-built Victoria, and no sooner had we done so than we saw the complete wreck of all our grandeur. With all the leaping and plunging and biting and kicking, in the vicinity of a handy lamp-post, the smash-up was fairly complete. Neither of the ponies was hurt, except by the lash of the whip, and I must say the little wretches looked rather funny; like very pretty and very bad children, sorry for what they had done. But their characters were established and they proceeded after that to live up to them.

'We never could have any confidence in them and my coachman was the only person who could do anything with them. He was a most unsatisfactory man in many ways and used often to call for us at dinner parties in a state of gay inebriety, but we didn't dare discharge him because everybody else in the stables stood in awe of the blacks while he seemed greatly to enjoy his constant and spectacular struggles with them.

The Filipinos are a most temperate people; there is no such thing as drunkenness among them; but coachmen seem to be an exception in that they allow themselves a sufficient stimulation of the fiery *vino* to make them drive with courage and dash, sometimes minus all care and discretion. The drivers of public vehicles seem to love their little horses in a way; they are inordinately proud of a fast paced or stylish-looking pony; yet they are, as a rule, quite harsh them. They overload them and overdrive them, and under all conditions they lash them continuously.

No Filipino *cochero* likes to have another *cochero* pass him, and the result is constant, indiscriminate racing, on any kind of street, under any circumstances,—and never mind the horse.

My children were driving with their governess to the Luneta one evening, when two *caromatas* came tearing down behind them, each driver hurling imprecations at the other and paying no attention to what was ahead of him. The result was a violent collision. The two *caro-matas* went plunging on, the *coclzeros* not stopping to see what damage they might have done—which was very characteristic—and the children narrowly escaped a serious accident. Charlie was hurled out and fell under the children's *calesa* and Robert and Helen both declare they felt a sickening jolt as a wheel passed over him. The baby, too, vowed that the *calesa* "went wight over me, wight dere," indicating a vital spot; but upon the closest examination we could discover nothing more serious than a few bruises. However, it made us very much afraid to trust the children out alone.

The gardener had two little boys, Jose and Capito, who were a few years older than Charlie, but about his size, and he took a tremendous fancy to them. They were clad, simply, in thin gauze—or jusi—shirts which came down a little below their waists, and I think Charlie envied them this informal attire. He used to order them around in a strange mixture of Spanish, Tagalog and English which made me wonder at my wholly American child; but it was an effective combination since he seemed to have them completely under his thumb and, as he revelled in his sense of power, he never tired of playing with them.

Maria and I soon adopted the universal habit of driving down to the Escolta in the early morning to do such shopping as was necessary. We found a variety of interesting shops, but with very little in them to meet the ordinary demands of an American woman. There were delightful Indian bazaars and Chinese *tiendas* where all manner of gaudy fabrics and strange oriental articles were on sale, while the Spanish shops upon which everybody had to depend in those days, and which had such grandly European names as Paris-Manila and La Puerta del Sol, catered largely to the Filipino taste for bright colours.

The Escolta at that time was full of saloons, established by the inevitable followers of a large army, and the street being very narrow and the old, rickety, wooden buildings being very wide open, the "beery" odour which pervaded the atmosphere at all hours was really dreadful. Mr. Taft decided that as long as this was the only street in town where women could go shopping, the saloons would have to be removed. There was opposition on the Commission to the bill which provided for their banishment, and it was fought from the outside with great vigour and bitterness, but a majority were in favour of it, so it passed, and the saloons had to move. There has not been a saloon on the Escolta from that day to this and, indeed, they have ever since been under such satisfactory regulation that there is little evidence left of their existence in the city.

I am afraid it is going to be very difficult to convey an adequate picture of Manila society during the first years of American occupation. There had been, in the old days, a really fine Spanish and rich *mestizo* society, but all, or nearly all, of the Spaniards had left the Islands, and the *mestizos* had not yet decided just which way to "lean," or just how to meet the American control of the situation. I may say here that most of the educated, high-class Filipinos are *mestizo;* that is, of mixed blood. They may be Spanish mestizo or Chinese mestizo, but they have in them a strong strain of foreign blood. Besides the Spanish- Chinese-Filipinos, there are a number of British mestizos who are very interesting people. Mr. Legarda, Chief Justice Arellano, Dr. Pardo de Tavera and Mr. Quezon, the Filipino delegate to the United States Congress, are Spanish mestizos, while Mr. Arafieta, the Secretary of Finance and Justice, as well as the Speaker of the Philippine Assembly and many able lawyers and successful business men are of Chinese descent. The mestizos control practically all the wealth of the Philippines; and their education, intelligence and social standing are unquestioned. It is the only country in the world that I know about—certainly the only country in the Orient—where the man or woman of mixed blood seems to be regarded as superior to the pure blooded native.

Dating back also to the Spanish days was quite a numerous foreign society consisting of a few consuls, some professional men, the managers of banks and large British and European mercantile firms, and their families. The leaders of the British colony were Mr. and Mrs. Jones—Mr. Jones being the manager of the Manila branch of the Hongkong and Shanghai Banking Corporation. Mrs. Jones, a very beautiful and charming woman, gave some very elaborate parties during that first winter. Bank House, the residence maintained by the bank for its manager in Manila, is a beautiful place in Uli-Uli, a district on the picturesque banks of the upper Pasig, and it is finely adapted for balls and large receptions. Then there were several German families who also entertained quite lavishly, and I remember, especially, one Austrian exile; indeed, I shall never be able to forget him because my husband took such joy in pronouncing his name. He was Baron von Bosch.

This was the "set" which entertained the Commission most cordially during our first season in Manila, while the Army officers, following the lead of their Commanding General, held themselves somewhat aloof. I kept up a constant round of parties of different kinds in my house, and gave a dinner at least once a week at which were gathered companies of a most interestingly cosmopolitan character.

And we did not fail to observe all the desirable forms. Both Filipinos and Europeans expect a certain amount of ceremony from the representatives of government and are not at all impressed by "democratic simplicity"; so believing in the adage about Rome and the Romans, we did what we could. Beside the spic and span guard at the outer gate of the illuminated garden, we always, on dinner party nights, stationed coachmen, or other stable boys disguised as liveried footmen, on either side of the entrance, to receive guests and conduct them to the dressing-rooms, and up the stairs to the reception room.

Our house was nicely adapted for a dinner of twelve and I usually tried to confine myself to that number. We always had an orchestra, orchestras being very plentiful in Manila where nearly every native plays some sort of instrument, and the music added greatly to the festive air of things, which was enhanced, too, by a certain oriental atmosphere, with many Japanese lanterns and a profusion of potted plants and great, hanging, natural ferneries and orchids which were brought in from the forests by the Filipinos and sold on the streets.

My husband is supposed to be the author of the phrase: "our little brown brothers"—and perhaps he is. It did not meet the approval of the army, and the soldiers used to have a song which they sang with great gusto and frequency and which ended with the conciliating sentiment: "He may be a brother of William H. Taft, but he ain't no friend of mine!"

We insisted upon complete racial equality for the Filipinos, and from the beginning there were a great many of them among our callers and guests. Their manners models of real courtesy, and, while their customs are not always like ours, wherever they are able they manifest a great willingness to be conforme,—to adapt themselves,—and their hospitality is unbounded.

I shall never forget my first call from a Filipino family. They arrived shortly after six in the evening: el senor, la senora and four senoritas. We went through a solemn and ceremonious handshaking all around. I received them first, then passed them on to my husband who, in turn, passed them on with a genial introduction to my sister Maria. We had been sitting on the verandah, and when a

115

semi-circle of chairs had been arranged, the six of them sat down; el senor noisily cleared his throat a couple of times while the ladies calmly folded their little hands in their laps and assumed an air of great repose. It was as if they had no intention of taking any part whatever in the conversation.

El senor explained in Spanish that they were our near neighbours and that they had called merely to pay their respects. Mr. Taft had been studying Spanish diligently ever since he left the United States, but he is not conspicuously gifted as a linguist, and he had not yet waked up—as he so often expressed a wish that he might—to find himself a true Castilian. However, his ready laugh and the cordiality of his manners have always had a peculiar charm for the Filipinos, and he was able on this occasion, as he was on many future ones, to carry off the situation very well. We all nodded and smiled and said, "Si Senor" and "Si Senora," to long and no telling what kind of speeches from our guests; then Maria and I complimented the ladies on their beautifully embroidered *camisas,* which started things off properly. They praised everything in sight, and what we didn't get through the little Spanish we knew, we got from gesture and facial expression. They got up and wandered all around, feeling of my Japanese tapestries and embroideries, breathing long "ahs!" of admiration over my gold screens and pictures and curios, and acting generally like callers who were being very well entertained. Then the children came in and they broke out afresh in voluble praise of them. I assumed the proper deprecatory mien in response to their laudation of my children, and altogether I felt that we were acquitting ourselves rather well in this first inter-racial social experience.

But at the end of half an hour the strain was getting a little severe and I was wondering what to do next, when our six callers arose and said they must be going. I breathed an inward sigh of relief and was making ready to escort them to the top of the stairs, when my husband cordially exclaimed:

"Why, no! *Porque? Tenemos bastante tiempo.* Why hurry?" And— they—all—sat--down!

I regretted then even the little Spanish Mr. Taft had learned, though, of course, he didn't expect them to heed his polite protest. He knew nothing at all about Filipino manners; he didn't know they expected to receive some sign from him when it was time to go and that they would consider it discourteous to go while he was urging them to stay. He kept up, without much assistance, a brave if laboured conversation, and the minutes slowly passed. Our dinner hour approached and I darted warning glances at him, for I had a horrible fear that he just might ask them to remain and dine. But at the end of another hour a strained expression began to spread itself over even his face, and there was not a word of protest from him when, at a quarter past eight, our little brown neighbours once more indicated an intention of going home. We entertained Filipino callers nearly every day after that, but never again did we urge them to reconsider their sometimes tardy decision to depart.

With regard to Filipino manners and customs; I am reminded that we were nonplussed, though greatly amused by the *costumbré del pais* which decreed that some return be made by a Filipino for any and all favours bestowed upon him. We grew accustomed to this before we left the Islands, and came to expect a few offerings of sorts almost any day in the week, but in the beginning it was usually most embarrassing.

One time, soon after our arrival, a very loyal *Americanista* was shot down in the street, during the peaceful discharge of his duty, by an *insurrecto*. His widow, with her children, came into Manila in a state of utter destitution, to secure some recompense from the government for her husband's services, and while her case was pending Mr. Taft, in great pity for her, sent her money enough to live on. The next day the whole family, from, the wide-eyed boy to the babe carried astride the mother's hip, came to call on their benefactor, bringing with them as a gift a basket containing a few eggs, some strange Philippine fruits and a lot of sea-shells. Mr. Taft was deeply touched, and with the brusqueness of a man who is touched, he told her he had given her the money to buy food for herself and her children and not for him, and he refused her offering. I know, by the light of a fuller knowledge of the character of the lowly Filipino, that she went away feeling very much cast down.

But in connection with such gifts there were always more laughs than sighs. We invited to luncheon one day a dashing Filipino named Tomaso del Rosario. Senor Rosario, a man of wealth and prominence who had a fine Spanish education and was well dressed in the high-collared, patent-leathered and immaculate-linened Spanish style, was quite self-confident and enjoyed himself very much. He seemed attracted to Maria and she, being linguistic, was able to talk to him in a mixture of many languages. The next day she received from Senor Rosario, not a floral offering, but a basket filled with nuts, a canned plum-pudding, some canned chocolates and preserved fruits. This attention did not seem so remarkable, however, when we learned, to our amusement, that he had sent exactly the same present to Alice Worcester, then five years old.

Our life, on the whole, was intensely interesting in its unusual atmosphere and curious complications, but throughout everything we were made to feel the deep significance of our presence in the Islands; and the work of the Commission was first, last and always to us the subject of the greatest moment. Even in our daily round of social affairs we dealt with tremendous problems whose correct solution meant the restoration of peace and prosperity to what then should have been, and what we knew could be made, a great country. That for which the American flag had always stood began to assume, for many of us, a broader and a finer meaning; and being so much a part of our flag's mission in a strange field a certain zest was added to our patriotism which we had never felt before. I believe, and I think all those who know the truth believe, that Americanism, in its highest conception, has never been more finely demonstrated than in the work done by the United States in the Philippine Islands; work, the broad foundation for which the Commission was engaged in constructing during the period of which I write.

So many were the problems to be met and dealt with that in the beginning the Commissioners were each given a set of subjects for investigation and study, their findings being submitted for debate and consideration in the general meetings.

Taxation, civil service, provincial and municipal organisation, currency and finance, police, harbour improvements, roads and railways, customs, postal service, education, health, public lands, an honest judiciary and the revision of the code of laws; these were some of the vital problems, but underlying them all was the immediate necessity for the establishment of tranquillity and confidence throughout the archipelago.

In order to make clear, in any degree, the Philippine situation as we found it, it is essential that, briefly, the position of the Catholic Church and its representatives, the Friars, be explained. For the first time in its history the American government found itself compelled to adjust a seemingly insurmountable difficulty between a church and its people.

With us the Church is so completely separate from the State that it is difficult to imagine cases in which the policy of a church in the selection of its ministers, and the assignment of them to duty could be regarded as of political moment, or as a proper subject of comment in the report of a public officer, but in the first reports of the Philippine Commission to Washington this subject had to be introduced with emphasis.

The Spanish government of the Philippine Islands was a government by the Church through its monastic orders, nothing less. In the words of the Provincial of the Augustinians, the Friars were the "pedestal or foundation of the sovereignty of Spain" which being removed "the whole structure would topple over." The Philippine people, with the exception of the Mohammedan Moros and the non-Christian tribes, belonged, during the Spanish dominion, to the Roman Catholic Church, and the Church registry of 1898 showed a total membership of 6,559,998. The parishes and missions, with few exceptions, were administered by Spanish Friars of the Dominican, Augustinian and Franciscan orders, and it was to the nature of this administration that Spain owed the insurrections of 1896 and 1898, the latter of which terminated only upon our assuming control of the islands.

In 1896 there were in the Philippines 1,124 monks of Augustinian, Dominican and Franciscan orders, which body included a company of Recolletos, who are merely an offshoot of the order of St. Augustine and differ from the Augustinians only in that they are unshod. In addition to these there were a few Jesuits, Capuchins, Benedictines and Paulists, but they engaged in mission and educational work only and did not share with the other orders the resentment and hatred of the people. Filipinos were not admitted to any of the orders, but they were made friar curates and served as parish priests in some of the smaller places.

When a Spanish Friar curate was once settled in a parish he remained there for life, or until he was too old for service, and because of this fact he was able to establish and maintain an absolutism which is difficult to explain in a few words. He was simply everything in his parish. As a rule he was the only man of education who knew both Spanish and the native dialect of his district, and in many parishes he was the only Spanish representative of the government. In the beginning, through his position as spiritual guide, he acted as intermediary in secular matters between his people and the rest of the world, and eventually, by law, he came to discharge many civil functions and to supervise, correct or veto everything which was done, or was sought to be done in his pueblo.

He was Inspector of Primary Schools, President of the Board of Health and the Board of Charities, President of the Board of Urban Taxation, Inspector of Taxation, President of the Board of Public Works, Member of the Provincial Council, Member of the Board for Partitioning Crown Lands, Censor of Municipal Budgets, and Censor of plays, comedies or dramas in the dialect of his parish, deciding whether or not these were against the public peace or morals. In a word, he was the government of his parish; and in addition to all things else, it was he who, once a year, went to the parish register, wrote on slips paper the names of all boys who had reached the age of twenty, and putting these into a receptacle, drew them out one by one and called every fifth man for military service. So hateful was this forced duty to the Filipino youths that many of them would run away into the mountains and hide, become outlaws in order to escape it. But the civil guard would go after them and when they were captured they would be put in jail and watched until they could be sent to their capital.

The monastic orders had behind them a powerful church organisation the heads of which took an active and official part in the administration of government. The Archbishop and the Bishops formed part of what was known in Manila as the Board of Authorities; and they, with the Provincials of the orders, belonged to the Council of Administration, a body analogous to the Council of State in Spain or France, charged with advising the Governor General on matters of urgent moment, or in times of crises. The Friars, Priests and Bishops constituted a solid, permanent and well-organised political force which dominated all insular policies, and the stay in the islands of the civil or military officer who attempted to pursue a course at variance with that deemed wise by the orders, was invariably shortened by monastic influence. Each order had in Madrid a representative through whom the Court of Spain easily could be reached without the intervention of any authority.

Upon the morals of the Friars I can only touch. That some of them brought up families of sons and daughters is beyond question. Such were guilty of violating their vows of celibacy rather than of debauchery. On this point the moral standard of the Filipino people was not rigid, and women were rather proud than otherwise of the parentage of their Friar-fathered children who were often brighter, better looking and more successful than the average Filipino. The truth is that this charge was urged with more eagerness and emphasis after the Filipinos began to appeal to the American government than during Spanish times, and when the standard of morality in the Filipino priesthood of the period was considered, it seemed as if the accusers thought the charge would have more weight with those they sought to influence than it did with themselves.

The three great orders of St. Francis, St. Augustine and St. Dominic owned, in different parts of the Islands, more than 400,000 acres of the best agricultural land, and this they rented out in small parcels to the people. Their income from these immense holdings was not what a prudent and energetic landlord would have realised, but they paid no taxes, while the Filipino was taxed in every possible way.

In the province of Cavite alone the Friar estates amounted to 131,747 acres, and it was in the province of Cavite, which is just across the bay from Manila, that the two insurrections against Spain, or rather against Friar domination, began.

When we arrived in Manila all but 472 of the 1,124 Friars had either been killed or had fled the country. In each of the uprisings many of them lost their lives, and many more were taken prisoners. Indeed, the last of them were not released until the rapid advance of the American troops in our own encounter with the *insurrectos* made it necessary for the insurgent army to abandon all unnecessary impedimenta. All the Friars remaining in the Islands had taken refuge in Manila.

Strange to say, this resentment against the Friars interfered in no way with the Filipino's love for the Church. With a strong and real emotion he loves the religion which has been given him; and the elaborate and beautiful forms of the Roman Catholic Church are calculated, especially, to make a powerful appeal to his mind. It is really an astonishing commentary on the character of these people that they should be able to rise against the men who administered the sacraments which they so deeply loved and revered. Or, is it more of a commentary on the conditions which caused the uprisings'?

*Without exception the Spanish Friars had been driven from their parishes, and the most burning of all the burning political questions which the Commission met and had to settle, was whether or not they should be permitted to return. It was impossible to make the people understand that the government of the United States and the government of Spain were two different matters, and that if the Friars were returned to their parishes they would exercise no secular functions of any kind. The people had the proverbial dread of the "burnt child" and no amount or kind of reasoning could move them from the position they had taken, nor could any of them, from the highest to the lowest, talk calmly and rationally about the subject.

The one point upon which the Filipinos were united was that the Friars should never be reinstated.

Universal agitation, uneasiness, fear, hatred, a memory of wrongs too recently resented and resented at too great a cost; these were the factors which made necessary the stand which the Commission finally adopted. The question with the Friars became one, largely, of getting value for their property, their title to which was never seriously disputed, and it was decided that on condition of their leaving the Islands, the insular government would undertake the purchase of their vast estates. The intention was then to make some arrangement whereby the lands might be sold back to the people in homestead tracts, and on terms which the poorest man might be able, in time, to meet.

It was to negotiate this transaction, involving the expenditure of $7,000,000 that my husband was sent to Rome the following year as an emissary of the United States government to the Vatican. This was in the time of Leo, and it made a most interesting experience which I shall detail in another chapter.

The first thing, really, that the Commission undertook when they arrived in Manila, was the settlement of a definite dispute between the Church and the People as to which had the right to administer the affairs of the Medical College of San Jose. Their manner of procedure in this case instituted in the Islands a new and never-before-thought-of system of evenly balanced justice, and made a tremendous sensation.

The case was called: "*T. H. Pardo de Tavera, and others, for themselves and other inhabitants of the Philippine Islands— against—The Rector of the University of Santo Tomas, a Dominican monk, and the Holy Roman Apostolic Catholic Church, represented by the Most Reverend, the Archbishop of Manila, and the Most Reverend, the Archbishop of New Orleans, Apostolic Delegate.*" Its importance, under the conditions then existing, can hardly be exaggerated.

San Jose was one of the oldest institutions in the Islands; it was founded, as a matter of fact, in 1601, by virtue of a legacy left by a

Spanish Provincial Governor named Figueroa who provided that it should always be managed by the head of the Jesuits in the Islands. It was originally a college for the education of Spanish boys, but through various vicissitudes, including the expulsion of the Jesuits in 1766, it had changed from one thing to another until, finally, it had become a college of physicians and pharmacists and was made a department of the University of Santo Tomas, the Rector of which was a Dominican Friar. One of the Philips had granted to the college a Royal charter, and within the last hundred years the Crown had asserted its right of control. So when the American government took over all the public property in the Philippines, General Otis closed San Jose, but he did not issue an order as to its management. The Church was petitioning for a restitution of what it regarded as its rights in the property, and the Commission was called upon to settle the controversy.

They conducted their examinations in open meetings so that, all might see the full and free workings of a wholly equitable system, and the Filipinos were enabled to behold, for the first time, the, to them, astonishing spectacle of high ecclesiastics presenting in open court the arguments upon which they based their claims.

The first hearing Mr. Taft describes as "an historic scene."

"There were the two Archbishops in their archiepiscopal cassocks," he writes, "with purple girdles and diamond crosses, accompanied by a Secretary of the Dominican order robed in white; while opposed was a Filipino lawyer, Don Felipe Calderon, who derived his education in the University of Santo Tomas. Accompanying him were a lot of young Filipino students and others of the Medical Association interested in wresting San Jose from the University. The Archbishop of Manila made a speech in which he was unable to restrain the feeling of evident pain that he had in finding the rights of the Church challenged in this Catholic country. He made a very dignified appearance."

And at the second hearing:

"Both Archbishops were again present, and the same scene was re-enacted except that we had rather more of a formal hearing. We had them seated on opposite sides of a table, just as we do in court at home, and had seats for the spectators.

"Senor Don Felipe Calderon, who represents the Philippine people, was given an opportunity to make the first speech. He had printed his argument and read it, having given us translated copies with which we followed him. His argument was a very strong one, lawyer-like and well-conceived, but he weakened it by some vicious remarks about the Dominican order. The Archbishop of Manila, once or twice, felt so much outraged at what he said that he attempted to rise, but Archbishop Chapelle prevented him from doing so. At the close of the argument Monsignor Chapelle asked for ten days in which to prepare an answer and we granted him two weeks. The scene was one I shall always carry with me as marking an interesting period in my Philippine experience."

The Commission did not settle the question. After careful consideration and many hearings, they left the property in the hands of the Dominicans, but appointed a Board of Trustees to prepare and present an appeal to the Supreme Court of the Islands, appropriating at the same time, five thousand dollars to pay the expenses of the litigation.

Archbishop Chapelle did not like this decision and telegraphed to Secretary Root asking him to withhold his approval. Then he asked the Commission to modify the law and give him an opportunity, in case the decision in the Supreme Court should go against the Church, to appeal to the Congress of the United States. This the Commission refused to do on good and sufficient grounds, whereupon the Archbishop cabled to the President, declaring that the decision as it stood would retard pacification. Although he had always been strongly opposed to the continuation of military government, we were much amused to learn that in his cable to the President he took occasion to remark, significantly, that "General MacArthur is doing splendidly."

But if Archbishop Chapelle was displeased with the action of the Commission, the Filipino press was delighted, and the editorial encomiums heaped upon them can only be described as brilliant. The *Diario de Manila,* the next morning, was absolutely unable to express itself, and it concluded a more or less incoherently eulogistic editorial with the words: "The decision satisfies everybody; it raises a question which threatened to drag itself over hot sands we tread, cleanses it of all impurities, and makes it the beginning and the end of a most transcendental principle of sovereignty and law." The Filipino or Spanish editor is nothing if he is not hyperbolic.

When we arrived in Manila it was a source of great worry to us that we could not send our children, eight and ten years old, to school. The Jesuits had a school for boys in the Walled City, and Mr. Taft considered for awhile the possibility of sending Robert there, where he might, at least, learn Spanish; but so strong was the feeling against the Friars that this would have been taken by the people as a certain indication that the President of the Commission was leaning toward the Church in his deliberations on the vital subject. As I have said, they could not look upon this question, in any of its bearings, in a reasonable light.

We eventually settled Helen in a convent where she made an effort to learn Spanish, and Robert we turned over to Mrs. LeRoy, the wife of Mr. Worcester's Secretary, who was a graduate from the University of Michigan and a most excellent teacher.

Mr. and Mrs. LeRoy went to the Philippines as bride and groom. They were classmates, graduated together, and this was their first big venture into the world. They were a valued part of our little pioneer circle, and it was with the greatest dismay that we learned, after about two years in the Islands, that Mr. LeRoy had developed tuberculosis. He had either brought the germs with him from the United States or had contracted the disease there, where, indeed, it is most prevalent. He continued to act as Secretary for Mr. Worcester beyond the time when he should have gone to another climate to devote himself to a cure, but finally, when he realised that the sentence was upon him, he decided to leave the Islands, and my husband was able to secure for him, because of his splendid efficiency, a position in the Consular service under Mr. Hay, at Durango, Mexico. This post was chosen because it is in a dry, mountainous region where the ravages of tuberculosis are supposed to be checked.

Mr. LeRoy was an exceedingly well-informed and studious man. He was a natural linguist, spoke Spanish with ease, and soon was able to acquire enough Tagalog to enable him to go among the people and get their point of view at first hand. He immediately became interested in writing a history of the Islands and wanted much to go to Spain to examine Spanish-Philippine documents at Seville and other places, but he was never able to do so.

In the days when death faced him in New Mexico, whither he had gone after leaving Durango, he wrote, as Grant wrote, on a book which he hoped might furnish some means to his wife after his death. He died before he was able to complete what Mr. Taft says is a very accurate, comprehensive and interesting history of the Archipelago from the beginning down to, and including, Dewey's victory, the taking of Manila and the work of the first Commission. He had planned to give a full account of the work of the second Commission, with which he was so intimately connected, but his pen dropped before his purpose was fulfilled. His history has been only recently published.

Mrs. LeRoy later went to Washington, and Mr. Taft appointed her to one of the few clerical positions not covered by the Civil Service law. This is in the Land Office where she signs the President's name to land patents. She is the only person in the government who has the right and power, given by special act of Congress, to sign the President's name to a document.

Throughout the autumn of 1900 the insurrection dragged itself along; behind any bush the American soldiers were likely to find a lurking "patriot"; and the uncensored reports of the "brave stand" of the Filipinos were being sent out daily by Democratic reporters, to help along the anti-expansionist cause, represented by Mr. Bryan, in the United States.

The *insurrectos* were being assured by their incitants to violence that the eyes of the world were upon them. They were being told that they were winning undying renown throughout the civilised universe; and they believed it. They read with avidity all the anti-imperialistic newspapers which came out to the Islands and accepted as a true estimate of themselves the laudations therein contained. Besides, the promoters of the insurrection pretended to translate from other languages still more extravagant praises, and they certainly were enjoying a most exalted opinion of themselves.

We understood that Aguinaldo was trying to concentrate for one spectacular move shortly before election, in order to add to the chances of a Democratic victory; and there was some cause for alarm. The Filipinos are born politicians and many of them knew much more about the campaign between Bryan and McKinley than the Americans in the Islands knew.

Apropos of this: Archbishop Chapelle told Mr. Taft that Aguinaldo had, through Archbishop Nozaleda, requested an interview with him. Monsignor Chapelle went to General MacArthur and asked that Aguinaldo be allowed to enter Manila. The General readily gave his consent, and even offered the revolutionary Dictator the hospitality of his own roof. Aguinaldo, in due military form, acknowledged this courtesy and fixed the time for his arrival in Manila. He clearly indicated that he was discouraged and had decided to solicit permission, through Archbishop Chapelle, to leave the Islands. But just then the news of Bryan's plan for calling an extra session of Congress to settle Philippine independence came out, so the insurgent general sent word that he had decided not to come. No American knew just where he was, but he probably got the papers and telegrams just as soon as any of us.

I remember the sixth of November as a very nervous day. We had received all manner of reports from home; we were so far away that mail and newspapers were a month old when they reached us; and the cable reports had been contradictory in the extreme. We really were on our tiptoes with excitement. And the worst of it was that because of the thirteen hours' difference in time between Washington and Manila, we lived through the day knowing that the United States was asleep, and went to bed just about the time voters began to go to the polls. We kept getting all manner of doubtful telegrams throughout the next morning—when it was night in the United States and the votes were being counted—but just at one o'clock, as we went to lunch, Mr. Taft received a despatch from General Corbin in accordance with his previous agreement. It read:

"Taft Manila McKinley Corbin." It had been sent from the War Department in Washington at eleven o'clock the night of the election and had taken just forty-five minutes in transmission. This was record time for a cablegram then between Washington and Manila, despatches having to be sent by numerous relays.

"DAYS OF THE EMPIRE"

THERE was a trying period of unrest and uncertainty in our early experience in the Philippines, during which we lived in a state of suspense which can hardly be described; a state of suspense which included among its various elements the excitement of an intermittent guerilla warfare and frequent threats of native uprisings in Manila. Established order and a fixed governmental policy, so necessary to the tranquillity of the normal citizen, were non-existent, and one experienced a sense of complete detachment which made plans for even the immediate future seem entirely futile. To unpack all one's things; to establish a satisfactory home and give one's attention to its ornamentation; to supply one's self with the necessities of a long residence in the tropics; in other words, to settle down to the pursuit of a usual mode of existence; all these things had to be done, but, needless to say, they were not done with the enthusiasm incident to a feeling of permanence, nor did such enthusiasm begin to manifest itself in the local atmosphere until after the re-election of Mr. McKinley in 1900 when it became certain that the American flag was in the islands to stay as long as its presence there should be deemed requisite to the peaceful development of the country and the fitting of the people for self government.

There were those who saw long years ahead,—not all Americans, by any means,—and soon the American spirit began to make itself felt in business, in schemes of civic progress, in social life, in everything. We were there for a purpose which was at last defined, so we cheerfully confronted chaos and went to work.

We were sorry to note that the election of Mr. McKinley and the consequent establishment of the American status in the Philippines did not change the military attitude toward the manner of solving the governmental problems. The Commission was definitely pledged to the rapid adjustment of affairs on a civil and generally representative basis, but the military authorities still maintained that military rule would continue to be a necessity for an indefinite period.

However, the Civil Commission went on its way mapping out a programme of peaceful pacification and carrying it into effect as promptly as possible, while its activities engaged universal attention and formed the chief topic of conversation wherever two or more people were met together. Society became frivolous enough, but nobody ever got very far away from the questions of absorbing interest with which many of us were so closely associated.

Our first Christmas surely would have saddened us in our peculiar exile had we been able to realise its approach, but this was not possible. The "Christmas spirit" does not thrive in a temperature of eighty-odd degrees, and I think I would have taken little interest in preparations for the holidays had not my children been there to remind me that Christmas is Christmas no matter what the thermometer may say about it. It was still the most important day in the year for them and it was almost pathetic to see them trying to defeat the climate through sheer force of their imaginations. It was a "green Christmas" with a vengeance, and very hot.

Our friends at home had not forgotten that we were more than a month's journey away and letters began to arrive as early as November in each of which some mention was made of a box which would be sent from Cincinnati in time to reach us before Christmas and, naturally, we began at once to imagine its contents. For weeks our children's favourite amusement was exchanging guesses as to what sort of gifts their affectionate relatives had sent them. Nor were their Aunt Maria and I any less excited. There were every two weeks in those days and we were not at all disappointed not to receive our box on the early December ship. There would be another one in on Christmas day and it would be much nicer, we thought, to get it then, and never a doubt did we have that it would come. Mr. Taft had a messenger ready to get it and bring it to the house as soon as it could be landed.

From our balcony we watched the transport steam up the bay; we felt the interest that only a Christmas box from home, ten thousand miles away, could excite; we forgot that it was eighty in the shade; it was really Christmas. We waited as patiently as we could for our messenger, but when he arrived he had only sympathy to offer us.

The box had not come. It was a most depressing disappointment, and the children were inconsolable. However, everybody cheered up about dinner time. I had done what I could with red ribbons and greenery, with cotton wool and diamond dust to create the proper atmosphere; then we had invited a number of homeless young secretaries and others to take Christmas cheer with us, and though the cold storage turkey was tough and the cranberry sauce and plum-pudding were from Commissary cans, we managed a near approach to a Yuletide air, and little Charlie went to bed with his Escolta toys quite as happy as he would have been had he been at home in his own country. I assured the three children that the box from home would come in on the next transport and promised that we would then have Christmas all over again. But I reckoned without knowledge of the shipping methods of the transport service. Transports came and transports went; our hopes were dashed to earth any number of times and it was endless weeks before our carefully prepared and holly-decked presents finally arrived.

On New Year's morning General MacArthur gave a reception at Malacafian Palace. It was such an affair as is spoken of in social circles everywhere as "the event of the season." It was a very special event to all the members of the Commission and their families, because not one of us had ever been invited to the Palace before.

There was much discussion of the serious subject as to what the civil government officials should wear at the New Year's reception and, if gossip can be relied upon, it came very near causing several family riots. The men naturally inclined toward the comfort of their white linens, but they were overcome by argument and it was eventually decreed that they should present themselves in frock coats and silk hats. This may sound reasonable, but it wasn't. It was intensely funny, however, and that helped some. A silk hat which has reposed in a box throughout a rainy season in the Philippines is a curious object. It is not the glossy, well turned and dignified article which a silk hat should be. Its rim is warped, its nap is dulled and roughed beyond repair; it is very sticky, and it has an odour all its own. In Judge Ide's hat some mice had made a nest and had eaten a small hole through its one-time shiny crown, but it was the only one he had and, as silk hats are not carried in Philippine shops, he had, perforce, to wear it.

My husband communed with himself during the process of getting into his heavy frock coat with all its stiff and its woollen accessories,—for the first time in seven months and in the bright white heat of a tropic morning,—but we were finally ready and on the way, in our diminutive Victoria behind the prancing black stallion ponies of uncertain disposition.

When we arrived at Malacarian, quite early as we thought, we found ourselves in a long block of carriages which moved up slowly and, one by one, discharged their occupants under the porte-cochere of the Palace. Considerations of rank and precedence had escaped our minds for the moment and this was evidently a very important matter. However, we found a capable staff of military aides who knew just where everybody belonged, and they adopted the method of marshalling the crowds into a room on the first floor and letting them out in the proper order of precedence. In consequence we found a more or less annoyed throng awaiting our arrival. We had plenty of rank, my husband being the ranking civil officer in the Islands, but as everybody in Manila had been invited, the process of forming the line was a long and laborious one and many were the caustic comments of the delayed and rankless multitude. It reminded one forcibly of similar receptions at the White House, except that in Washington everybody knows the rules of precedence governing diplomatic circles and recognises the necessity for following them, while in Manila it was a departure which did not meet with full and general approval.

General MacArthur and his staff were receiving at the head of the grand staircase on the second floor, and, as the spacious rooms became filled with military men in dress uniforms, with gaily attired women and black-coated civilians, the scene was sufficiently dignified to make one feel that a brilliant local society was an established fact. But there was no denying that it was hot and that the Army officers in trim white duck had the frock-coated, camphor-ball-scented and profusely perspiring civil government officials at a disadvantage.

Nowdays—and always after that first experiment—the man in a temperate-zone costume is a sadly conspicuous figure at a social gathering in Manila. The accepted formal evening dress is white linen with either a short mess jacket or a dinner coat of the usual pattern, while for morning or afternoon affairs a man may wear anything his laundryman can turn out for him. As a matter of fact, in the early days in Manila women, as well as men, enjoyed emancipation from the tyranny of clothes. It was a case of discovering how unnecessary many supposed necessities are. There were no fashionable gowns to be had, therefore simplicity, or a more or less rundownedness of one-time respectability, became the fashion. There were no hat shops, so women ceased to wear hats. We went shopping on the Escolta in the early morning hatless; we went to luncheon parties hatless, and in the later afternoon we made our calls and drove on the Luneta minus the millinery which is considered so dear to a woman's heart. I do not say that the women liked it; there were many plaintive protests; but it was one of the crosses of their environment which saved them numerous jealous pangs as well as much expense. It is different now. The importer of fashionable millinery and sumptuous garments has invaded the field and the women in Manila to-day are about as finely gowned and hatted as they are anywhere, but I doubt if they are as care-free and comfortable as we were in "the days of the Empire."

It was expected that the New Year's reception at Mala-cafian was intended to inaugurate a gay season of hospitality at the Palace, as General MacArthur announced a dinner and reception to follow early in January. But they were unquiet times; for various reasons there were many postponements; then came the death of Queen Victoria, whereupon the British community went into mourning, and, as it was deemed courteous to observe a period of social inactivity, it was many weeks before we again went to Malacafian.

The campaign of pacification, due to the election of McKinley, the activity of the army, and the actual legislation and organisation work of the Commission, was making great progress throughout the Islands and hardly a day passed that did not bring news of the capture or surrender of insurgent officers and forces in the provinces, while in Manila they were being arrested and imprisoned by the hundreds. They were given an opportunity to take the oath of allegiance and those who persisted in their refusal to do so were banished to Guam. This vigorous policy was having marked effect upon the spirit of the insurrection and it was rapidly approaching total collapse.

The peace movement was greatly assisted, too, by the activities of the Federal party, a strong political organisation, pledged to the acceptance of American control and American principles, which numbered among its leaders and adherents many of the best men in the Philippines. In its directory were Chief Justice Arellano, Don Benito Legarda, Dr. Pardo de Tavera and General Ambrosio Flores, a one-time leader of the insurrection.

Perhaps the most extraordinary demonstration any of us ever saw in Manila took place on Washington's birthday in 1901. The Commission had already begun its long task of instituting provincial and municipal governments and its members had just returned from a trip into the country north of Manila where they had been received with great enthusiasm, and where the people had shown every indication of a glad determination to stop all hostilities and settle down to peaceful pursuits under the representative and democratic system which the Commission was inaugurating.

On the evening of February 20, General MacArthur gave a splendid reception at Malacarian, where Americans and Filipinos mingled together in perfect amity, the Filipinos being in the majority. They seemed greatly pleased with the spirit of the occasion which served to demonstrate in a particular manner the fact that America was in the Philippines as a friend rather than as an arbitrary ruler; that there was to be none of the familiar colour or race prejudice, so far as we were concerned, in the association of the two peoples; that the best thing to do was to acknowledge a mutual aspiration and strive for its fulfilment in friendly co-operation; and there was a heart-lift for us all, Americans and Filipinos alike, in the whole tone of the evening. On the night of the 21st, the Partido Federal gave a famous dinner at a new hotel where a French chef prepared the menu.

Before this my husband had jokingly written to Secretary Root that he thought some sort of pension should be provided for the widows and orphans of the men who fell in action before the fearful onslaughts of native hospitality, but at the banquet of the Federal party there were none of those mysterious viands to which the Commissioners had been trying to accustom themselves in the provinces, and in consequence the quality of mutual enjoyment was not strained, the Filipino, unlike the Japanese, being as fond of foreign cookery as he is of his own. The speeches were all of the friendliest character and the "dove of peace," verily, seemed to be hovering near.

The next morning, the 22nd of February, the Federal party, many thousands strong, marched through a flag-decked city to the Luneta where a speakers' stand had been erected for the celebration of the day. There were scores of bands, each, as usual, playing its own tune in its own way regardless of what the others were doing; the populace, in its gayest attire, crowded in the wake of the procession; the spirit of festivity was rampant; and altogether it was a most interesting scene.

As close as ten thousand people could get to a speakers' stand ten thousand people massed themselves, and they listened in respectful silence to the words of both the American and Filipino speakers, each one of whom made a spirited appeal for peaceful co-operation in the solution of the problem which America had acquired through no fault or desire of her own and which she could not, in honour, abandon. General Wright was the American speaker of the day and the frank friendliness of his speech was translated, paragraph by paragraph as he delivered it, by Mr. Arthur Fergusson, the Secretary-interpreter for the Commission, whose extraordinary command of Spanish made it possible for him not only to translate the words themselves, but to infuse into them the poetic fervour of the Spanish tongue. Never was Washington's birthday so celebrated, and it marked a new era of mutual toleration which was to grow into sympathetic understanding disturbed only by the agitation of the few whose aspirations were in no way in those days shared or condoned by the many.

The method adopted by the Commission for organising provincial governments was extremely simple. The people were instructed to send delegates from all the towns in a province to meet the Commission on a given date at the provincial capital. Having gathered this popular assembly in the largest available hall Mr. Taft, or some other member of the Commission, would proceed to read and explain the new Provincial Code which covered every governmental function and which provided for the appointment by the Commission of a provincial governor, a treasurer and a secretary. It was the intention of the Commission to name a Filipino for governor in each province, thereby giving them an immediate opportunity for the exercise of self-government, but in several instances they were almost unanimously petitioned by the people to appoint to this office the American Army officer who had been in command in the district. Considering the attitude of the Filipinos toward military rule and their eagerness to substitute a purely civil form of government, it was really astonishing that they should have wished to retain any representative of the hated regime, but personality counts for a great deal with the Filipinos, and the Army officer who displayed tact and kindly justice in his dealings with them was sure to win for himself a peculiar popularity.

For treasurer an American was almost invariably chosen. During Spanish times the Filipinos had not learned much about the proper use of public funds and they have had to be very painstakingly taught that government money is for government purposes only. To our poignant and everlasting shame object lessons had to be given them by the drastic punishment meted out to certain American treasurers who were unable to resist temptation. The penalty prescribed in Philippine law for the misuse of public funds or the falsification of a public document is terribly severe, and there is a little band of white men in Bilibid prison in Manila to-day because of their venality and breach of trust. Our mission in the Philippines is based upon the highest principles and we have always striven to maintain a high moral tone in the government personnel, so it is particularly painful to the small American community when, as happened too often at first, an American went wrong.

Though the Commission proceeded with the establishment of civil government in a conspicuously simple manner as much cannot be said of the Filipinos. They were bent upon making the most of a rare opportunity for the enjoyment of great and ceremonious festivity.

On the 23d of February, following the extraordinary celebration of Washington's birthday, the Commission, accompanied by a considerable number of prominent Filipinos and by several of the ladies, took a government launch and steamed across the Bay to the town of Balanga, the capital of the province of Bataan which lies directly opposite Manila where the sun goes down in tropic splendour behind the Meriveles Mountains. This trip was a new experience for me and was the beginning of my long acquaintance with Filipino hospitality.

As we approached the Bataan shore there were splashes of brilliant colour all over the surface of the Bay, which, on nearer view, turned out to be the decorations of a great fleet of *bancas* coming out to meet us. There must have been a hundred or more and, while they were of all sizes, some of them were large enough to hold twenty and thirty rowers. The *banca* is a long, narrow dugout which usually looks as if it were just about to sink. Some of these had outriggers, some had not, but each and every one of them was loaded to capacity, and each was covered with the most gorgeous decorations. Bunting and paper flowers of every hue were mixed with long palm leaves and branches of bamboo and everything in the nature of an ornament that could possibly be used, while from every angle and at every point fluttered small American flags, some of them home-made and only approximately correct. Then there were two huge flat affairs with decorated awnings over them which we found were nothing less than rafts prepared for our own use, the water in the little harbour being too shallow for our big steam launch. These rafts were made of split bamboo flooring lashed to the tops of large *bancas* and, though they looked exceedingly unsafe, we found they would hold as many as could stand upon them without being pushed over the edge.

In ten minutes this gay and unusual fleet had surrounded us; the rafts came alongside and over our rails clambered the reception committee, a half dozen Filipinos in more or less nondescript, heavy black clothes with silk hats! Where these garments came from I have no idea. Most of the hats looked like heirlooms, just as the silk hats of our own husbands looked, but the chief concern of their owners seemed to be their protection. Never have I seen silk hats so cautiously handled.

Having got safely aboard the launch each man went through a deliberate process of straightening himself out and carefully adjusting his attire before he advanced to the stern of the launch where we waited to receive him. Then there were some set speeches of welcome in which the chief sentiment seemed to be that never had the province of Bataan been so highly honoured and that, therefore, it and all it contained was, with feelings inexpressible, laid at the feet of the honourable Commission. Mr. Fergusson translated the flowers and figures of oratory and all the soaring flights of sentimental generosity into literal English, then, with equal solemnity and impressiveness, he rendered Mr. Taft's matter-of-fact, though cordial, replies into a marvellous flow of Spanish eloquence.

This formality disposed of, the reception committee invited us to step upon the pavilioned raft and be wafted ashore. It sounds like a dignified proceeding, but of course it was not. We had to climb over the rails of the launch and, more or less, slide to a secure footing on the frail floor of the curious craft. Contrary to my secret expectations it kept afloat and we were soon landed at a little fishing village down on the beach, where Army ambulances waited to take us to the town of Balanga, a mile inland. Just outside of Balanga we passed under a great bamboo arch, the sort of thing the Filipinos erect and ornament with great skill and ingenuity. This one was so thickly decorated, however, with small American flags that little of its intricate frame-work was visible. A piece of white bunting stretched across the top of it bore, in large letters, the inscription: "Glory Honor to the Commission."

We drove into the town and found the place *en fete*. I never saw so many American flags in one place in my life. Four thousand of them had been bought in Manila for the occasion; and four thousand flags go a long way in decorating a small provincial town. There was not much of the town left uncovered.

When we got to the provincial building where the meeting was to be held, we found all the delegates gathered from the different villages a-tiptoe in an atmosphere of intense excitement. Bataan had never been a rich province and we discovered that few of the Filipinos understood Spanish. They spoke only Tagalog. This was due to the fact that the province had been for generations under the control of the Dominican Friars who did not believe in encouraging the natives to learn Spanish. In consequence, all the speeches had to be translated from English to Spanish, from Spanish to Tagalog, and vice versa. Felipe Calderon, the Manila lawyer who handled the San Jose College case for the People, acted as Tagalog interpreter, and I have often wondered just how much of the familiar Spanish hyperbole was convertible into the phrases of that primitive language. It made the proceedings very long and tedious, but we sat through them and they finally came to an end with much cheering for the newly appointed officials.

The Filipinos were greatly pleased at having the Commissioners bring their wives and daughters along. It was new to them and they were not slow to grasp its significance. Much to the disgust of the military authorities present, we all shook hands with everybody and assumed the friendliest kind of attitude. That the Army officers did not approve of our cordiality toward the Filipinos can hardly be wondered at. They had been subjected to the risks of a campaign of ambush and assassination for many months, and even then they were trying to bring in a band of about one hundred and fifty insurrectos, with as many rifles, who were hiding in the Meriveles Mountains and preying upon the people; so, it was natural for them to think that a policy of disdain and severity was the only one suited to the apparent unreliability and deceitfulness of the native. However, these same officers very shortly admitted to us, though rather unwillingly, that our mode of dealing with the people had had an extraordinary effect on the general tone in Bataan.

It was about this time that President McKinley communicated through Secretary Root the intention of the Administration to abolish the military governorship and to install a civil Governor under the power of the President as Commander-in-Chief, and to create civil departments also. When Mr. Taft received a cable from Secretary Root advising him of this fact, he went to see General MacArthur for the purpose of discussing with him the mode of procedure and to get his ideas as to how and when the transfer of power should be made.

The General had begun to look upon the work of the Commission from a somewhat less prejudiced angle and was by this time freely admitting that the establishment of provincial and municipal governments was having a good effect. He, of course, did not wish to surrender his power as military governor and remain in the Islands in a less important position, but he thought somebody would soon be named to succeed him and that the proper time for the transfer was after his successor arrived. Mr. Taft was going, with the other members of the Commission, on a long organising trip through the southern islands, and he thought he could not be ready for the adjustment of affairs before the end of June, so it was decided that the civil Governor should be inaugurated on the 4th of July, and my husband soon received assurances that he would be asked to serve in that capacity.

AN HISTORIC TRIP

THE Philippine Islands as mere territory do not seem to have impressed themselves very forcibly upon the general American mind, and the average person one talks with really has but a vague conception of their importance as regards number and area. There are enthusiasts who do not hesitate to declare for the edification of wondering friends that there are more than three thousand islands in the group, but it is necessary to explain that a vast majority of these are mere dots upon the map not to be considered in the sum total of habitable area. And yet the archipelago is one of the finest on earth and not much smaller in point of arable land than the whole Japanese island empire with its fifty-odd millions of inhabitants.

It is a rather widely distributed territory and its population, some seven millions six hundred thousand in number, comprises a variety of peoples, each of which has its own language and its own traditions, though all Christian Filipinos are much alike in general characteristics.

Personally to superintend the establishment of civil government throughout the Islands at a time when many of the people were still in sympathy with armed resistance to our authority was a tremendous task for the Commission to undertake, but it was thought that only through direct contact could anything like sympathetic understanding be obtained. Tranquillity had, as speedily as possible, to be restored, and while the ungentle persuasion of armed force continued for some time to be a necessity, the methods adopted by the civil officials never failed to make a visible and lasting impression.

It was decided in the beginning that the ladies should accompany the Commissioners on their long organising trip through the southern islands and the success of our visit to Bataan proved to us that as members of the governmental party we could make ourselves distinctly useful.

We wanted to get away much earlier than we did but the exigencies of the still active military operations made it impossible for the

Commanding General to supply us with a transport, so it was not until the tenth of March that we started out on what proved to be one of the most unique expeditions of my life.

It begins to get very hot in the Philippines in March and this being our first "hot season" in the Islands we felt it particularly. It is always warm enough but there is a variety in the temperature which one soon begins to appreciate. From November to February it is almost always delightful, just warm enough; and sometimes, in the evenings, cool enough for light wraps. But in March the heat becomes intense and not until the rains begin in June or July can anything pleasant truthfully be said about the climate.

However, this southern island trip was not a pleasure jaunt and it was of such historic interest that none of us was willing, out of consideration for personal comfort, to forego the privilege of making it.

General MacArthur assigned to the Commission for the southern trip the transport *Sumner,* which contained sufficient cabin space to accommodate in comfort a large party. Besides all the ladies in the civil government, the Commission had invited some newspaper men and a number of prominent Filipinos who were pledged to the restoration of peace under American control. Among them were representatives of all the peoples in the southern islands to be visited. Then, too, we all took our children. We had to; and it was fortunate for us that they were such experienced and adaptable little people else they might have proved a great nuisance in such a mixed party and on a trip where we to stop at twenty-odd different towns and attend innumerable meetings, *banquetes* and *bailes.* But, as it was, they gave us little trouble. Mrs. Moses' little daughter, who had just come out from San Francisco, my daughter Helen and my son Robert, Mr. Fergusson's son Arthur and young Jack Branagan, were all about the same age, and they never tired of devising games that could be played around such parts of the decks as were not infested with grown-ups. Then, to while away the hours when their elders were attending ceremonies on shore, they explored bays and rivers in a sailboat which was rigged out for them by Captain Lyman, of the *Sumner,* a most fatherly man who seemed to enjoy this unusual opportunity to indulge his love for children. On the beaches they collected an infinite variety of shells, corals and malodorous marine curiosities, but these they kept on the lower decks where they could enjoy them in peace. Charlie was, of course, the ship's baby. He was younger than either of the Worcester children and, I am afraid, somewhat less well behaved. He scorned their rather quiet amusements and led a strenuous and independent existence which gave me some uneasiness. He rushed around over the ship with the utmost carelessness, delivering orders in a strange jargon to his little Filipino nurse, who was always rushing after him just far enough behind to be utterly useless in case anything should happen to him. It was a certainty that should he fall overboard she would reach the rail just in time to see him sink. Some of the deck rails were low, but strange to say he came through without accident. I think Charlie must have acquired some of the surefootedness of a cat. He had been twice around the world before he was eight years old, and that he managed to grow up into an unscarred and quite decorous young man was certainly not due to natural caution on his part nor to over-restraint on ours.

It was an interesting party gathered on the *Sumner*.

Among others were the Atkinsons. Mr. Atkinson was the Superintendent of Public Instruction who had recently come out from Springfield, Massachusetts, and who was making this trip for the purpose of seeing what steps should or could be taken to introduce a system of public instruction in a practically schoolless land. The Commission had appropriated just as much for the establishment of public schools as the treasury could spare, this being the natural American thing to do under the circumstances, and no time was to be lost in getting down to practical work. And, I should like to note, that in no enterprise which America has undertaken in the Philippines have we received such enthusiastic support and co-operation from the Filipinos as in this. That they were tremendously alive to the value of the educational privileges offered to them is proved by the phenomenal success attained by the public school system which was introduced. District schools, village and town schools, the high school and the normal school are to-day as much a cherished part of Philippine life as such institutions are a part of the great "American idea" in the United States. And in addition to these a University has been founded which promises to become one of the finest institutions of learning in the whole East. Whatever may be said about the American Constitution there can be no dispute about the fact that education follows the flag.

The Filipinos in our party, who were invited to go in order that they might give the Commission information and advice and also, in some measure, explain to their own compatriots the intentions of the American Government, included Chief Justice Arellano, the two Supreme Court Judges, Llorente and Araneta, •and the originators of the Federal Party, Don Benito Legarda, Doctor Pardo de Tavera and General Flores. The Federal Party expected to organise in the far provinces and it was hoped this would have a healthy effect on insular politics. There were sixty of us in all and I think we must have seemed rather a formidable host to some of the nervous reception commit-tees that were forced to encounter us.

It was all wonderfully interesting. Our first stop was at Lucena in the Province of Tayabas. We arrived there in the late afternoon so we had to lie at anchor until next morning, but while the daylight lasted we gazed eagerly at the shore through our field glasses and were astonished to see the crowds of Filipinos not only lining the beach but wading in throngs out into the Bay, as far as they safely could. It was as if they had decided to walk out to meet us. And the town was decorated, decorated magnificently. There were bamboo arches a-flutter with flags and flags flying everywhere, to say nothing of bunting and palm leaves and myriads of gay paper streamers.

Bright and early the next morning the reception commit-tee came out in a steam launch, accompanied by Colonel Gardiner, the American Army officer in command of the garrison. The Filipinos, immaculate little ex-insurrectos to a man, proudly climbed the gangway, stopped to adjust their attire, then proceeded to bid us welcome with the utmost grace. Their spokesman made the usual cordial speech, which Mr. Fergusson solemnly interpreted. He laid at our feet everything to which he or the town of Lucena had any claim, and assured us that the honour of our visit was most deeply appreciated by the entire community; then he and his companions stood smiling before us while Mr. Fergusson turned my husband's simple words of thanks and appreciation into Spanish metaphor and hyperbole.

I have often thought that America never could have won the friendship of the Filipinos if it hadn't been for Mr. Arthur Fergusson's clever tongue. My husband's smile and frank geniality accomplished much, but his interpreter's suavity struck a deeper and more familiar chord and together they created harmony. They were a remarkable pair as they stood side by side. Neither of them weighed less than three hundred pounds, but Mr. Taft was blond and ruddy, Anglo-Saxon no less in appearance than in manner and speech, while Mr. Fergusson was dark and rather dashing and seemed naturally to assume the lofty mien of a Spaniard when he spoke the beautiful Spanish tongue. Mr. Fergus-son became Executive Secretary of the Islands when Civil Government was established and continued in that office until his death about six years ago. His loss to the men who were then doing America's work in the Philippines was incalculable and the whole community, Filipinos and Americans alike, joined in the warmest tributes to his memory that have ever been paid to an American in the Islands.

When we arrived at the landing in Lucena we found a motley throng of vehicles awaiting us, and were greeted by a roar of vociferous speech from the *cocheros* which sounded like imprecations, but which turned out to be the Filipino equivalent for the deafening "Cab, lady! Cab, sir!" with which travellers are welcomed at so many American railway stations.

Mr. Taft and I, who seemed, in the opinions of our hosts, to be the only persons of real importance present, were ceremoniously escorted to a diminutive Victoria decorated with flowers, while the rest of the party indiscriminately clambered into the nearest conveyances. Then started a mad race down an execrable road, where the holes and ruts were so filled with dust that there was no way of foreseeing or preparing for the bumps. Our carriage, being a sedate "flower parade" all by itself, was soon left far behind by the sportier two wheel vehicles, and when we arrived at the Municipal

Building, where ,the meeting was to be held, confusion reigned. I have no doubt that several private secretaries had been greeted as the honourable "Presidente del Commission," but if so, their fleeting honours detracted nothing from the welcome we received.

The streets were crowded with men, women and children waving flags and shrilly cheering, and just in front of the hall were drawn up two Filipino bands dressed in gorgeous, heavy uniforms decorated with such scraps of gold lace as they had been able to procure. Together they struck up the "Star Spangled Banner," but they kept together for just about two bars, each leader having his own fixed idea as to the proper *tempo*. One band finished several bars ahead of the other, and immediately, without so much as a lowering of instruments, it hurled itself into "A Hot Time in the Old Town To-night," whereupon the uplift of "Don't you hear those bells go ding-a-ling" collided merrily with the solemn sentiment of "Long may it wave!" Yet nobody laughed. We were cultivating a sobriety of demeanour because we knew we were dealing with a people whose ears heard not and whose eyes saw not as we hear and see.

The meeting which followed our spectacular reception was exceedingly interesting. The questions of the Commissioners elicited the information that Tayabas had been completely pacified for more than a year, although the surrounding provinces, Cavite, Laguna and Batangas, were among the most unruly in the Archipelago. This happy state of affairs seems to have been produced by Colonel Gardiner, in command of the garrison, who had displayed great tact in dealing with the peacefully inclined Filipinos and absolute military rigidity in his attitude toward the insurrectos. That his methods had gained popular approval was evidenced by the fact that every town in the province petitioned the Commission to make him Governor. The requisite permission to do this having been obtained from General MacArthur, who, as Military Governor, had specially to detail army officers for such service, it was done amid general rejoicing made violent by brassy discords from the jubilant bands which nearly drove me out of the building.

There were many speeches and Mr. Taft, as usual, read and explained the Provincial Code to the assembly. After I had listened almost daily for more than six weeks to that dry-as-dust document I was sure that I could repeat it backward if I tried. Mr. Taft finished his speech with a neat little summing up of conditions in general,— mellifluously embellished by Mr. Fergusson,—then he introduced Chief Justice Arellano as the ablest lawyer in the Islands and a man whom any country would be proud to own; which was literally true. The Chief Justice spoke for some time, earnestly, appealingly, and with great dignity, and he was listened to with reverence. I had hoped that his speech would end the proceedings, but this was only the beginning of my experience with the Filipino love of oratory and I never thereafter entertained any optimistic ideas with regard to time limits.

But, as all things must, the meeting came to an end and, stretching our weary bodies, we accepted an invitation to view the town. Our progress was triumphal. In our flower-decked Victoria, with the municipal *presidente* on the little seat in front of us, Mr. Taft and I moved slowly along, one band in front of us blaring out "A Hot Time in the Old Town" with all the force of its lungs, and the other behind us doing its best to make itself heard and appreciated in a wholly original rendition of "Ta-ra-ra-ra-boom-de-ay." Then came the other members of our party in nondescript vehicles which jolted and creaked.

Speaking of Filipino bands, it may be thought that my partial description of those in Lucena is exaggerated. Not at all. There are more bands in the Philippines, perhaps, than any other one thing. The Filipinos as a people are extremely musical and, in many instances, have proved themselves capable of reaching a high point of musical proficiency, but in the early days of American occupation a vast majority of the musicians were the rankest who played "by ear" only. They had never been taught, but they could play, after a fashion, anything that anybody could whistle, sing or pick out for them on any instrument. They had listened to the American regimental bands and they had made selection for their own repertoires of such pieces as were easiest to play, hence the popularity of "A Hot Time in the Old Town," "Ta-ra-ra-ra-boom-de-ay," "Won't You Come Home, Bill Bailey" and things of like character. They did not know the words, or the "sentiment" of the songs; they knew only the tunes, and these they played at all times, for occasions either solemn or gay. Of my own experience I can testify that "A Hot Time in the Old Town" makes a perfectly good funeral march when reduced to a measure sufficiently lugubrious.

It didn't take us long to see the town and when my ears could endure the discords no longer I explained to the pleasant little *presidente* that I thought it was necessary for the ladies to return to the transport for a rest before it was time to dress for the evening festivities. He protested that the town was ours, that his house and everything in it belonged solely to us, but I was backed up by my husband and the ladies finally were permitted to go out to the *Sumner* for a short respite. No such luck for the men. They had to attend a prodigious luncheon, an afternoon *banquete* really, and then continue, for the rest of the day, their interviews with Lucena citizens and American Army officers. And, be it remembered, it was insufferably hot.

The *banquete* and *baile* that evening were typical Filipino entertainments, novelties to me then and intensely interesting. It was a procession, a meeting, a *banquete* and a *baile* every day for nearly seven weeks unless by a happy turn of events it became necessary for us to sail for our next port in the afternoon instead of at midnight as we generally did. Under such circumstances, if any special entertainments had been prepared for the evening, such as torchlight processions, illuminations, or fireworks, they were duly produced in broad daylight, thereby losing much in general effect no doubt, but nothing in their proof of friendly intentions.

Processions and meetings may be just processions and meetings, but *banquetes* and *baffles* are not just banquets and balls, and that is why I always refer to them by their Spanish names.

We arrived at the *banquete* in Lucena at seven o'clock and found, in a great open room in a public building of some sort, a long table laden with mysteries. In the centre was a tremendous ornament, made entirely of toothpicks, built up to represent a flower garden. Whoever made it was a genius with both imagination and delicacy of touch. All along both sides of the table were strange, highly ornamental and formidable looking dishes which were evidently meant to be eaten. I didn't know what they were, but having acquired a cosmopolitan attitude toward food I was not at all dismayed. My chief concern related to the fact that a Filipino host expects one to eat at least a little of everything that is served and through endless courses of elaborately prepared meats one's appetite naturally becomes jaded.

The most important and distinguished Filipinos did not sit down at table with us. It is *el costumbre del pais* for the Filipino host to wait on his guests, to hover about and see that he enjoys what is given him, and until one gets used to it it is most disconcerting. The *presidentes* and *fiscals* and generals and other *illustrados* were not as skilful as trained servants and I found myself leaning this way and that in momentary expectation that one of them, in his excitement, would accidentally slip some sticky mixture down my back. There were speeches of course; there always are; and then more speeches, but we had to get to the *baffle,* so they were not too long drawn out.

The *baile* was given in the Municipal Building where the meeting of the morning was held, and when we arrived we found the hall quite filled with guests. The Filipino women didn't display so many jewels and fine garments in those days as now because, in certain quarters, the insurrectos were still levying tribute, but the girls and women, many of them quite pretty, were very gay in long, trailing calico skirts and *jusi, sinamay* or *pina camisas,* while the men were attired in all manner of garments from calico and white linen to black cloth.

The men are nearly all excellent dancers, but the women are hampered somewhat in the ordinary "round dances" by their foot gear. They don't wear shoes,—nor stockings either. At least, they didn't in those days. They thrust their bare toes into little slippers called *chinelas* and *cuchos,* which look for all the world like fancy bed-slippers. There are two kinds: *cuchos* being considered very "dressy" and having heels which clatter on the floor, while *chinelas* are heelless and make a scuffing, shuffling noise.

The first dance of the evening at any *baile* is the *rigodon* which is really the national dance of the Philippines. I am not going to try to describe it because I know I can't, though I have danced it hundreds of times. It is the real ceremony on such an occasion. It can be likened to an old-fashioned quadrille, but the square is made up of as many couples opposite each other as there is space and there are couples. There are a number of graceful and somewhat intricate but stately figures. It is a dance unique and, as far as I know, confined to the Philippine Islands. I'm afraid we made but a poor display in our first attempts at the *rigodon,* but by dint of watching others night after night both my husband and I became most proficient at it. I always had for my partner the most conspicuous *illustrado* in any community, while Mr. Taft conferred the honour of his attendance upon the lady of highest rank. This was important as a recognition of the established formalities.

We left Lucena pretty much exhausted and slightly aghast at the prospect of sixty consecutive days of such strenuous festivities. Our route on the map lay like a tangled thread throughout the archipelago, and its immediate trend was toward the Equator, further and further south. Every point marked as a stopping place meant a full programme of business and festivities, but, hot as it was, not one of us willingly would have turned back. There was strong fascination in the very names of the places we were bound for.

First came Soak on the island of Marinduque. Who wouldn't endure a little discomfort for the sake of seeing Soak? This province could not yet be organised because it was not sufficiently peaceful for the successful introduction of civil government. The Commissioners, after endless interviews with Army officers and with leading Filipinos who were eager for the restoration of normal conditions, promised to return to the province on the way back to Manila and complete its organisation if, by that time, certain stipulations should have been complied with. This meant the bringing in of a couple of hundred insurrecto rifles and the gathering together of properly accredited representatives of the people from all parts of the island. We left behind us a disappointed but a determined town, and when we returned nearly seven weeks later we found such a difference as proved the wisdom of delay.

The Commissioners were really walking in the dark. Only through personal investigation could they learn the exact conditions in any town or province and this investigation had always to precede any definite action on their part. This made the proceedings long and arduous for them and drew the days out endlessly for the rest of us.

Romblon, Masbate, Iloilo, Bacolod; each with its distinct problem, each with its own impassioned orators, and each offering boundless hospitality; we left them all in better condition, we hoped, than we found them and, certainly, we carried away from each in turn a feeling of great friendliness and gratitude for the courtesies they so enthusiastically extended.

From Bacolod, in oriental Negros, we set our course straight south to Jolo, to the Sulu Islands, to the realm of the comic opera sultan, and we woke up one brilliant morning to find ourselves in the prettiest harbour imaginable and in the midst of scenes which we could not believe belonged to the Philippine world. We were in Moroland. Straight before us, in the curve of the beautiful bay, lay a little white city, surrounded by bastioned walls which looked age-old, and backed by soft green hills and groves of tall cocoanut palms. A high white watch tower at the end of a long pier reminded one of piratical days and of Spain's never-ending troubles with her Mohammedan subjects. Off to the right, against the farthest shore, was the strangest collection of habitations I had ever seen. To be told that the Moros live on the water is to imagine them living in boats, but these were houses built far out in the water, perched up on frail wooden stilts and joined together by crooked and rickety bamboo bridges.

The harbour was full of curious small craft; high prowed and beautifully carved war junks, long, graceful *praos* and slender canoes with bamboo outriggers, nearly all carrying sails of fantastic design and brilliant hues. Indeed, there was colour everywhere. Everything afloat was decorated in gaudy silks and pennants, the American flag predominating, while all the Moros who wore anything except a loin cloth were attired in costumes which were lively and strikingly original. These were made, for the most part, of rich silks of native weave in stripes or plaids of vivid, crude greens, reds and yellows, and from neck to ankle the more elegant ones were so tight that one wondered how they stood the strain. Around his waist each man wore a bright silk sash under which was thrust a long cruel looking knife in an ornamental and curiously shaped scabbard.

The picturesque fleet quickly surrounded the *Sumner* and while we watched the lithe, naked boys diving into the clear depths of the bay for coins that were thrown overboard for the purpose of testing their prowess, the American Army officers came aboard to bid us welcome to Jolo.

They explained that the Sultan of Sulu had given them some diplomatic difficulties which, they were glad to say, they had been able to overcome. He had at first decided to play the haughty monarch and to extend a royal invitation to the American officials to pay their respects to him at his "palace." But a little reasoning had convinced him that the Commissioners were the accredited representatives of the President of the United States whose sovereignty he acknowledged and that it was therefore his duty to call on them, so, it was announced, he was on his way to the landing where the officers' launch waited to bring him out to the *Sumner*.

Several large war junks carrying different chiefs, or *dattos,* preceded the imperial visitor and these men came aboard without waiting for His Majesty. We found them extremely entertaining. They were by far the most picturesque figures we had seen, and utterly unlike Filipinos. They were of a different build, lithe, active and graceful, with a free and defiant gaze which offered a strong contrast to the soft-eyed modesty of the Christian tribes. In their sashes they all carried long knives called *barongs, campildns* and *krises,* which Mr. Worcester induced some of them to exhibit to our delighted eyes. They were of the most exquisite workmanship and design, inlaid, some of them, with gold and silver, and with hilts of hardwood beautifully carved.

Finally the officers' launch put out from the dock and we knew that the Sultan was approaching. As he came alongside the *Sumner* he received a salute of seventeen guns while we all stood by holding our ears and stiffening our nerves against the deafening shock. We were expecting some one similar in appearance to our friends the *dattos,* except that we were sure he would be accoutred in three times as much barbaric splendour. Fancy our disappointment then, when there emerged from the low awning of the launch a figure quite commonplace; a very short, very black little man in a heavy uniform of black cloth embroidered in gold braid, not unlike the uniform of a British Consul. He was awkward and homely and he had shiny black teeth; that is how I remember him. He had two attendants who served only to accentuate his own insignificance. The Commission got nothing out of him either. He had none of the polish and gentlemanly manners of the Filipino leaders, and conversation of any kind with him was found to be extremely difficult. Almost the only interesting remark he made was to invite the ladies of our party to call on his many wives, a thing I should have greatly enjoyed, but which was impossible because the Sultan's "palace" was back over the hills, on the other side of the island, a long way from Jolo.

The problem of the government of the territory inhabited by the Moros in a measure adjusted itself. These Mohammedans have always been unruly and independent and were never wholly conquered by the Spaniards, and they absolutely refused, as they have since continued to do, to be placed under Filipino control. So it was decided to detach them from the general organisation and to place them under a semi-military system with an American officer of high rank in charge in the dual capacity of Governor and Commanding General of Troops in the Moro Province. This system was developed to a point where a high state of efficiency obtained in the government to the complete satisfaction of nearly everybody. To solve the problem of *juramentado,* or religious fanatic outbreaks, a general order for the disarmament of Moros had to be enforced, but only a comparatively small number of natives took part in the armed resistance. For all of them it was hard, no doubt, to have to surrender their beloved and time-honoured weapons, but the wisest among them recognised the necessity of obedience for the sake of the general good. If this had not been so it would have been vastly more difficult to make the order effective. These wise ones are to-day everywhere busy upholding the American policy of establishing markets and schools and honest trade relations, and in preaching to their people that, for the first time in their history, they are being fairly and justly dealt with. They cling to American protection with determined faith, telling us in plain words that if we leave them they will fight their neighbours. So, whatever we may do with the Philippine Islands we cannot abandon the Moros, and this adds a grave complication to our Philippine problem.

At Jolo we received the news of the capture of Aguinaldo and his reception by General MacArthur at Malacañan Palace. General Funston, then a Colonel of Volunteers, was a conspicuous member of a small company of Army officers known locally as "the suicide squad," who risked their lives in one exploit after another with the utmost unconcern, not to say glee, so we were not surprised at anything he might do. But there was a real thrill in the story of his daring venture into the remote and isolated camp of the insurrecto general and Dictator, and we cheered his performance with heartfelt enthusiasm, though our ardour was somewhat dampened by doubts as to what the arch-conspirator would do in Manila. General MacArthur was not a politician; he was a soldier,—an officer and a gentleman, —and in his treatment of his captured enemy he was not likely to take into consideration the nature of the people with whom he was dealing.

However, that story has been told, well and often. We know that General Aguinaldo also was "an officer and a gentleman," proving himself worthy of all the courtesy extended to him and accepting defeat with great dignity. He is the most striking figure in the Philippines even today, though one only hears of him as a peaceful and unambitious farmer in his native province of Cavite whence he emerges only on rare occasions to be present at some important social event in Manila where, among Americans in particular, he is most highly regarded. But, it must be remembered that at the time of his capture the Islands were still in a state far from satisfactory; that he had lieutenants in all parts of the archipelago endeavouring, under his orders, and by methods not counted as "civilised," to keep alive the spirit of rebellion, and that he had an extraordinary genius

155

for conspiracy and organisation. So it cannot be wondered at that my husband was deeply concerned and that he wished he were back in Manila where he could keep his large but gentle hand upon the delicate situation.

From Jolo we sailed to Zamboanga, capital of the Moro province, and thence to Cottabato. At Zamboanga we met an entirely different class of Moros, more refined, better educated and less spectacular than those in the Sulu Islands, and were entertained by the American Army officers in the ancient Fortress del Pilar, which still bears the marks of many a conflict between the Moros and the Spaniards. We met here two very interesting men, Datto Mandi, a Moro, and Midel, a leading Filipino. Mandi was said to be, and looked, part Spaniard, though he denied the Spanish blood. He was the chief of tribe of many thousands of people and wielded a wide influence which the American Government never sought to curtail. He was a good business man and intensely loyal to the Americans, giving substantial demonstrations of his loyalty whenever opportunity offered. He told the Commission what has since proved to be the truth about Moro customs relative to slavery, the administration of justice and other matters, and displayed, altogether, a genuinely friendly and helpful attitude. Midel, the Filipino, was himself made a *datto* by Mandi and seemed inordinately proud of his rank. He was an odd individual with a doubtful record behind him. Sometime before we met him he had sent his son to be educated at the University of California, and it was he who delivered the province over to the American troops as soon as they arrived, having previously disposed of a couple of insurgent rivals of his own race who attempted to keep it out of American hands.

At Cottabato, a long day's sailing from Zamboanga across Illana Bay, we met the Moros who inhabit the valley of the Rio Grande del Mindanao, a large and sinister looking river. We communicated with these people through their *dattos,* Piang and Ali. Piang is the most powerful *datto* in the province. He is the son of a Chinese carpenter and a common Moro woman, and he won his position through shrewdness, generosity to his people and native ability.

Ordinarily a peaceful conservative he was not always at peace with Ali, who is inherently warlike and a *datto* of royal descent, but a couple of American Army officers, Colonel Brett and Major MacMahon, in charge of the post at Cottabato, not only adjusted their differences but induced the royal Ali to marry the commoner Piang's daughter. Colonel Brett was Ali's "best man," while Major MacMahon stood sponsor for the bride. There are American Army officers who have seen strange service in our Far Eastern possessions.

A few years after the time of which I write a daughter of Datto Mandi was married at Iligan in northern Mindanao and, to quote from Foreman's "History of the Philippines": "Several American officers were present on the occasion, accompanied by a Spanish half caste who acted as their interpreter. The assembled guests were having a merry time when suddenly the festivities were interrupted by the intrusion of a *juramentado* Moro fanatic, who sprang forward with his *campilan* and at one blow almost severed the interpreter's head from his body. Then he turned his attention to the other natives, mortally wounded two, and cut gashes in several others before he fell dead before the revolver shots fired by the American officers. After the dead and wounded were carried away and the pools of blood were mopped up, the wedding ceremony was proceeded with and the hymeneal festival was resumed without further untoward incident."

We were very fortunate that, disturbed as conditions were, no "untoward incident" of this nature occurred to mar the serenity of our first great trip through the Islands.

To illustrate Datto Piang's intense desire to establish his status as a loyal friend of the United States Government I think I must relate, in part, the conversation my husband had with him in regard to the gutta percha industry. The forests in the Rio Grande Valley and around Lake Lanao, in the northern part of the island were thought to be almost inexhaustible in their supply of gutta percha trees, and Piang was found to be a large dealer in the product. But inquiry elicited the information that the most primitive methods were employed in gathering the gum and that every year thousands of trees were destroyed, no idea of scientific conservation ever having entered the heads of the Moros. Mr. Taft asked Piang whether if we sent him an expert who knew how to have the trees treated he would undertake to enforce regulations which such an expert would frame. He said he acknowledged the sovereignty of the United States Government and held himself subject to its orders, every one of which he would obey. Moreover, he would make all the other *dattos* obey the same orders whether they were willing to do so or not. Then Mr. Taft explained that the United States Government might desire to lay a cable from San Francisco to the Philippines and that one of the great items of expense in such an enterprise was the gutta percha. He was merely trying to impress upon Piang's mind the immense value of his product and the necessity for its proper handling, but Piang immediately offered to make the United States a present of all the gutta percha it needed for a Pacific cable, declaring that all he wanted was a note from the authorities indicating the amount required. He would see that it was promptly gathered and delivered. Mr. Taft then told him that the United States always paid for whatever it received from any person, whether subject to its sovereignty or not, whereupon Piang declared that, anyway, he preferred to sell his gutta percha to the United States, and at a much lower price, too, than he was receiving from the Chinese dealers. He is just a clever, crafty Chinaman himself, is Datto Piang, but an interesting figure. After a thorough investigation of Cottabato and a right royal entertainment provided by a number of gorgeously attired *dattos* and sultans, of greater or less degree, who had gathered in the town to greet us, and gaze in wide-eyed curiosity upon us, we went on our way around the great island of Mindanao.

At Davao we saw thousands of acres of the highest hemp in the world, and a number of beautiful bead-bedecked hill tribes who had come down into coast civilisation for the purpose, no doubt, of seeing what we looked like.

These hill tribes are very interesting people. They are, perhaps, more picturesque than any of the other non-Christians, and they have developed to a fine point the of making bead embroidered clothing. So beautiful and so unusual are these garments that the ladies in the party, forgetting everything else, made a grand rush to purchase some of them from the various tribesmen. Our eagerness, indeed, had finally to be restrained in order that attention might be given to the efforts of the Commission to enlighten the people as to our mission, but having patiently awaited the termination of business we returned to our search for the bead-work, only to find that the finer specimens could not by any process of cajolery be secured. Money meant nothing to the hillmen and we had no substitutes in the way of gewgaws to offer them. The only one of us who succeeded in getting a really good suit was Miss Anne Ide, and her success was the result of a curious incident. She met a chieftain gorgeously arrayed, and at a venture tried upon him the Samoan greeting and a Samoan song which she had learned in her childhood when her father was Chief Justice of the Samoan Islands. To her great surprise the Bogobo answered and seemed greatly pleased. He had already had conveyed to him the fact that the only thing the ladies wanted was bead clothing, so he indicated to Miss Ide that he would present to her his coat and pants, and without further ado, and much to her astonishment, he began to divest himself of these garments which she accepted with delight. The incident awakened natural curiosity on our part as to the relation between the Polynesian language of Samoa and the vernacular of the hill tribes around the Davao gulf.

From Davao we proceeded on our journey around Mindanao, sailing out into the open Pacific and up to the province of Surigao in the northeast corner of the island.

The town of Surigao lies six miles up a swamp-bound, sluggish river and we experienced, as we so often did in the whole course of the trip, a sense of being in uncharted and therefore dangerous waters. We embarked in a launch

when the tide was high and had no trouble in getting up to the village, but we were earnestly entreated by the officer in charge of the launch to hurry with our business in order that we might start back before the tide went out. He assured us that it would be very difficult, if not impossible, to cross the bar at the mouth of the river at low tide. His entreaties were in vain. The Commissioners were engaged in interviews with Surigao citizens which they could not or would not cut short, so the ladies and children, having seen everything and met everybody, went back to the landing and sat in the launch patiently waiting while the daylight slowly disappeared. The launch captain was visibly agitated, and told us time and again about what a hard time we were sure to have getting back to the *Sumner*. And he was quite right.

The launch was not large enough to accommodate the entire party so it towed a cutter which also was fairly well loaded. When the men finally arrived, full of explanations and good-natured apologies, it was pitch dark, but, being optimists, we shoved off into the river, feeling sure that the fears of our commanding officer were groundless.

After steaming merrily along for a few miles, becoming more and more confident all the time, we suddenly got a shaking bump and found ourselves fast in the mud. It didn't take so long, however, to get afloat again, and we were just congratulating ourselves that the captain's bugbear of a sandbar was behind us when we felt a violent impact followed by a terrifying sensation as if the keel were grinding over rocks.

The captain swore softly and said something about striking "the ruins of that old Spanish bridge," then hurried forward to see what damage had been done. The people in the cutter, riding the short waves in our wake, were thoroughly alarmed and were clamouring to know what had happened to us. We couldn't tell them, but it sounded very much as if we had torn the whole bottom out of the launch. The engine had stopped; it was inky dark; the children all began to cry; and, to add further discomfort to the situation, it began to rain in torrents. The launch swayed sickeningly this way and that, then the engine started again, whereupon came a most furious clatter aft. There is no denying that it made us blanch with fear, but it proved to be only a blade of the propeller which had been bent and was striking the boat with each revolution.

Three times more we slid into the mud; the last time we stuck and no effort that could be made would get us out, so we were forced to abandon the launch and wedge ourselves altogether into the little cutter. You may picture for yourself the scene of men, women and children, in the rain and with no light save the faint flicker of lanterns, dropping off a big launch into a small rowboat over an inky stream supposed to be filled with crocodiles.

When we reached the mouth of the river the captain began to show signs of nervousness, though he had been entirely self-controlled throughout the worst of our troubles. We couldn't see where we were going, but we could distinctly feel that the open bay lay not far ahead of us. What we wanted was to have the *Sumner's* searchlight turned on our path, but the only thing we had with us with which to convey this desire to the ship's officers were red rockets,—the last resort of the sailor in distress. There was nothing else to do; the launch captain began firing them off, and a weirder scene than was revealed by their momentary glare can hardly be imagined. They produced the desired effect, however, and in less than ten minutes a great shaft of light, straight from the bridge of the *Sumner,* was sweeping the banks of the river and bay shore and affording us just the kind of assistance we required.

But that was not the end. Less than half-way to the *Sumner* we met a lifeboat, equipped with all the paraphernalia for rescuing us from a watery grave, and manned by an excited crew in oilskins, who, under the sharp commands of an almost frantic officer, were pulling in mad haste for the river's mouth. When they saw us they lapsed into a state of utter disgust. They turned and rowed sadly back to the ship, and afterward I overheard them exchanging very definite opinions as to the possible future of a sailor who would burn red rockets when all he wanted was a searchlight.

After calling at Cagayan Misamis, Dapitan, Iloilo, San Jose Antique and Capiz, we made straight for Cebu. Cebu is, in rivalry with Iloilo and next to Manila, the most important town in the Philippine Islands. It is a receiving station for exports from all parts of the southern islands and is altogether what is known as a "live" town. It is the capital of the province of the same name which consists of a single long island some two thousand square miles in area and with a population (at that time) of nearly seven hundred thousand.

At Cebu we were rejoined by Chief Justice Arellano, who had left us sometime before to go back to Manila. We were greatly interested in

161

his account of the effect of Aguinaldo's capture and subsequent treatment. The erstwhile insurgent leader was still in prison, but his prison was made an honourable abode where he was permitted to be with his family and to receive his friends. The mass of the people would not, for a long time, believe he really had been captured. They thought the report was an American fabrication to delude them and to destroy their faith in Aguinaldo's *anting-anting,--or* magic charm against defeat. The shattering of that faith gave vast impetus to the general peace movement and, though a few hundred rifles and several insurrecto officers were still unaccounted for, and though occasional outbreaks and the activities of marauding bands of outlaws continued for a considerable length of time, actual organised insurrection had suffered a complete collapse.

The Commission kept Cebu on tenterhooks for a time as to whether the condition of order in the province was such that they could go on with the establishment of government there, and it was interesting to watch the effect of this uncertainty. To be included in the general organisation became at once the warmly expressed wish of a majority of the people, and there was great excitement throughout the town. Eventually Justice Llorente, of the Supreme Court of Manila, a member of our party, and himself a Cebuano, was appointed Governor of the province under the simple American form, and because of his integrity and real patriotism, because of the high regard in which he was held by the people, and because of the enthusiasm and complete faith with which he entered upon his duties, it was hoped that he would be able soon to lead his province into the sensible paths marked out for it.

With Cebu and the problems of Cebu behind us, we felt that our long trip was nearly finished. Bohol, Leyte, Samar, Albay, the Camarines and Sorsogon, each in its turn brought us nearer to our comfortable homes in Manila and to relaxation, for which we were beginning to long.

Each district expected us to give them at least a day for business and an evening for festivity, but this was not always possible. At Sorsogon we found a veritable riot of decoration, with fine arches and many flags and every indication that the town had spared no effort to make our visit there a memorable event. In the evening, beside the *banquete* and *baile,* there was to have been a torchlight procession, with a triumphal car and a Filipino maiden as the Goddess of Liberty. It was a great pity that we couldn't stay, but we had to sail that afternoon for Soak, so the programme had to be advanced several hours.

The extraordinary car, or float, which had undoubtedly cost weeks of skilled workmanship, came forth into the blistering sunlight bearing the pretty brown girl in tinsel and white muslin, her long, black hair almost wholly enveloping her as she held aloft the flickering symbol of Enlightenment. It was a Filipino adaptation of the "sacred torch" which we had ourselves been carrying throughout the islands, and I felt that its production was a fitting climax to our laborious progress.

Two days later when we landed in Manila, after organising Marinduque and Batangas, we were able to look back upon a singular experience, an expedition perhaps unique in history, with which was ushered in a new era, not to say a new national existence, for the people of the Philippine Islands.

THE WILD MEN'S COUNTRY

I SHOULD like to say here, by way of explanation, which may or may not be necessary, that I am not trying in this narrative to pose as a woman endowed with an especial comprehension of such problems of state as men alone have been trained to deal with. I confess only to a lively interest in my husband's work which I experienced from the beginning of our association and which nothing in our long life together, neither monotony, nor illness, nor misfortune, has served to lessen; and it would be practically impossible for me to write a record of memories in which he did not figure very largely.

In the settlement of American control in the Philippine Islands Mr. Taft, first as President of the first legislative Commission and, later, as Civil Governor, had to contend with a varied and complex resistance which it would be difficult for one not experienced in politics to comprehend. If it had been Filipino resistance only it would have been fairly easy to overcome, but Filipino resistance was indirectly sanctioned and directly assisted by a strong opposition in the United States to what seemed to us who were on the ground to be the only sensible and really patriotic measures possible under the circumstances.

For reasons which I have tried to convey, as clearly as I am able, my husband was not in favour of a continuation of military rule in the Islands beyond the time when military activity was imperative, nor was he in favour of abandoning a problem which grew daily more difficult and more complicated. So he and his colleagues persisted in the tremendous task of settling a whole people under a sane and sensible form of government.

The trip through the southern islands was valuable to them in that it gave them first-hand, working knowledge of existing conditions in every province. They immediately set about revising their original Provincial code in accordance with requirements which they were able to discover only through personal investigation, and at the same time they took up the grave business of establishing a sound judiciary.

There was always something new to be talked over at our family table, or during the long evening hours on the verandah overlooking the Bay and, in spite of the fact that much of our "news" presented itself in the form of fresh delays and exasperating difficulties, life was very entertaining.

Not long after we returned from our trip through the South Mrs. J. Franklin Bell invited my sister Maria and me to go with her on an expedition, on which she expected to accompany her husband, through the mountains of northern Luzon which are inhabited by non-Christian tribes only. General Bell was commander of troops in the North and this was to be an inspection trip. It meant several weeks on horseback, over dangerous trails where, in parts at least, no white woman had ever been, but we were most anxious to go. The trouble was that I had never ridden in my life, so I looked with considerable trepidation to the prospect of a long and necessarily intimate association with a horse. I brought the proposition up in family council and my husband advised me, by all means, to go. I should probably have gone without this advice, but it was comforting to have it because if anything happened I could "blame it all on him." In fact, I began to do this even before I left. When my courage dwindled a little I promptly told him that it was all his fault; that if he hadn't urged me to go I never should have thought of such a thing; but that as long as I had promised I should have to see the adventure through, though I knew I should never survive it. He only and assured me that we would have a glorious time and that the trip would do us "all the good in the world."

Major Stevens, who expected to accompany us, brought me an American horse, of formidable dimensions, and volunteered to superintend my first encounter with him. He was as gentle as a lamb. I wouldn't let him go faster than a walk the first evening and the fact that I was pretty stiff at the end of my ride made me almost hopeless. The second evening I let him out a little, and began, much to my surprise to enjoy the exhilaration of the exercise. By the third evening I had progressed so far that I decided for myself that the poor old beast had no speed in him at all.

We took a Spanish steamer, the *Salvadora,* from Manila up to Vigan, where General Bell was stationed, and, though I am glad to have had the experience, I shouldn't care to repeat it. When we got on board we were shown at once to a most promising-looking stateroom, quite spacious, and with four berths in it. The trip to Vigan was to take from Thursday to Saturday and we were glad to note that we were going to be quite comfortable. But our self-congratulations came to a sudden end. Upon inspection we found the room was indescribably dirty, the beds were without sheets, the pillows were like rocks, there were insects galore, and the thermometer stood at 110 degrees. Ventilation was out of the question because the room opened into a sort of public saloon where innumerable Filipinos, in various states of undress, slept, stretched out on the floor, on the tables, on chairs, on anything that could serve as a resting place. The second night I got the Captain's permission to sleep on the bridge, since the decks, too, were covered with a miscellaneous crowd and were rendered additionally uncomfortable by odoriferous strings of cabbages and other vegetables which hung from the awnings.

The food on the ship was all Spanish; indeed, I might say, terribly Spanish; still, I was rather used to it and didn't mind much as long as I could get into a wind-swept corner of the deck to eat it. But there were some American women on board who had just come out from the United States and they complained violently.

We were put ashore early Saturday morning; much earlier, in fact than we had been expected to arrive. We had to drive three miles before we reached the Bells' house, and when we did get there we were delighted to find that they were just having breakfast. They were eating real, human food and, however heroically we had adapted ourselves to the peculiarities of Spanish cookery, there was nothing we stood so much in need of. They were a most homelike and comfortable-looking party. Besides the General and Mrs. Bell there were two young officers, Mr. Wilcox and Mr. Nolan, and a young lady whose name was Miss Bubb, a daughter of General Bubb, and whose general characteristics had won for her the nickname of "Bubbles."

The first thing we learned was that Mrs. Bell would, after all, be unable to go with us on the trip through the mountains. She was not at all well and the doctor had forbidden it. We were greatly disappointed. Mrs. Bell is so jolly and full of fun that she is an addition to any party, and on such an expedition as we were contemplating we were sure to miss her tremendously. But, the party was all made up. General Bell was to take command; "Bubbles" was going; then, in addition to my sister and me, there were Major Rice, Major Stevens, Captain Shearer and Captain Haight—eight in all.

First let me say that the northern part of the island of Luzon bears just about as much resemblance to the rest of the archipelago as the Alps bear to the plains of Nebraska. We began to notice the difference even at Vigan, though Vigan is at sea-level and is as hot as a sea-level town is supposed to be in that latitude. But it feels and looks like a little foreign city; foreign, that is, to the Philippines. Its houses are well built of ancient-looking stone, with heavy red-tiled roofs; its streets are narrow and crooked and it has a fine plaza filled with fire-trees which, when I saw them first, were in full bloom. There is no way to describe the magnificence of a grove or avenue of fire-trees. They make a veritable cloud of flame which, seen against a background of blue hills, or overhanging the mouldy, old-world grace of a Spanish church and convent, fairly "takes one's breath." The world-famed cherry trees of Japan, wonderful as they are, seem pale and soulless in comparison. I wonder the Spaniards didn't line the streets of Manila with fire-trees and make for themselves the reputation of having created the most amazing city in the world.

While we were at Vigan, and before starting on the long trip, we made an excursion to Bangued, in the province of Abra. Mrs. Bell went with us. This town, a short time before, could be reached only by raft up the Abra River, no launch ever having been built that could go through the rapids, but the establishment of an Army post made necessary the building of a piece of road which shortened the journey at the Bangued end. The first part of the trip, however, had still to be made by water and all the supplies for the soldiers were sent up on a fleet of twenty or more rafts which started out together every morning. When there was a breeze each of them would run up a sail of bright, striped Igorote cloth.

We had a grand raft with a bamboo awning. And there were comfortable rattan chairs, to say nothing of a picnic luncheon and a carefully wrapped and jealously guarded box of ice. Ice was the rarest of all luxuries in the provincial towns of the Philippines in those days.

We moved very slowly against the current of the swift-flowing river, but we had no desire to hurry. It was really enchanting. From narrow, pebbly beaches on either bank rose rugged cliffs which seemed to tower mountain high, throwing deep shadows into the canyon and leaving only a narrow ribbon of sky above us. And these cliffs were hung with a tangled undergrowth through which small, white waterfalls rushed and rustled. Where the river broadened, here and there, we came upon groups of bright-clad natives who regarded us with great curiosity, and at one place we saw half a dozen women starting up the steep bank with graceful brown water-jars balanced on their heads. Each one was carrying at least six, one on top of another, and all of them full. How they managed it was beyond comprehension. We watched them until they were out of sight and not one of them ever raised a hand to her head. As a matter of fact, they were nonchalantly smoking and chattering away as if they were quite unconscious of their burdens, though the slightest unrhythmical motion would have spelt disaster for them all.

At eleven o'clock we reached the village where the road begins and the whole population gathered around in curious groups and gazed at us. White women were still a novelty in that region and I'm sure we looked much more peculiar to them than they looked to us. There were crowds of school children from the new American school, and one very much embarrassed little girl, who had had her English book only about four months, read some English for me very nicely. Likely as not that same little girl has by this time won a normal school certificate and is herself teaching English in an "American" school. Such is the history of many of her generation.

When we reached Bangued the young men in the command of Major Bowen, who was our host, gave up their house to the ladies, and we had three comfortable beds, with mosquito nets, in a large, airy room. It was a fine afternoon for a *siesta* because it rained in torrents for the rest of the day and the patter of rain on nipa thatch is a soothing sound. The young men's house was just across from the

Major's and by evening the street was such a river that we had to be carried over for dinner. But nobody minded; and we enjoyed even the music of the native band which stationed itself down under our windows and enlivened the occasion with a wonderful medley of sound. When the bandmen came upstairs for refreshments Mrs. Bell and two of the young officers ran down and tried their powers on the instruments, and I can only say that the result was joyful pandemonium.

The next morning we left our hospitable hosts and, escorted by Lieutenant Ingram, made the return trip all the way down the river. The water was high and, though it had taken us an interminable time to go up, it took only three hours and a half to go down; and some of the rapids were most exciting. We took our lunch basket and chairs ashore on a lovely, green, shaded knoll and dallied there for several hours. Only a month before nobody, who was not compelled to, ever went over this route on account of the danger of being shot, but the last of the Abra insurgents had surrendered, and so safe did we feel that we were absolutely unarmed.

If I should try to write a detailed account of this expedition I am afraid I could not avoid conveying the idea that we encountered nothing but a continuous downpour. It was the "rainy season" and we were wet most of the time, but Mr. Taft was right when he promised that we would have a glorious time and that the trip would do us a "world of good." Down in the heat and the political turmoil of Manila I was taking things much too seriously, while up in the far-away north there was nothing to do but dismiss all worry and accept things as they came along. After we left Vigan on the long trail the only way we could get even a letter through was by messenger who had to travel hundreds of miles through a most difficult country. So I enjoyed myself thoroughly, as did every one else in the party, hardships and physical discomforts seeming only to add to our gaiety.

At first I thought that my riding lessons in Manila were not going to do me much good. We had had a most luxuriously easy time in the beginning. We left General Bell's house in an Army ambulance, instead of on horses, for our first day's journey on the "long trail." General Bell was in command and he knew what he was doing. All he had to do was to issue orders; we obeyed. That is what it is to go camping with a soldier. One learns what discipline means.

We were permitted to take with us only such things as were absolutely necessary. Even then, the "absolute necessities" which we eventually discarded as useless impedimenta would have made a long list. Everything was done up in waterproof bundles and when we started out these were stuffed so full that they would hardly fasten, but they grew slimmer as time went on. The most important articles, we found, were our slickers and wraps. It was wet and cold and we had to have them, but all our toilet appurtenances together went easily into Miss Bubb's saddle-bags.

The first day we forded a river—the same river—several times, and, finally, we had to cross it on a raft which was so small that it could carry only one thing, or one person at a time. My sister, Miss Bubb and I sat on the bank above the ford for more than two hours waiting for all our things to get across. While we waited many natives came along driving carabaos, and it was amusing to see the two-wheeled, awkward carts hustled onto the swaying raft—one thing after another falling into the river—while each poor old carabao was forced to swim, dragged along by his master who held fast to a string attached to a ring in the animal's nose. If I had been able to speak the dialect I would have said: "Your friend the Carabao, being a water-buffalo, could probably swim the river much more easily without your assistance." I have had to look on and suffer at many things in the Philippine Islands merely because I was unable to speak a dozen-odd different dialects. In the provinces Spanish was seldom of any use because the common *tao* knows little or nothing of it, and it is with the common *tao* that one wishes there to communicate.

On our first day's journey we did thirty-seven miles in a jolting Army wagon, but the air was so invigorating, and we were having such a good time, that we were not exhausted. We didn't even murmur when we were told to be ready to start at four the next morning.

This was at Candon and we were joined there by Major Stevens, which made our party complete. The next evening, at Concepcion, we camped in a lovely, new nipa-thatched house which had been built by a man who was known generally as "Windy" Wilson, an Army captain. We were extremely thankful for the shelter, because it was raining as it can rain only in northern Luzon and we had every reason to believe that this would be the last house we would be permitted to occupy for many a day. We were striking straight into the mountains and our shelter-to-be was a small field tent slung on the cargo saddle of a commissary mule.

Captain Wilson's house was quite spacious. It had two rooms; one small and one large one. The ladies slept in the smaller room on Army cots, while the four stalwart officers of our military escort stretched themselves out on blankets and slickers on the split bamboo floor of the larger room. The walls and partitions were of woven nipa palm leaves, known locally as *suali,* while the two windows were made of braided bamboo and were set in grooves so, when we wanted to open them, all we had to do was to give them a gentle shove. There were no "trappings of civilisation," but we managed to be perfectly comfortable.

The next day, before the sun was very high, we found ourselves in the midst of mountain-tops, on a trail which rose in great upward sweeps around the densely wooded slopes, an altitude of 5600 feet. By this time we were all on horseback with eight Igorrote boys behind us carrying a sedan chair to be used in case of accident or a dangerous washout on the trail. I wish I could describe the magnificence of the scene which lay all about us when we reached that amazing summit. General Bell, who had been all through the Rocky Mountains, the Yellowstone, and the Yosemite Valley, said there was nothing that he had ever seen which could compare with it. And its grandeur is accentuated by vivid colouring. The Igorrotes have, for hundreds of years, been building extraordinary rice-terraces and these have gradually climbed the mountains until, in some places, only the rugged crests are left uncultivated. The terraces are as symmetrical as honeycomb and are built in solid walls of finely laid masonry out of which grow ferns and tangled vines. The brilliant colour of the young rice fairly glows against the dark greens of pine trees, of spreading mangoes, and of tropic forest giants whose names I do not know. And wherever one looks there are peaks, jagged sunlit peaks which rise from sombre valleys upward into a strange light whose every ray seems to shine in its own individual hue. In the far distance we could see the ocean, with white breakers dashing against the cliffs; while in the valley below the Santa Cruz River, though actually foaming and dashing through its winding, rocky bed, seemed to us to be lying still, without motion of any kind, or sound.

In my diary, which I kept on that trip, I find that at each stopping place I have solemnly set down the observation that: "the scenery to-day was the finest we have yet found"; and when we reached Sagada I took the trouble to record for my own future reference that: "I shall not rest until Will has seen it." He never has.

At Sagada we found ourselves quite far up in the Igorrote country, where Filipinos as a rule, do not go. We had come from Cervantes over a trail where the horses kept to the inside, and where we were told to let go of our inner stirrups so, in case a horse went over the edge of the precipice its rider would have a chance of falling clear on the *terra-firma* side instead of being hurled out into open space. There are a great many people who have to be taken over such trails blind-folded, but there were no dizzy-heads among us, and as each turn of the way revealed to us different and more wonderful views, we filled the day with exclamation points.

Here and there we met bands of Igorrotes, marching "Indian file," carrying great bundles of rice up short-cut mountain trails, which wound through the rice terraces and were "as steep as the side of a house." All the men had long, murderous-looking spears, while the women were evidently the burden-bearers. Along the main trail we came, now and then, upon a company of men leading home a whimpering and pitiful little pack of very thin dogs. We knew these were to be killed and eaten and, naturally, the thought was sickening, but in the Igorrote country the dog-loving white man has to get used to this. Some day, perhaps, it will be different, but not until herds and flocks have been substituted and entirely new ideas have patiently been instilled into the minds of these people. For the time being dog flesh is their most cherished article of diet.

I wish it were known just where these curious wild tribes came from; just what their race history is. They are as unlike Filipinos as American Indians are unlike Englishmen. They have but one thing in common with the Filipinos, and that is their colour, which is a soft, dark brown. There is hardly an American who has ever lived among them for any length of time who has not a real admiration and affection for them and yet, to all intents and purposes, they are naked savages. They are most amenable to civilising influences. They take to education eagerly. They are, in their physical development, beautiful to look upon—when they are cleaned up— perfectly formed, straight and muscular, with features strongly marked and with wide, clear eyes which inspire confidence. They are entirely fearless; and they are loyal to the "last ditch." Also, it is these same incomprehensible "naked savages" who have built the thousands of acres of rice terraces which are a marvel and a mystery to every irrigation expert or technical engineer who has ever seen them.

Bontoc, which we reached after a day's weary, wet riding over slippery trails from Sagada, is the capital of what is now known as the Mountain province. For the first time in their known history the Igorrotes are united under one central government, each tribe having its lieutenant governor—an American always. There are the Benguets, the Bontocs, the Ifugaos, the Ilongots, the Kalingas and others, and they have been engaged in inter-tribal warfare since time began, their chief pleasure being derived from the taking of each other's heads. When I went into the Igorrote country headhunting was still in full force and houses were still decorated with festoons of human skulls, while no man ever ventured forth, even to his rice-fields, without his spear and shield and head-axe. They all carry spears even yet, but head-hunting, having been made by the American government a capital offence, is not so popular. Mr. Dean C. Worcester, as Secretary of the Interior, in direct charge of all wild tribes, actually succeeded in introducing substitutes for the sport in the form of baseball and other inter-tribal athletic contests and peaceful, though rough and strenuous pastimes. For fourteen years Mr. Worcester was to these children of the hills a most highly respected *Apo-apo,—chief* of chiefs.

Miss Bubb, my sister Maria and I were the first white women who ever set foot in Bontoc and to say that we created a sensation is to describe our reception too mildly. We were the guests of three American miners who had a comfortable house and who, having lived among the Igorrotes for a long time—one of them for more than a year without visiting civilisation—could give us much interesting firsthand information. The people gathered around us in hordes, but they kept at a respectful, not to say a reverential, distance. I think they were afraid of us; especially the women, not one of whom would let us look at her baby. But we were used to that. Many Christian Filipinos believe firmly in the "evil eye." There was one little dwarf who was bolder than the rest and who followed us everywhere we went. He was like a little, brown, toy-child, beautifully formed, and looking not more than one year old, but we were told that he was at least fourteen.

Everybody wanted to give us things. The evening I arrived I received a present from one of the headmen, of three live chickens, and the next day, as we were picking our way through the native village, another man ran after me and, very graciously and gracefully, presented me with two fresh eggs. We learned to say *"mapud,"* which means "good," and, in connection with smiles and gestures, found it served us famously for all purposes of social intercourse.

Bontoc is in a deep valley, on the bank of a wide, swift river and surrounded by close sheltering hills, so it is not as cold as it is in Sagada and some other places we visited; but it is cold enough, and I failed to understand how the natives could live in a state of almost complete nakedness. But they do and, in fact, all these people do, even in the coldest regions. The Bontoc Igorrote wears a very bright-coloured clout called a "G-string" with a heavy, brass chain around his waist, while his long, black hair is tucked into a little, flat, straw hat which is fastened, in some mysterious way, on the back of his head. They nearly all wear heavy, brass earrings which make their ears unsightly, and the Bon-toc "dandy" usually has a long, black, homemade and half-smoked cigar tucked behind one ear for all the world like the pencil of an absentminded bookkeeper.

We had *can yaos,* or bonfires with "head-dances," and all the strange varieties of entertainment provided by the village headmen. The musical instrument of the Igorrote is called a *ganza,* which is a round brass gong with a handle made of a human jaw-bone, upon which the "musician" beats a rhythmical measure with a soft, padded mallet as he whirls and twists in his fantastic dance. These *ganzas*—some of them very old,—are tribal rather than individual property and it is very difficult to induce their owners to part with them. Their value is computed in carabaos instead of in rice, or in dollars and cents. If you should ask an Igorrote how much he would take for his *ganza,* especially if it were one associated with tribal history, he would very likely look smilingly solemn and say: "One hundred carabao," or any other prohibitive number that might happen to occur to him. This is a form of racial pride and deserves respect.

We went from Bontoc back through Sagada to Cervantes, and then started down the long, narrow trail straight through the mountains to Baguio. At Cervantes we received our first messages from Manila and, among other things, was an order to Major Stevens to report for duty. His going gave us an opportunity to send letters down and report ourselves alive and not at all anxious to get home, but we didn't like losing the Major. We had, by this time, become a very well-acquainted, well-disciplined and congenial party and we disliked seeing the beginning of the end of our expedition. General Bell directed everything and joined in our sports and foolishness whenever he could do so without endangering the dignity of the "corps," but, while he was kindness itself, he was so strict with the young officers that we had sometimes to steal our opportunities for relaxation.

A few hours' riding south from Cervantes are some famous copper mines which were owned by a Spanish syndicate. We turned off in their direction and came into a most extraordinary country. The whole face of the landscape looks like corroded copper, and the great, scarred gulches where the ore has been taken out make one think of chaos, or dreams of an inferno. I don't know how to express an idea of bigness in a mere touch of description as I pass on through the story of this trip, but I want to convey an impression of overwhelming size in everything. It is a great, wild world where one sees miles in every direction and where nature seems to have done everything on a gigantic scale.

A mile or so beyond the copper mines we came upon a veritable mountain paradise,—from our point of view, at least. It was the home of Don Jose Mills, a Spaniard who, for 'some unknown reason, had banished himself to this out-of-the-world spot and, with what labour and pains can only be imagined, had made for himself a civilised abode. I was shown to a room all by myself, which had in it a real bed with springs and a mattress. It was the first one I had seen for I don't know how long. I regarded it with great curiosity at first, then I sat down on it most respectfully. I lay down and stretched myself out; then I pulled up a soft blanket and, though it was only midday, nothing short of the gravest emergency could have induced me to move. The emergency presented itself, finally, in the form of luncheon and I discovered that Don Jose had returned hurriedly from Candon in order to entertain us and that he had brought with him everything in the form of food and liquid refreshments that he could find. The result was a triumph, and we decided that we should like to remain under his hospitable roof indefinitely.

That night, amid much merriment, we initiated our host into the mysteries and secrets of a little society we had formed and which we called the Earring Club. Our insignia was a big, brass Igorrote earring, and we had signs and pass-words, to say nothing of a song which nobody but ourselves could sing. We appropriated the Cavalry tune of "For Seven Long Years I've Courted Nancy," but the words were our own and it was not difficult to supply a new verse to fit each incident or occasion as it came along. The song began:

For twelve long days we've hiked through mountains, Heigh ho!
Cross roaring rivers!

For twelve long days we've hiked through mountains, Ha! Ha! While
on our way through wild Lepanto!

Up at Sagada we came upon the only bed of mint that any of us had
ever seen in the Philippines, and as General Bell had almost an
inspired knowledge as to what mint was originally intended for, this
gave us material for three new verses:

One rainy day we reached Sagada,

Heigh ho! Among the rice fields!

One rainy day we reached Sagada,

Ha! Ha! As we toiled along o'er the hills of Bontoc!

A place most sweet with fragrant mint-beds, Heigh ho! How did it
get there'?

A place most sweet with fragrant mint-beds,

Ha! Ha! 'Way high up in the hills of Bontoc!

We didn't do a thing but make a julep,

Heigh ho! Without the cracked ice! We didn't do a thing but make a
julep,

Ha! Ha! With the mint we found in the hills of Bontoc!

It was a free-for-all composition contest; anybody was likely to
produce a new verse, or even a whole new song with a different tune,
at any moment, and we shortened many a long mile with such
nonsense.

At Don Jose's we not only sang all our songs for the benefit of our
host, but one of our number produced a harmonica, on which he
played very well indeed, and we had an impromptu *baile*. Then we
"dropped the handkerchief," "followed the leader," gave some
original renderings of German Grand Opera, played Puss-in-the-
corner, and finished the evening with our feet on a fender before a

great, open fire, recounting, with much appreciated embellishments, our interesting experiences.

We knew we should not find any place as delightful as Don Jose's again,—not even in Manila, because Manila would be hot,—so it was with great reluctance that we obeyed orders to be ready to leave the next morning at six. This meant getting out of our comfortable, civilised beds at five o'clock, while the stars would still be out, and when the ashes of our evening's fire would be cold and grey on the hearth. It was a cheerless thought, but we had to "get to Loo" said General Bell.

It was raining—of course—and there was not much scenery visible except when the clouds would float upward, now and then, like veils lifted off grand panoramas, but by this time we had ceased to consider the weather. When we got to Loo we found the "town" consisted of just two empty log huts, one with a plaited reed floor, the other with no floor at all, and neither of them with any sort of partition. We stretched a rope across the middle of the better one, hung Igorrote blankets on it by way of a screen, and prepared to make ourselves comfortable on the, fortunately flexible, floor; ladies on one side, gentlemen on the other. But along late in the afternoon a pack train of mules and Igorrotes and orderlies arrived from the south bringing us the astonishing news that the Commissioners were only a few miles behind and expected to camp that night at Loo!

The rain had settled down into a dreary, soaking patter; it was cold; we were all wet; there was no place for a fire; and, altogether, we were fairly uncomfortable.

The Commissioners, Mr. Worcester and Mr. Moses, with their private secretaries and a doctor—five in all—came along about an hour behind their pack train. They straggled in one by one, very grumpy, and we decided right away that they had not been taught, as we had been, to make the best of everything and to cultivate sociability on the trail. They had had a much more difficult day's riding than we because the trail up is much harder than the trail down, but we were pretty certain, on the whole, that we were much the better managed party.

178

With more Igorrote blankets we arranged another partition in the hut to make room for them, then we gave them a good hot dinner—cooked in the tent which had been put up for kitchen purposes—and immediately a social thaw set in. We got all the news from Manila that we were so anxious for, and all the latest gossip. The news was disquieting. A cablegram had come announcing that the Supreme Court had decided there should be no duties in Porto Rico against United States imports, and instructing the Commission to suspend all legislation in the Philippine Islands until further notice. This might mean anything, but whatever else it meant it certainly meant renewed uncertainty and the possibility that no change in the government would be made until after Congress met.

The politics of the situation were extremely complicated and seemed to revolve around a question which, because of a rather pugnacious manner of expressing it, had become a popular clamour. The question was: "Does the Constitution follow the Flag?" In other words, really, could duties be collected on imports from one American port to another? In any case, the question in respect to us was one for Congress to answer and it seemed to me we were facing another long period of uneasiness and delay.

We knew the entire Commission had expected to make a trip in June for the purpose of organising the Christian provinces in the far north beyond the Mountain Province, but they were halted by the order to suspend definite activities, and Commissioners Worcester and Moses had taken advantage of the "breathing spell" to run up into the mountains and inspect proposed routes for roads and railways. That is how we happened to encounter them at Loo. We shared their opinion that one of the greatest things that could be done for the country was to make the mountains of central Luzon, with their glorious climate, easily accessible. The trails as we found them were mere paths worn by the feet of Igorrotes and, besides being very narrow, were at such grades as to make them in many places all but impassable. The party, highly representative of American authority in the Islands, as it was, sat around on the bamboo floor, huddled up in blankets, and talked long into the night about hopes and fears and governmental problems of great difficulty and importance.

We left Loo at six o'clock in the morning and after eight straight hours of the hardest work we had yet been called upon to do, we arrived at Cabayan. According to my own diary: "I was completely tired. The greater part of the way we rode through beautiful pine forests, but up and down hills as steep as the side of a house; across rivers, and up a waterfall." This sounds like pretty heavy going, but my account of it written at the time was, I am sure, only slightly exaggerated. I remember distinctly that from Loo to Baguio, five full days, we walked a great part of the way; and not only did we walk, but we rendered necessary assistance to our horses which, giving out one by one, had to be dragged up the steep grades and "eased" down the opposite sides in a way that would have been highly ludicrous had we been engaged in anything but a very serious business. Only the steady old mules plodded along "without a word," and found their own way in safety around the dangerous turns.

After leaving Bontoc we travelled down through Nueva Viscaya and into Benguet, the southermost division of the Mountain province. At Cabayan we had for camping quarters a large *presidencia* and schoolhOuse ˉcombined, while a tent was put up and rudely equipped for bathing purposes. This was luxury indeed, and we began to think that we had left all hardship behind us; but the next night, after a seven hours' "hike" over a terrible trail, we found shelter in a miserable hut with only one room which we all had to occupy, with Igorrote blankets for partitions:

The Igorrotes grew less and less interesting as we went along and displayed few evidences of the industry and thrift which characterise the more northern tribes. The mountains are higher and the scenes are broader and more wonderful at the southern end of the range, but the only cultivation we came upon was in the villages and along the banks of the little rushing streams. It was evident that we were approaching "civilisation." Here and there we went through small groves of coffee trees, beautiful in a wealth of snow-white blossoms, but evidently' deserted, and wretchedly ragged and unkempt.

Baguio, now the summer capital of the Philippine Islands, the "Philippine Simla," as it is so often called, lies at the top of what has become justly celebrated as "the magnificent Benguet Road," the building of which has been the subject of more controversy than almost any other one thing that American authority and enterprise has accomplished in the Islands. The Benguet Road when I first saw it was known as "Mead's Trail," so named in honour of the engineer who made the original survey for it, and in some places it was nothing more than a thin line drawn against perpendicular cliffs to indicate where cutting was to be done.

Let somebody else argue the question as to whether or not this road has justified the faith of the men who built it. My husband and his colleagues were responsible for the beginning of it and Mr. Taft authorised the payment of the large sums of money which went into it, but he does not in the least object to honest criticism of the project. His only question is: "How else could we have accomplished what we did?" For which there is no satisfactory answer. I have ridden over it since it was completed and, in common with a majority of those who have enjoyed this privilege, I am strongly prejudiced in its favour. There are few, if any roads in the world more spectacular, or which represent a greater triumph of engineering skill. Fairly hewn out of the almost solid, but too crumbling, walls of the Bued River Canyon, it winds for about seventeen miles through constantly changing scenes of extraordinary grandeur, then it strikes the foothills of the mountains and rises in a succession of splendid upward sweeps to an altitude of more than five thousand feet in less than six miles.

The Benguet Road was originally a railway project and was to have been built by the British company which owns the Manila and Dagupan Railway. But this syndicate wanted a perpetual grant and a guarantee from the government which could not then be given. It was necessary, in any case, to build a wagon-road before railway construction could be started and Captain Mead, who was sent out at the head of a surveying party, reported that such a road would cost at least $50,000, or $75,000. The Commission appropriated the $50,000 and issued orders to have the work begun, fully expecting to have to add another $25,000 before the road was finished. Nobody knows what character of road Captain Mead had in mind when he made his estimate, but it transpired that nothing short of first-class construction would last through even one heavy rain. Besides, the Bued River Canyon had to be spanned six or eight times with tremendous suspension bridges, and before the project was completed an unwilling government had spent something like $2,500,000 on it. This was spread over a period of years, of course, and much of it went for necessary improvements or for the replacement of storm-wrecked bridges and graded sections, but its enemies like to refer to it as our two and a half million dollar road.

The Manila and Dagupan Railway company extended its road up to the point where the Benguet Road begins and thus a way was opened into the only region in the Philippines where one may find really invigorating air. And while the road was building Baguio development began. A United States Army Camp was established on a ridge overlooking a wide range of pine-covered hills, and a hospital was erected for the accommodation of invalid soldiers who, before these facilities for taking care of them were provided, had always, at great expense to the government, to be sent back to the United States. A civil hospital and tuberculosis camp were opened; good hotels under private ownership soon took the place of field tents and rough board shacks; markets and stores were started, bringing in supplies in wholesale lots, and fair-sized buildings soon began to go up in a substantial business section; people began to build houses as rapidly as builders could be found to do the work; churches and schools began to appear where nothing was before; a summer camp for the recuperation of thousands of public-school teachers was started in a high valley carpeted with pine-needles, and lecture courses for vacation instruction were instituted; a country club was organised with golf links, a baseball diamond, polo grounds, tennis courts and everything that goes to make a country club successful. The plan of the city was drawn by Architect Burnham of Chicago, who visited Benguet for the purpose, and a great central plaza was provided with artistic, but inexpensive buildings for the accommodation of the two branches of the government. Cottages in rows went up almost overnight; rich Filipinos and a few Americans built fine homes; beautifully metalled drives began to wind in and out and over and around the hills, and a high-class government automobile

'bus line was put on the Benguet Road which is the delight of every American or other foreigner in the Islands, as well as of many hundreds of Filipinos who annually take advantage of this wholly novel opportunity to reach a salubrious climate in their own land, and by a route which in any European country would attract scores of thrill-seeking tourists.

And so the Philippine Simla was begun. Its friends, or, in other words, most people have dreams of a great future for it when it shall be a thriving, prosperous city and a health resort for everybody "east of Suez" who needs to seek near by a temperate and invigourating climate.

It is six years since I saw Baguio, for I visited it the last time in 1907, but even then I could not believe that it was built on the ground that I had ridden over and found practically uninhabited only six years before. At that time a provincial government had been organised, and an American, Mr. Phelps Whitmarsh, who was a writer and had lived among the Igorrotes a long time, was appointed governor. But he was governor of a wild-tribe province which did not then boast any greater signs of civilisation than winding foot trails and a few groups of low-thatched huts which were known as towns.

We rode in from Trinidad, not many miles from Baguio, on the morning of the 23rd of June and went straight to the governor's "mansion." We were welcomed by Mrs. Whit-marsh into a nipa-roofed, *suali* house which, though it was quite large, had no partitions except such as were made of bamboo screens and hangings of bright-coloured Igorrote cloths. But it had a big, open fireplace and a fine blaze from odorous pine boughs was crackling up the chimney. This seemed particularly cosy and delightful to us because we had just been camping in native huts in which the only place for a fire was a square of earth in the middle of the floor and we were not only quite frozen but we were thoroughly smoked.

At Baguio we got letters and telegrams from Manila and one of the telegrams announced my husband's appointment as Governor of the Islands, so I knew that an adjustment of state affairs had been made and that I should reach Manila to begin a new era in my Philippine experience. Mr. Taft wrote me that the plans for his inauguration were practically complete and that he was issuing cards for a big reception in honour of General MacArthur at our house on the evening of the Fourth of July. This filled me with something like panic, because I didn't expect to reach Manila until after the first of July and I didn't see how I could get ready on such short notice to entertain hundreds of people. However, it was not for me to enter a protest on such a score, so it was decided that we would go down as soon as we possibly could.

We spent two days enjoying the delightful hospitality of our friends in Baguio and in exploring the country round about, and I, after listening to builders' dreams of what was to be and now is, proceeded to select a site for my own future summer home.

We sat around a roaring fire of an evening and sang all our songs, rather ruefully; we recounted our many adventures, and expressed our sincere regret that our holiday was over; then on the morning of the 25th of June, at the dreary hour of half past four, we mounted our refreshed and rested horses and started down the long Naguilian trail to the coast. I wish only to add that the heat in the lowlands, after our long breath of white man's air in the mountains, was almost more than we could stand, and I made the fatal mistake of leaving Baguio in a heavy flannel riding shirt and with no thin blouse handy to take its place.

GOVERNOR TAFT

THERE is no denying that the arrangements made, during my absence in the north, for my participation in the events attending my husband's induction into the office of Governor of the Philippines were enough to fill me with dismay.

Mr. Taft had issued two thousand invitations for the reception at our house in honour of General MacArthur, and on my way down from Baguio I had been spending my time wondering how I should take care of the three or four hundred I imagined had been asked. I had received no information more definite than the simple statement that invitations had been sent out, and it was not until I reached Manila that I learned the startling number. I thought my husband knew something about the limitations of our house, but I found that he had not taken this important matter into consideration at all.

Fortunately we had a large garden in fairly good condition by this time, so I immediately went to work and had it decorated with long lines and festoons of Japanese lanterns; I ordered a large refreshment tent put up in the middle of the wide lawn; then I sat down and prayed for fair weather. It was the rainy season and I knew that only a specially importuned Providence could keep the afternoon of the Fourth of July clear.

The inauguration of the first American Governor was an occasion of great dignity and interest. The ceremony took place on a platform erected at one end of a large square in the Walled City which is enclosed on one side by the Ayuntamiento, or Insular Capitol, and on another by the Cathedral. The foundations of the Inaugural stand were of historic interest in that they were originally intended to support a magnificent residence for Spanish Governors-General and were on the site of the ancient gubernatorial mansion which was destroyed by an earthquake in 1863. The rebuilding had never progressed beyond the laying of the massive granite base, and this still stands as a mute reminder to progressive Americans of the dilatory and otherwise questionable methods which once obtained in the Philippine government.

The Cathedral Plaza—since renamed Plaza McKinley—presented a memorable scene that Fourth of July morning. The architectural grace and time-mellowed colours of the old Spanish buildings blended with the rich luxuriance of many-hued tropic plants and the green of spreading acacias. American flags covered the canopied platforms and floated from every possible point of vantage. Americans and Filipinos, all in gala attire, were pressed close together in the spectators' stands which extended on either side of the central pavilion; the plaza below was thronged with Filipinos of every rank and condition, in all manner of bright *jusis* and calicos; while above the crowd towered many American soldiers and sailors in spic-and-span khaki or white duck.

The programme was much like other programmes. General MacArthur and his staff occupied the centre of the platform. A well trained and finely conducted Filipino band played several numbers; there was a prayer and an invocation; then my husband, looking larger even than his natural size in his crisp white linen suit, stepped to the front of the platform and stood gravely looking down upon the stocky little Chief Justice of the Archipelago, Senor Arellano, who administered the oath of office. Afterward Mr. Taft and Mr. Fergusson stood together and delivered, in English and Spanish, paragraph by paragraph in translation, the Inaugural address.

I think only one unfortunate incident occurred to mar the complete harmony of the occasion, and that was furnished by a United States Congressman of the Military Committee of the House, who was visiting Manila at the time.

Tickets of admission to the central pavilion had been sent to him, but he had forgotten to bring them with him. However, when he arrived at the plaza he started, with several ladies who were with him, to mount the steps of the Inaugural platform on which no ladies were allowed. He was stopped, naturally, and a guard offered to conduct his guests to seats on a side pavilion, telling him at the time that the central stand had been reserved for government officials and representatives, among whom he, of course, was included. This separate seating of the ladies seemed to annoy him for some reason, and he announced his intention of remaining with

186

his party. He was then shown to the best available seats and the incident seethed to be closed. But he was by no means satisfied with his position, especially when he found that the wives of some of the Commissioners had seats in front of him. I think the heat must have been affecting him for he called the Naval Lieutenant, who was in charge as usher, and made audible protest against "those wives of clerks" being put before him and his wife. The young naval officer was polite, but quite firm in his refusal to take any steps to remedy matters.

"You don't seem to know who I am!" he exclaimed, with manifest indignation.

"No, sir, I do not," mildly replied the Lieutenant.

"Well," said the angry man, "I'm a member of the Military Committee of the House of Representatives. I helped to make this Army out here and I've come out to see what kind of work I did. I don't like it, and I'm going home and unmake it. This treatment of me here is of a piece with the treatment I've received ever since I've been in these islands."

This didn't sound quite fair. He had been treated with marked courtesy by everybody and had accepted rather lavish hospitality from both Army officers and civil officials. In fact, he had received every possible attention in a most unusually hospitable community. The young Lieutenant bristled up and said:

"Sorry, sir, but I'm obeying orders; and I'd just like to tell you that I consider your remarks exceedingly impolite."

Upon which the gentleman from Washington left the pavilion and went down to stand in a place which the guards had been ordered to keep clear.

The rest of the story I heard afterward. It seems that both General Barry and General Davis saw him and took pains to go down and ask him up into the central pavilion, but he refused to go. Then one of the guards came up and politely informed him: "Orders, sir, you'll have to stand back." By this time he was infuriated and he turned on the guard and, after identifying himself, repeated his remarks about having made the Army and being determined to go back to Washington and unmake it.

"Well," said the guard, "I guess you can't unmake me. I've just been mustered out of the United States Army and am a plain American citizen. I don't understand that Congress can do much about unmaking American citizens." Which all goes to show that it doesn't do much good to lose one's temper. The gentleman took his party and stalked out of the plaza.

My hopes for the evening were blasted. About five o'clock the heavens opened and such a sheet of water descended upon my refreshment tent and my strings of gay paper lanterns as one never sees in the Temperate Zone. It was raining in torrents when our guests began to arrive, and if many of those invited had not been kept at home by the weather I don't know what I should have done with the crowd. I had a wide hall, a small reception-room, a dining-room and the verandah, but two thousand people are a good many, and I'm sure a large majority of them came in spite of the weather. It was a "crush," and a warm, moist crush, but it was a gala occasion, everybody was in good humour and the evening passed much more pleasantly than I had any reason to expect. This was the first entertainment of such proportions that I had undertaken in Manila, and I saw at once that, as the Governor's wife, I should need all the spaciousness of Malacarian Palace.

I think General MacArthur was pleased with our farewell hospitality to him; he seemed to be; and I think his feelings toward Mr. Taft, when he left the Islands the next day, were exceedingly friendly. But we heard later that letters had come from companions of his on the ship which said that he very keenly resented the fact that the new Governor had not seen fit to mention him with praise in his Inaugural address. Mr. Taft said he was very sorry, but, in view of the relations which were known to exist between the Military government and the Commission, he thought it would have been very difficult to find the tactful words which would have satisfied the General, and in uttering which he would not have stultified himself.

I am quite sure that General MacArthur never disliked my husband personally. His resentment was against the Commissioners in their

188

official capacity, whereby his own authority was diminished. In later years, as Secretary of War, Mr. Taft met him very often and their relations were always perfectly cordial. After his death there was considerable newspaper comment to the effect that he had been very badly treated. There was no refutation of the charges, but everybody familiar with the facts knew they had no foundation. When Mr. Taft was Secretary of War, on his recommendation General MacArthur was given the highest rank in the United States Army, that of Lieutenant-General, and at his own request was sent by Mr. Taft on a mission to travel through China with his son, an Army officer, as his aide, and to make a military report upon the country. On his return, at his own request, he was not assigned to command, but was ordered to his home at Milwaukee to prepare the report on China, and there he remained by his own choice until his retirement.

On the morning of July 5, we moved to Malacañan, and General Chaffee, who succeeded General MacArthur, took our house on the Bay. There was a great deal of contention with regard to this exchange of houses. Mr. Taft knew that to the mind of the Filipinos the office of Governor, without the accustomed "setting" and general aspects of the position, would lose a large part of its dignity and effectiveness. He also knew that a Civil Government, unless it were quartered in the Ayuntamiento, the recognised seat of government, would inspire but little confidence or respect. The outward semblance is all-important to the Filipino mind, yet knowing this the Military authorities clung with dogged tenacity to every visible evidence of supremacy, and it took an order from Washington to get them to vacate the Ayuntamiento in which they had, in the beginning, refused the Commission adequate office room. An official order also turned the Governor's residence over to the new Governor and, at the same time, relieved Mr. Taft of the necessity for deciding what to do with our house in Malate. It was the best available house in the city and every man on the Commission wanted it, so if the War Department had not taken it for the Commanding General somebody's feelings surely would have suffered. Mr. Taft had about decided to toss a coin in the presence of them all to see which one of his colleagues should have it.

In some ways we regretted that the move was necessary, for we were very comfortable in our "chalet," as Senor Juan de Juan had editorially called it, and invigourating dips in the high breakers of the Bay had become one of our pleasantest pastimes. But we knew that no amount of executive orders could turn our homely and unpalatial abode into a gubernatorial mansion, so we needs must move for the effect on the native mind, if for nothing else. Not until we did, would the Filipinos be convinced that Civil Government was actually established.

Not that I wasn't well pleased with the idea of living in a palace, however unlike the popular conception of a palace it might be. I had not been brought up with any such destiny in view and I confess that it appealed to my imagination.

Malacarian is old and rather damp and, in my time, some of it had not been furnished or finished according to modern ideas, but in size and dignity it leaves nothing to be desired, and it has historic associations which give it an atmosphere that I found to be quite thrilling. It contains many fine, old-world Spanish portraits, and there is one large canvas of especial interest which hangs at the head of the main stairway. It depicts the ceremony through which Magellan made peace with the natives of Cebu when he landed on that island in April, 1521. This consisted of drawing blood from the breasts of the principal parties to the contract, the one drinking that of the other. The Spaniards called it the *Pacto de Sangre,* or the Blood Pact, and so the picture is named. In our own day the Katipunan League, the strongest and most sinister of all the insurrectionary secret societies, are said to have adopted this ceremony in their rites of initiation, and members of the League could be identified by a peculiar scar on the breast.

The grounds at Malacarian contain, perhaps, twenty acres, and in those days there were fields and swamps in the enclosure as well as lawns and fountains, flower-beds and kitchen gardens. There were five or six good-sized houses in the grounds for the use of secretaries and aides, and the stables were very large.

I would not care to hazard a guess as to the number of *parientes* we sheltered in the quarters of our employes. Mr. Taft called these quarters our "Filipino tenement" "Calle Pariente," but screened with shrubbery and spreading down the sides of a twenty-acre lot the colony did not seem as conspicuous as our huddled tribe had been in Mal-ate.

The Palace is architecturally Spanish, yet it lacks the large patio, having two small courts instead. The lower floor, on a level with the ground, is really nothing more than a basement and has no usable spaces in it except some raised offices and cloak rooms. Frequently during bad typhoons I have seen water two and three feet deep in the entrance hall, but it always receded very rapidly and seldom gave us any inconvenience. The entrance, which is paved with marble, is very broad, and there is a wide and imposing staircase of polished hardwood leading to the reception hall above. The great living-rooms open one into another, giving a fine perspective, and they lead, through a dozen different doorways, on to a splendid, white-tiled verandah which runs out to the bank of the Pisig River. There is a picturesque, moss-covered river landing on the verandah below.

There are about twenty rooms on the one floor, all of them good sized and some of them enormous, and it took a great many servants to keep the place in order. The floors were all of beautiful hardwoods and it required a permanent force of six *nzuchachos* to keep them in a proper state of polish. The Filipino method of polishing floors is interesting. Your *muchacho* ties either banana leaves or some sort of bags on his bare feet, then he skates up and down, up and down, until the floors get so slick that he himself can hardly stand up on them. It is easy to imagine that six boys skating together in the spaciousness of the Palace might cut fancy figures and have a delightful time generally, if they thought they were unobserved. Filipinos of the *muchacho* class always play like children, no matter what they are doing, and they have to be treated like children.

The Palace furniture, which must have been very fine in Spanish days, was of red *narra,* or Philippine mahogany, handsomely carved and displaying on every piece the Spanish coat-of-arms. But during the changing Spanish regimes some one with a bizarre taste had covered all the beautiful wood with a heavy coat of black paint. The effect was depressingly sombre to me.

The porcelain, however, or what was left of it, was unusually good. The Spanish coat-of-arms in beautiful colours was reproduced on each plate against a background of a dark blue canopy. I must say there were quite as many reminders of Spanish authority as I could wish for and I frequently felt that some noble Don might walk in at any moment and catch me living in his house.

But, it didn't take us long to get settled down in our new domain, and I soon ceased to regret the sea breezes and the salt baths of Malate. Malacanan enjoyed a clean sweep of air from the river and our open verandah was in many ways an improvement on´ the gaudily glazed one that we had gradually become accustomed to in the other house. The Malacanan verandah, being much of it roofless, was of little use in the daytime, but on clear evenings it was the most delightful spot I have ever seen. I began to love the tropical nights and to feel that I never before had known what nights can be like. The stars were so large and hung so low that they looked almost like raised silver figures on a dark blue field. And when the moon shone—but why try to write about tropical moonlight? The wonderful sunsets and the moonlit nights have tied more American hearts to Manila and the Philippines than all the country's other charms combined. And they are both indescribable.

When I lived in Malate and could look out across the open, white-capped bay to far-away Mt. Meriveles, I sometimes forgot I was in the Tropics. But at Malacanan when we gazed down on the low-lapping Pasig, glinting in the starlight, and across the rice fields on the other side where swaying lanterns twinkled from beneath the outline of thatched roofs, there was little to remind us that we were Americans or that we had ever Telt any air less soothing than the soft breeze which rustled the bamboo plumes along the bank.

Our household was in every way much enlarged on our change of residence and circumstances. There were eight or nine *muchachos* in the house, two extra Chinese helpers in the kitchen, and the staff of coachmen and gardeners increased on even a larger scale. Our stable of ponies multiplied to sixteen, and even then there were too few for our various needs. It is difficult for the dweller in the Temperate Zone to realise how small an amount of work the native of the Tropics, either man or beast, is capable of.

We thought at first that the salary attached to the office of Governor of the Philippines was quite splendid, but we soon gave up any idea we might have had of saving a little of it for a rainy day. Our rainy day was upon us. It rained official obligations which we had to meet. The mere cost of lighting Malacanan was enough to keep a modest family in comfort. I don't know about conditions at the Palace now, but I imagine they have not changed much, and I do know that Manila is a more expensive place in which to live than it was in my time. And yet there is serious talk of reducing the salary of the Governor-General. It seems a pity. This would place the office in a class with Ambassadorships which nobody but rich men can accept. The present salary, with nice management and a not too ambitious programme, will just about cover expenses, but I feel sorry for the wife of the Governor who must try to do what is expected of her on less.

My cook, who had been quite independent of me at Malate, became at Malacanan wholly unapproachable. I don't know why, but so it was. He occupied quarters opening on one of the courts below and connected with the dining-room by an outside staircase up which I was never able to inveigle him. I had to deliver my orders from the top of the stairs and when he had listened to just as much as he cared to hear he would disappear through the kitchen door, and no amount of calling would bring him back. As the kitchen was an ante-chamber to a sort of Chinese catacombs, extending over a good part of the basement, I never ventured to follow him and I had to swallow my wrath as best I could.

But he was a jewel despite his eccentricities. He could produce the most elaborate and varied buffet suppers I ever saw and I never knew a cook who could make such a wonderful variety of cakes and fruit tarts and cream-puffs. He took a real delight in their construction, and for two days before a reception he would spend all his time filling every pan in the house with *patisseries* elaborately iced in every imaginable colour.

193

I began at once to give an afternoon reception every week and if it hadn't been for my disagreeable, but capable, old Ah Sing I should have been in a constant turmoil of engagements with caterers and confectioners. As it was, I never had to give an order, really. "Reception Wednesday, Ah Sing," was all that was necessary, and except for a glance now and then to see that the *muchachos* were giving the floors and the furniture a little extra polish on Wednesday morning, the only preparations I had to make for receiving two thousand people were to put on an embroidered muslin gown and compose myself.

These afternoon receptions were public, our only form of invitation being an "At Home" notice in the newspapers, and considering the unsettled state of Manila society in those days, it is really remarkable that we had so few unwelcome guests. There were a great many derelicts and generally disreputable people, both American and European, trying to better their fortunes or add to the excitement in our agitated community, but we suffered no unpleasant consequences from our open hospitality, though every Wednesday the Palace was thronged and every Wednesday many new faces appeared. Army and Navy people, civilians of every occupation and many foreigners—Germans and British mostly—came nearly always. I remember especially the first instalment of American school teachers. They were, for the most part, a fine lot of men and women who had come out with high hopes and ideals and an enthusiastic desire to pass them on. There were some pretty girls among them and a number of very clever looking men. I believe they used to enjoy my parties as much as anybody in Manila. They were homesick, no doubt, especially the girls, and I suppose the sight of so many friendly American faces cheered them up.

The Filipinos had to have a little coaxing before they began to avail themselves very freely of our general invitation. But by asking many of them personally and persistently to "be sure and come Wednesday" we prevailed on a good number to believe they were really wanted; and after a little while there began to be as many brown faces as white among our guests.

Speaking of school teachers reminds me that it was just about this time that our minds were relieved of all anxiety with regard to Bob's and Helen's education. My husband had wanted to send our ten-year-old son back across the Pacific and the United States, all by himself, to his Uncle Horace's school in Connecticut, and I had opposed the idea with all my might without being able to offer a satisfactory substitute plan. But now a school for American children was opened and they were as well taught as they would have been at home. Moreover, Bob and Helen found a large number of congenial companions, and I don't think I ever saw a happier set of boys and girls. They lived out of and did everything that children usually do, but their most conspicuous performance was on the Luneta in the evenings, where they would race around the drive on their little ponies, six abreast, or play games all over the grass plots which were then, and always have been, maintained chiefly for the benefit of children, both brown and white.

My husband's change in title and station made very little difference in the character of his duties, but it gave him increased authority in the performance of them. The onerous necessity for submitting legislation to an executive whose point of view was different from that of the Commission came to an end, and he was able to see that such laws as the Commission passed were put in operation without delay. Under General Chaffee the feeling on the part of the Army against the encroachments of civil government gave way, slowly but surely, to an attitude of, at least, friendly toleration. It was as if they said: "Well, let them alone; we know they are wrong; but they must learn by experience, and, after all, they mean well."

General Chaffee and General MacArthur were two quite different types of men. General Chaffee was less precise, less analytical. General MacArthur had always been given to regarding everything in its "psychological" aspect and, indeed, "psychological" was a word so frequently on his lips that it became widely popular. General Chaffee was impetuous; he was much less formal than his predecessor both in thought and manner, and Mr. Taft found co-operation with him much less difficult. He made no secret of his conviction, which was shared by most of the Army, that civil government was being established prematurely, but he was not unreasonable about it.

He refused at first to listen to the proposition for the establishment of a native Constabulary. This had been the Commission's pet project ever since they had been in the Islands, and it was a great disappointment to them to find that the opposition which they had encountered in the former administration was to be continued.

What they wanted was a force of several thousand Filipinos, trained and commanded by American Army officers, either from the regular Army or from the volunteers. The same thing had been done with success by the British in India and the Straits Settlements, by the Dutch in Java and by our own General Davis in Porto Rico, and as the insurrectionary force had dwindled to a few bands and to scattered groups of murderers and ladrones, so acknowledged by everybody, there was no reason why a native constabulary should not be employed to clear these out.

This plan was among the first things submitted to General Chaffee, but he was evidently not impressed. "Pin them down with a bayonet for at least ten years" was a favourite expression of Army sentiment which sometimes made the Commissioners' explanations to the natives rather difficult.

General Wright, on behalf of the Commission, called on General Chaffee and was much surprised to learn that he had not even read the Constabulary bill which had been passed some time before and held up pending the hoped for opportunity to carry it into effect. When General Wright explained the purport of the measure General Chaffee said,

"I am opposed to the whole business. It seems to me that you are trying to introduce something to take the place of my Army."

"Why, so we are," said General Wright. "We are trying to create a civil police force to do the police work which we understood the Army was anxious to be relieved of. You have announced your purpose to concentrate the Army in the interest of economy, and to let our civil governments stand alone to see what is in them and we consider it necessary to have a constabulary, or some such force, to take care of the lawless characters that are sure to be in the country after years of war, and especially in a country where the natives take naturally to ladronism. The Municipal police as now organised are not able to meet all the requirements in this regard."

"There you are," said General Chaffee, "you give your whole case away."

"I have no case to give away," replied General Wright. "We are trying to put our provincial governments on a basis where they will require nothing but the moral force of the military arm, and actually to preserve law and order through the civil arm. The people desire peace, but they also desire protection and we intend through the civil government to give it to them."

The Commissioner then suggested the names of some Army officers whose peculiar tact in handling Filipinos had marked them as the best available men for organising and training native soldiers, but General Chaffee was not inclined to detail them for the work, so General Wright returned to the Commission quite cast down and communicated to his colleagues the feeling that they were to have a continuance of the same difficulties with which they were required to contend under the former administration.

But a peacemaker came along in the person of General Corbin. He spent some time with General Chaffee and then came to Malacanan to visit us. He made a hurried, but quite extensive trip through the Islands and gave the whole situation pretty thorough inspection. After he left, a change was found to have come over the spirit of affairs, and it was thought that he had managed to make clear to everybody concerned that, while there was a military arm and a civil arm of the government in the Philippines, they represented a single American purpose and that that purpose had been expressed by the administration at Washington when the Commission was sent out to do the work it was then engaged upon.

After that General Chaffee seems not only to have been amenable to reason, but to have been imbued with a spirit of cordiality and helpfulness which was most gratifying to the long-harassed Commission. To facilitate co-operation, a private telephone was installed between the offices of Mr. Taft and the Commanding General, and it seemed to me that my husband suddenly lost some of the lines of worry which had begun to appear in his face.

The Constabulary, as everybody knows, was eventually established and perhaps no finer body of men, organised for such a purpose, exists. It took a long time to get them enlisted, equipped and properly drilled, but to-day they are a force which every man and woman in the Philippines, of whatever nationality, colour, creed or occupation, regards with peculiar satisfaction. They include corps enlisted from nearly every tribe in the Islands, not excepting the Moros and the Igorrotes. The Moro *constabulario* is distinguishable from the Christian in that he wears a jaunty red fez with his smart khaki uniform instead of the regulation cap, while the Igorrote refuses trousers and contents himself with the cap, the tight jacket, the cartridge belt and a bright "G-string." To the Ifugao Igorrote uniform is added a distinguishing spiral of brass which the natty soldier wears just below the knee. It is difficult to imagine anything more extraordinary than a "crack" company of these magnificent bare-legged Ifugaos going through dress-parade drill under the sharp commands of an American officer. The Constabulary Band of eighty-odd pieces, under the direction of Captain Loving, an American negro from the Boston Conservatory of Music, is well known in America and is generally considered one of the really great bands of the world. All its members are Filipinos.

Press clippings and some correspondence which I have before me remind me that even at this period there began to manifest itself in the Taft family, and otherwheres, mild interest in the possibility that my husband might become President of the United States. Mr. Taft himself treated all such "far-fetched speculation" with the derision which he thought it deserved, but to me it did not seem at all unreasonable. We received first a copy of the Boston *Herald* containing two marked articles in parallel columns, one of which, headed by a picture of Mr. Taft, stated that in Washington there had been serious suggestion of his name as a Presidential candidate and the other giving a sympathetic account of an anti-imperialistic meeting at Faneuil Hall. We thought the two articles as "news items" hardly warranted juxtaposition, and it seemed to us the editor was indulging a sort of sardonic sense of humour when he placed them so. Not that my husband was an "imperialist," but that he was generally so considered. Indeed, he was the most active anti-imperialist of them all. He was doing the work of carrying out a thoroughly anti-imperialistic policy, but he recognised the difference between abandoning the Philippines to a certain unhappy fate and guiding them to substantial independence founded on self-dependence. It took a long time to get the shouters from the house-tops to accept this interpretation of our national obligation, but there was reassurance in the fact that where our honour is involved Americanism can always be trusted to rise above purely partisan politics.

Mr. Taft's mother, who took an active and very intelligent interest in her son's work and who sent him letters by nearly every mail which were filled with entertaining and accurate comment on Philippine affairs, took the suggestion of his being a Presidential possibility quite seriously. And she did not at all approve of it. Having seen a number of press notices about it she sat down and wrote him a long letter in which she discussed with measured arguments the wisdom of his keeping out of politics. At that time the idea appealed to nothing in him except his sense of humour. He wrote to his brother Charles: "To me such a discussion has for its chief feature the element of humour. The idea that a man who has issued injunctions against labour unions, almost by the bushel, who has sent at least ten or a dozen violent labour agitators to j ail, and who is known as one of the worst judges for the maintenance of government by injunction, could ever be a successful candidate on a Presidential ticket, strikes me as intensely ludicrous; and had I the slightest ambition in that direction I hope that my good sense would bid me to suppress it. But, more than this, the horrors of a modern Presidential campaign and the political troubles of the successful candidate for President, rob the office of the slightest attraction for me. I have but one ambition, and if that cannot be satisfied I am content to return to the practice of the law with reasonable assurance that if my health holds out I can make a living, and make

Nellie and the children more comfortable than I could if I went to Washington."

This letter is dated August 27, 1901, and was written on a Spanish steamer which the Commission had taken from Aparri, on the north coast of Luzon, after they finished the last of the long trips they had to make for the purpose of organising civil government in the provinces.

It was just after they returned from this trip; just when things were at their brightest; when everything seemed to be developing so rapidly and our hopes were running high, that we were shaken by the appalling news of the attack on President McKinley. We had kept luncheon waiting for Mr. Taft until it seemed useless to wait any longer and we were at table when he came in. He looked so white and stunned and helpless that I was frightened before he could speak. Then he said, "The President has been shot."

I suppose that throughout the United States the emotions of horror and grief were beyond expression, but I cannot help thinking that to the Americans in the Philippines shock came with more overwhelming force than to any one else. Mr. McKinley was our chief in a very special sense. He was the director of our endeavours and the father of our destinies. It was he who had sent the civil officials out there and it was on the strength of his never failing support that we had relied in all our troubles. It might, indeed, have been Mr. Root in whose mind the great schemes for the development of the islands and their peoples had been conceived, but Mr. Root exercised his authority through the wise endorsement of the President and it was to the President that we looked for sanction or criticism of every move that was made. Then, too, the extraordinary sweetness of his nature inspired in every one with whom he came in close contact a strong personal affection, and we had reason to feel this more than most people. Truly, it was as if the foundations of our world had crumbled under us.

But he was not dead; and on the fact that he was strong and clean we began to build hopes. Yet the hush which fell upon the community on the day that he was shot was not broken until a couple of days before he died when we received word that he was recovering. We were so far away that we could not believe anybody would send us such a cable unless it were founded on a practical certainty, and our "Thank God!" was sufficiently fervent to dispel all the gloom that had enveloped us. Then came the cable announcing his death. I need not dwell on that.

Mr. Taft and Mr. Roosevelt knew each other very well. They had been in Washington together years before, Mr. Taft as Solicitor General, Mr. Roosevelt as Civil Service Commissioner, and they had corresponded with some frequency since we had been in Manila. So, in so far as the work in the Philippines was concerned, my husband knew where the new President's sympathies were and he had no fears on that score. At the same time he was most anxious to have Mr. Root continued as Secretary of 'War in that there might not be any delay or radical change in carrying out the plans which had been adopted and put in operation under his direction. All activities suffered a sort of paralysis from the crushing blow of the President's assassination, but the press of routine work continued. We were very much interested in learning that a great many Filipinos, clever politicians as they are, thought that after Mr. McKinley's death Mr. Bryan would become President, and that, after all, they would get immediate independence.

Then came the awful tragedy of Balangiga. It happened only a few days after the President died, while our nerves were still taut, and filled us all with unspeakable horror intensified by the first actual fear we had felt since we had been in the Philippine Islands. Company "C" of the 9th Infantry, stationed at the town of Balangiga on the island of Samar, was surprised at breakfast, without arms and at a considerable distance from their quarters, and fifty of them were massacred. About thirty fought their way bare handed through the mob, each man of which had a bolo or a gun, and lived to tell the tale. It was a disaster so ghastly in its details, so undreamed of under the conditions of almost universal peace which had been established, that it created absolute panic. Men began to go about their everyday occupations in Manila carrying pistols conspicuously displayed, and half the people one met could talk of nothing else but their conviction that the whole archipelago was a smouldering volcano and that we were all liable to be murdered in our beds any night. Of course this made the Army officers more certain than ever that the Islands should have remained under military control indefinitely, and I cannot deny that, at the time, their arguments seemed to have some foundation. It was a frightful nervous strain and it took several months of tranquillity to restore confidence. If it had been a regular engagement in which the Americans had sustained a reverse it could have accepted with some philosophy, but it was a plain massacre of a company of defenceless men by many times their number who had gotten into the town with the consent of the American authorities, and in conspiracy with the local headman and the native parish priest, on the pretext of bringing in for surrender a band of insurrectos.

The man, Lucban, who was in command of the Samar ladrones who committed this atrocity, is now a prominent politico in Manila, and it is interesting to know that only last year, in a campaign speech, he referred with dramatic intensity to "our glorious victory of Balangiga." He was appealing to an ignorant electorate, many of whom, as he knew, wore the scar of the awful Katipunan "blood pact," but it is just to record that the average Filipino is not proud of the Balangiga "victory."

Shortly before these unhappy events my sister Maria was called back to America by the illness of our mother, and I was left to face the tragic excitements of the month of September without her comforting companionship. By October I began to feel that I would have to get out of the Philippine Islands or suffer a nervous breakdown, so my husband and I agreed that it would be well for me to "run up to China," as they express it out there. Running up to China at that time of year meant getting out of tropic heat into bracing autumn weather with a nip of real winter in it, and there was nothing that I needed more.

Mrs. Wright and Mrs. Moses were both anxious to see something of China before leaving the Orient, and as this seemed an excellent opportunity to make the trip, they decided to go with me. The Boxer Insurrection had just been suppressed and the Dowager Empress had not yet returned from the West, whither she had fled during the siege of Peking. We were used to the alarums of war and we thought we were likely to see more of China "from the in- side" than if we visited the country during a period of complete calm. Then there were wonderful tales of valuable "loot" which interested us. Not necessarily illegitimate loot, but curios and art treasures in the hands of Chinese themselves who were selling things at ridiculously low figures and, sometimes, with a fascinating air of great mystery. There is some allurement in the idea of bargaining for priceless porcelains, ivories, silks and Russian sables behind closed and double-locked doors, in the dark depths of some wretched Chinese hovel. Our Army officers who had helped to relieve Peking brought us stories of this kind of adventure, and I secretly hoped that we should be able to have just some such experience. But being the wives of American officials I thought likely we should be "taken care of" every hour of every twenty-four. And so we were.

We sailed to Shanghai and went from there straight to Peking, where we became the guests of Colonel and Mrs. Robertson, who had gone in with the American troops in the Allied Armies and were quartered in no less a place than the Temple of Heaven. The casual tourist looking now upon that glorious collection of ancestral shrines would find it difficult to believe that they once served as barracks for American soldiers. Most people who visit the Temple of Heaven find in it an atmosphere of peace and serenity such as is achieved by few structures in the world, and to have this deep calm invaded by business-like "foreign-devil" troops must have ruffled the spirits of the high gods. But the soldiers had to be quartered somewhere and this great, clean, tree-sheltered enclosure in the heart of the Chinese city offered ample space.

Mr. Conger was then our Minister to China, and after spending a few very busy days sightseeing we went to the Legation to visit him. The Legation quarter, which had been laid in ruins during the Boxer troubles, had not begun to assume an aspect of orderliness, and many were the evidences of the weeks of horror through which the besieged foreign representatives had lived.

As the Empress Dowager and her court had not yet returned, we hoped to be able to see all the mysteries of the Forbidden City, but order had been restored to a point where it was possible to make the palaces once more "forbidden," so we were shown only enough to whet our curiosity. But the wonderful walls and the temples, the long, unbelievable streets and the curious life of the people were sufficient to save us from any feeling of disappointment in our visit. At a dinner given for us by our Minister we met a number of men and women who had been through the siege, and I sat next to Sir Robert Hart, of the Imperial Chinese Customs, the most interesting man, perhaps, that the great occidental-oriental co-operation has ever produced.

When we returned to Shanghai on our way down from Peking I was greeted by two cablegrams. It just happened that I opened them in the order of their coming and the first one contained the information that my husband was very ill and said that I had better return at once to Manila, while the second read that he was much better and that there was no cause for alarm. There was no way of getting to Manila for several days, because there were no boats going. So I decided to take a trip up the Yangtse River on the house-boat belonging to the wife of the American Consul. If I had been doing this for pleasure instead of for the purpose of "getting away from myself" I should have enjoyed it exceedingly, but as it was I have but a vague recollection of a very wide and very muddy river; great stretches of clay fiats, broken here and there by little clumps of round mounds which I knew were Chinese graves, and bordered by distant, low hills; an occasional quaint grey town with uptilted tile roofs; and a few graceful but dreary-looking pagodas crowning lonesome hill-tops. And in addition to all of this there was a seething mass of very dirty and very noisy humanity which kept out of our way and regarded us with anything but friendly looks.

I had left my husband apparently perfectly well, but I subsequently learned that the night after I left Manila he developed the first symptoms of his illness. It was diagnosed at first as dengue fever, a disease quite common in the Philippines which, though exceedingly disagreeable, is not regarded as dangerous. It was about two weeks before a correct diagnosis was made, and it was then discovered that he was suffering from an abscess which called for a serious emergency operation. He was taken to the First Reserve Army hospital and the operation was performed by Dr. Rhoads, the Army surgeon who afterward became his aide when he was President.

The children must have been much frightened. They had never seen their father ill before, and he told me afterward that he should never forget the way they looked as he was being carried out of Malacarian on a stretcher borne by six stalwart American policemen. They were all huddled together in the great hall as he passed through, and while Bob and Charlie were gazing at the proceedings in open-eyed astonishment, Helen was weeping.

For twenty-four hours after the operation the doctors were not at all certain that their patient would live, nor did their anxiety end at that time. The abscess was of long growth, the wound had to be made a terrible one, and there was great danger of blood poisoning. Mr. Taft rallied but a second operation was necessary. By the time I reached Manila he was well on the way to recovery, though even then there was no prospect of his being able to move for many weeks to come.

He used to lie on his cot in the hospital and recite to his visitors a verse of Kipling's which he thought fitted his case exactly:

> "Now it is not well for the white man
> To hurry the Aryan brown,
> For the white man riles and the Aryan smiles,
> And it weareth the white man down.
> And the end of the fight is a tombstone white
> With the name of the late deceased,
> And the epitaph drear: 'A fool lies here
> Who tried to hurry the East.'"

It was decided at once by everybody, including the doctors, Mr. Root and President Roosevelt, that Mr. Taft must leave the Islands as soon as he was able to travel, and there were several reasons, besides those connected with health, why it seemed best for us to return to the United States. The principal one was that Congress was becoming very active with regard to Philippine matters, and as Mr. Taft was anxious that the right kind of legislation should be passed, he wished to go to Washington and present the facts about the situation as he had found them during his long hand-to-hand struggle with the problem. Mr. Root cabled him that his presence in Washington was necessary and granted him a three months' leave of absence from his duties as Governor, while General Wright was appointed vice-Governor to fill his place for the time being.

Mr. Worcester was the ranking member of the Commission, but my husband felt that he had not quite the same talent for genially dealing with every kind of person, whether evasive Filipino or dictatorial Army officer, which General Wright so conspicuously displayed, and, moreover, Mr. Worcester was entirely engrossed with the problems of his department, which included health and sanitation and the satisfactory adjustment of the difficulties connected with the government of the non-Christian tribes. These were matters which appealed to Mr. Worcester's scientific mind and which he vastly preferred to the uncongenial task of administering the routine of government, so he was only too willing not to be encumbered with the duties of Governor. This, I understand, was Mr. Worcester's attitude throughout his thirteen years as Secretary of the Interior, during which time he was always the ranking Commissioner with the first right, under a promotion system, to the Governorship whenever a vacancy occurred in that office.

The transport *Grant* was assigned for our use by General Chaffee, and we made our preparations for an extended absence.

One incident of my husband's convalescence in the hospital I think I must relate. In an adjoining room General Frederick Funston was recovering from an operation for appendicitis and he was sufficiently far advanced to be able to walk around, so he used to call on Mr. Taft quite often. Now General Funston, for the benefit of those who have no mental picture of him, is by no means gigantic. He has the bearing of a seven-foot soldier, but the truth is he is not more than five feet three or four inches in height.

One day there was an earthquake of long duration and extended vibration which would have been sufficient to destroy Manila had it not lacked a certain upward jerk calculated to unbalance swaying walls. One gets used to earthquakes in the Orient in a way, but no amount of familiarity can make the sensation a pleasant one.. My husband was alone at the time and he had decided to hold hard to his bed and let the roof come down on him if it had to. The hospital was a one-story wooden building and he really thought he was as safe in it as he would be anywhere. Moreover, he was quite unable to walk, so his fortitude could hardly be called voluntary, but he had scarcely had time to steel himself for the worst when his door was thrown open and in rushed General Funston.

"We must carry out the Governor!" he shouted; "we must carry out the Governor!"

"But how are you going to do that, General?" asked Mr. Taft.

He knew quite well that General Funston, in his weakened condition, would be incapable of carrying an infant very far.

"Oh, I have my orderly with me," responded the doughty General, and by this time he had begun to get a firm grasp on the mattress while behind him hurried a soldier, shorter even than his chief, but with the same look of dauntless determination in his eye.

In spite of the straining on the rafters, Mr. Taft burst out laughing and flatly refused to let them try to move him. Fortunately for them all the upward jerk necessary to bring down the roof didn't occur, so there is no way of telling whether or not, for once in his life, General Funston started something that he couldn't finish.

We sailed from Manila on Christmas Eve, 1901, and, much as I had enjoyed my life and experiences in our new world of the Philippines, I was glad to see the tropic shores fade away and to feel that we were to have a few months in our own land and climate, and among our own old friends, before I sighted them again.

A TRIP TO ROME

THE winter of 1902, the greater part of which we spent in Cincinnati, is memorable only as a period of bereavement and protracted illnesses. Perhaps such a record has no place in a narrative wherein it is my wish to dwell on pleasant memories only, or, at least, to touch as lightly as possible upon those incidents which, for one's peace, may better be forgotten, but a whole winter filled with grief and worry is not so easily torn from the leaves of the calendar rolled back.

In the first place, when I left Manila in December, 1901, I was very near to a nervous breakdown.* This was due to the long strain of a peculiarly exacting official life in a trying climate, and an added weight of uneasiness about my husband's illness.

*[A remarkable statement that modern First Ladies would be unlikely to make.]

Then, too, my mother was very ill. She had suffered a stroke of paralysis the year before from which she had never rallied and I was extremely anxious to be with her in Cincinnati.

When we arrived in San Francisco a terrible mid-winter storm was sweeping the country from one end to the other and we were strongly advised to delay our trip across the continent, but we were both eager to go on so we started East at once over the Union Pacific.

When we passed Ogden we found ourselves in the midst of the worst blizzard I ever saw. The snow piled up ahead of us, delaying us hour by hour; the bitter wind fairly shook the heavy train; and to turn mere discomfort into misery the water pipes in the cars froze solid and we were left without heat of any kind. There was nothing to do but to go to bed; but even so, with all the blankets available piled on top of us, we shivered through interminable hours while the train creaked and puffed and struggled over the icy tracks.

When we reached Omaha I received a telegram telling me that my mother had died the day before, and I found it no longer possible to brace myself against the inevitable collapse. We hurried on to

Cincinnati and arrived in time for my mother's funeral, but I was too ill to be present. It was two months before I began to recover.

In the meantime Mr. Taft left us and went on to Washington for consultation with the President and Mr. Root and to appear before the Philippine Committees of the House and Senate which were then conducting minute inquiries into conditions in the Islands preparatory to passing a much-needed governmental bill. For a whole month he was subjected to a hostile cross-examination, but he was able to place before the Committees more first-hand and accurate information on the subject of their deliberations than they had theretofore received. This was exactly what he wanted to come to the United States for, and he would greatly have enjoyed it had he been in his usual form, but he was not. During his stay in Washington he was the guest of Secretary and Mrs. Root and only their friendly care and solicitude enabled him to continue so long. In March he was compelled to return to Cincinnati for another operation, the third in five months. Everything considered, it seemed to me the Taft family had fallen upon evil days.

However, the weeks passed, I began to improve, and as soon as my husband had fairly set his feet on earth again we began to make plans for our return to the Philippines. There could be no thought of abandoning the work in the Islands just when it was beginning to assume an ordered and encouraging aspect, nor was it possible just then to shift the responsibility to other shoulders. This would have been too much like "changing horses in the middle of a stream."

My husband was able while he was in Washington to present to President Roosevelt and Secretary Root a very clear outline of Philippine affairs, together with such details as could never be conveyed by cable, and the inevitable conclusion reached was that no solution of the problem was possible which did not include the settlement of the Friar controversy. The four monastic orders, the Franciscan, the Dominican, the Augustinian and the Recoleto, which held four hundred thousand acres of the best agricultural land in the Islands, had won the lasting enmity of the Filipino people and it was absolutely impossible to establish permanent peace while the Friars remained and persisted in an attempt to return to their parishes.

Hundreds of them were living in practical imprisonment in the monasteries of Manila, and that they should not be allowed to return to their churches throughout the Islands, from which they had been driven, was the one stand taken by the Filipinos from which they could not by any form of persuasion be moved.

The solution of the difficulty proposed by Mr. Taft and his colleagues in the Philippine government was that the United States purchase the Friars' lands and turn them into a public domain on the condition that the orders objected to by the people be withdrawn from the Islands.

As soon as President Roosevelt recognised the importance of accomplishing these things he decided, with characteristic directness, that somebody should go at once to Rome and open negotiations with the Vatican, and after considering various men for this delicate mission he concluded that Mr. Taft was the man best fitted to undertake it.

The prospect of another novel experience was exceedingly gratifying to me and I began at once to look forward with interest to a renewal of my acquaintance with Rome and to the trip back to the East by the Suez Canal, the Red Sea and the Indian Ocean which, according to Kipling, "sits an' smiles, so sof', so bright, so bloomin' blue." So my feet no longer lagged in my preparations for a long trip with my three children and another extended residence in the tropics.

To assist Mr. Taft in his negotiations with the Vatican, and to make up a dignified and formidable looking Commission, the President appointed Bishop O'Gorman of the Catholic diocese of South Dakota, and General James F. Smith, at that time a member of the Philippine judiciary and in later years Philippine Commissioner and Governor-General of the Islands. His rank of General he attained as an officer of volunteers in the Army of Pacification in the Philippines, but, a lawyer in the beginning, after he was appointed to the Bench he became known as Judge Smith, and Judge we always called him. He is an Irish Catholic Democrat and a man of very sane views and exceptional ability. Major John Biddle Porter was made Secretary-Interpreter to the Commission, and Bishop Brent, Episcopal Bishop of the Philippines, on his way to Manila, decided to go with Mr. Taft, wait for him until he had completed his business at Rome and then continue with him the journey to the Philippines. This was the beginning of a warm friendship between Bishop Brent and ourselves, and no one can have lived in the Philippines since, or have been familiar with the affairs of the Islands, without knowing what a blessing his work and presence have been to the Philippine people, and how much he has aided the Government in its task.

We engaged passage on the steamship *Trave,* sailing from New York to Gibraltar about the middle of May; the day for our departure was close at hand; many good-byes had been said; and, altogether, the immediate future was looking bright, when suddenly I found myself once more within the orbit of my unlucky star. My son Robert chose this opportune moment to develop a case of scarlet fever. Of course that left me and the children out of all the plans and I was compelled to accept a hastily made arrangement which provided for my remaining behind and following my husband and his interesting party on a later ship. Fortunately

Robert was not with the other children when he contracted the disease. He was visiting friends in another part of town and I had him removed immediately to the Good Samaritan Hospital, then settled down to my vigil which might be long or short as fortune decreed.

My husband's mother was in Millbury while all these things were transpiring and he called her up on the long distance telephone to tell her about Bobby's illness and to say good-bye.

"Then Nellie cannot go with you'?" said Mrs. Taft. "No, I'm sorry to say she can't," said my husband.

"But you have now an extra stateroom, have you not?" "Yes, Mother."

"Well, Will, I don't think you ought to make such a trip alone when you are so far from strong, so I just think I'll go with you in Nellie's place," said my mother-in-law.

And she did. The intrepid old lady of seventy-four packed her trunks and was in New York ready to sail within twenty-four hours, and my husband wrote that she acted altogether with an energy and an enterprise which filled him with pleasure and pride. On the steamer, and later at the hotel Quirinal in Rome, she presided with dignity for more than a month over a table at which daily gathered a company composed of a Colonial Governor, a Supreme Judge, a Roman Bishop, an Anglican Bishop and a United States Army officer.

Her activity and fearlessness kept her family and friends in a state of astonishment a good part of the time. She went wherever she liked and it never seemed to occur to her that it was unusual for a woman of her age to travel everywhere with so much self-reliance. She thought nothing of crossing the American continent every year to visit her daughter or sister on the Pacific Coast, and out in Manila we used to laugh at the possibility of her appearing on the scene at any moment. In fact, she very seriously coming at one time. I was glad that she could go with my husband to Rome because she really could be a comfort and a help and not at all a responsibility.

Robert was not nearly as ill as we expected he would be and in a few weeks I was able to make definite plans for joining my husband. My sister, Mrs. Anderson, was going to Paris so I took advantage of the opportunity to enjoy her companionship on the voyage and sailed with her on the fourth of June, landing in France and going by train to Rome.

That the record of our ill-luck may be quite complete I must add that on the way across the Atlantic my son Charlie managed to pick up whooping-cough, and that by the time we reached Rome he had passed it on to Helen. Her first remark to her father was a plaintive query: "Papa, why is it we can never go anywhere without catching something?"

I devoutly hoped that we had caught everything there was to catch and that we might now venture to predict a period of peace.

I found my party very comfortably bestowed. They were occupying a whole floor at the Quirinal, the largest hotel then open in the city, and were keeping what appeared to me to be considerable "state." It looked as if they had the entire building to themselves, but that was because it was midsummer when few tourists visit Rome and when all Roman society is supposed to flock to its mountain homes and to northern resorts. However, midsummer though it was, a good many members of the "Black," or Vatican division of society, still lingered in the city and I found them evincing every desire to make our stay both pleasant and memorable. Before I arrived Mr. Taft had already "met, called upon, taken tea with and dined with Cardinals, Princes, counts, marquises, and distinguished Englishmen and Americans resident in Rome," to quote from one of own letters, but he had a good many things to do over again in my honour. He had also had an audience with Pope Leo XIII, and was deep in the rather distracting uncertainties and intricacies of his negotiations.

He did not have the pleasure of seeing the King of Italy whom he had a great desire to meet, because, even though the American Ambassador had made all the arrangements, etiquette did not permit such an audience until his relations with the Vatican had terminated, and by that time the King had gone to the military manoeuvres in North Italy.

My husband's position was one of very great delicacy. By the nature of our national institutions it is not possible for us to send a representative to the Vatican in a diplomatic capacity no matter what the emergency may be, and Mr. Roosevelt in sending this Commission to Rome had no intention that its office should be construed into a formal recognition of the Vatican, which could not fail to raise a storm of protest and opposition in this country. So the instructions given to Mr. Taft by Secretary Root were made very definite on this point. After reviewing the necessity for taking such action on the part of our government and covering the favourable reports on the proposed negotiations submitted by the Philippine Committees of the House and Senate, the instructions began with paragraph one:

One of the controlling principles of our government is the complete separation of church and state, with the entire freedom of each from any control or interference by the other. This principle is imperative wherever American jurisdiction extends, and no modification or shading thereof can be a subject of discussion.

Following this in numbered paragraphs, a tentative plan for the adjustment of the Friar difficulties is outlined and the instructions end with paragraph nine:

Your errand will not be in any sense or degree diplomatic in its nature, but will be purely a business matter of negotiation by you as Governor of the Philippines for the purchase of property from the owners thereof, and the settlement of land titles in such a manner as to contribute to the best interests of the people of the Islands.

These instructions were easier to receive than to carry out, since from the beginning the Vatican made every possible effort to give the mission a diplomatic aspect and to cast upon it the glamour of great official solemnity, and Mr. Taft had constantly to keep his mind alert to the danger of accidental acquiescence in a misinterpretation of his position. To take a position which would soothe the feelings of American Catholics and yet not shock the conscience of any Protestant was something like being ground between the proverbial millstones. However, Cardinal Rampolla very graciously met the businesslike ideas of the Commission and arranged a private audience with Pope Leo at which the propositions of the Philippine government were to be outlined to him.

My husband's memory of this now historic mission to Rome seems to include little which was not directly connected with the business in hand, but Judge Smith displays a more impressionable bent. In answer to ari inquiry as to what he recalls of the visit he wrote Mr. Taft a most interesting letter. All his memoranda of the trip, including letters, journals and souvenirs, were destroyed in the San Francisco fire, but he says:

"After our arrival there was a long wait that arrangements might be made for an audience with the Holy Father, but finally the date was fixed and the Commission, at high noon, in evening dress and top hats, went to the Vatican and passed up the long staircase, lined with Swiss Guards, which leads to the State apartments. 'We were received by the Chamberlain and several other functionaries and

214

were conducted from one apartment to another until finally we were ushered into the presence of Leo XIII, to whom you made a statement of the matters which were to be made the subject of negotiation.

"This statement had been previously translated into French by Bishop O'Gorman and Colonel Porter, and you will remember there were some things about Bishop O'Gorman's French which did not meet with the entire approval of Colonel Porter. Whether you arbitrated the matter and selected the appropriate phrase which should have been used I do not know, but I do know that at one time there was danger of the severance of the friendly relations which had theretofore prevailed between the good Bishop and the good old Colonel.

"My recollection of the Holy Father is that his face was like transparent parchment, that he had the brilliant eyes of a young man and that he was wonderfully alert of mind, although bent over by the weight of years.

"Of course, none of us could forget Cardinal Rampolla, —tall, slender, straight, vigorous in both mind and body, impenetrable, and cold as fate. A man evidently of wonderful intellect and fully equal to any demands that might be put upon him as the diplomat of the Vatican."

I might add that the first part of my husband's speech, a copy of which I have, consisted of a few remarks appropriate to the presentation of a gift from President Roosevelt to the Pope. This gift was a specially bound set of Mr. Roosevelt's own works.

When the formal interview was at an end the Pope came down from the dais on which he sat and indulged in a fifteen or twenty minute personal conversation with the members of the Commission. "He asked for the pleasure of shaking my hand," writes my husband to his brother Charles, in the usual vein of humour which obtains between them, adding, "a privilege which I very graciously accorded him." He also joked about Mr. Taft's proportions, saying that he had understood he had been very ill, but from observation he no reason to suppose that the illness had been serious. He poked gentle fun at

Bishop O'Gorman and made kindly inquiries of Judge Smith and Major Porter; then he walked with the party to the door and bowed them out, a courtesy which I believe was unprecedented.

"He had a great deal more vigour of motion," writes Mr. Taft, "and a great deal more resonance of voice than I had been led to suppose. I had thought him little more than a lay figure, but he was full of lively interest and gesture, and when my address was being read he smiled and bowed his head in acquiescence."

"We visited the catacombs," says Judge Smith, "St. Peter's, St. Paul's beyond the walls, and a few of the basilicas of ancient Rome now dedicated to Christian worship. The Borghese and various other art galleries left their impression, as did some of the interesting old palaces, notably the one which was then threatening to fall into the Tiber, and the ceiling of which bears the famous fresco of Cupid and Psyche.

"One day during our first wait we had dinner out at the American College as guests of Monsignor Kennedy, where you (Mr. Taft) made a speech which brought much applause from the students in red cassocks, and everybody was happy. After dinner some of us made a visit to a villa by the Orsini on the hills overlooking the Campagna, which villa had recently been purchased by the college as a summer home.

"You will remember our call on Cardinal Martinelli and the dinner we had with good old Cardinal Satolli who took such a pride in the wine produced by his own vineyards, a wine, by the way, which was not unreservedly approved by the owners of other vineyards. One of the most delightful experiences of all was our dinner with the good Episcopal Rector, Dr. Nevin, when ox-tongue done in the Russian style was served as the *piece de resistance*. You cannot for- get how shocked were some of the circles in Rome to find Bishop O'Gorman and myself at such a festal board under such circumstances, and how Pope Leo showed his thorough understanding of American institutions by saying that American Catholics might very properly do things which would be very much misunderstood if done by Romans. The Episcopal Rector was a mighty hunter, a great traveller, and gifted with a fund of anecdote which made him a most delightful host."

I found this highly social and sociable party rather impatiently awaiting a reply to their formal, written proposals to the Vatican which had been turned over to a Commission of Cardinals. They were giving a fine imitation of outward leisurely poise, but among themselves they were expressing very definite opinions of the seemingly deliberate delays to which they were being subjected. Mr. Taft was anxious to sail for Manila on the 10th of July, and already had his passage booked on the *Koenig Albert*, but the immediate prospect seemed to be that he would be held in Rome for the rest of the summer.

He did not have the greatest confidence that he would succeed in the mission which meant so much to his future course in the Islands, and, indeed, it was quite evident that he would not succeed without prolonged effort to be continued after he left Rome. The various Cardinals lost no opportunity to assure him that the Vatican was in full sympathy with the proposals made and that he might expect a very early and satisfactory termination of the business, but he decided not to believe anything until he should see the signatures to the contract. The factions and the politics of the Vatican were most perplexing. The monastic orders were the conservative element in the negotiations, being willing enough to sell the Friars' lands at a valuation to be decided upon by a board of five members, two representing the church, two representing the United States government and the fifth to be selected from some other country, but they were not willing to consent to the withdrawal of the Friars from the Philippine Islands. Then there were wheels within wheels; Papal candidates and candidates for Cardinals who thrust into the negotiations considerations for agreeing or not agreeing which greatly puzzled the purely business-like representatives of the American government.

But I was not particularly annoyed by the delay. I found much to interest me in Rome, and I saw my husband improving in general health and gaining the strength he needed for a re-encounter with the difficulties in tropic Manila. Prominent Republican leaders had aroused his impatience at different times by publicly announcing that, in all probability, he was "going out to the Philippines to die." He wrote to his brother from Rome:

"I dislike being put in such an absurd position before the country as that of playing the martyr. I'm not asking any favours on account of health or any other cause, nor am I taking the position that I am making any sacrifice. I think that a great and unusual opportunity has been offered me and if I can improve it, all well and good, but I don't want any sympathy or emotional support."

He was easily aroused to resentment on the subject, but, just the same, it was gratifying to observe him quite rapidly regaining his normal vigour and buoyancy.

My mother-in-law was having a most wonderful time. She was comfortably established at the Quirinal in rooms next to ours, and was enjoying the devoted attention of every man in the party whether he wore ecclesiastical frock, military uniform or plain citizens' clothes. She went everywhere and saw everything and was as indefatigable in her enjoyment as any of us. She met old-time friends whom she had known when she and Judge Taft were in the diplomatic corps abroad, and with them she indulged pleasant reminiscence. After I arrived she became more energetic than ever and led me a lively pace at sightseeing and shopping, because, as she wrote to another daughter-in-law, Mrs. Horace Taft, "Nellie is not at all timid and as she speaks French we can go anywhere."

I soon found that in spite of official and personal protest to the contrary we were considered quite important personages, and the elaborate hospitality we were offered kept us busy at nearly all hours when hospitality is at all in order. There were teas and luncheons, dinners and receptions, and functions of every description, and we met a great many renowned and interesting people, both Roman and foreign. Mr. W. T. Stead, the correspondent for the London *Times* who was lost on the *Titanic,* was one of them. Then there was Mr. Laffan; proprietor of the New York *Sun,* and Mrs. Laffan, and Dr. Hillis of Brooklyn who was in Rome with his son. An attractive personality, who interested us very much and whose hospitality we enjoyed, was Princess Rospigliosi, the wife of an Italian nobleman, who lived in an enchanting house. She had a very beautiful daughter who was at that time keenly interested in the controversy as to whether or not Catholics should vote in Rome. She was strongly in favour of their doing so and, with extraordinary directness, carried her advocacy straight to the Pope and insisted that it was a great mistake for Catholics not to take advantage of the ballot and by that means secure the political rights to which they were entitled. Pope Leo, although very much impressed by what she said, insisted that it was not yet time to urge the reform suggested, and wound up by saying, "My good daughter, you go altogether too fast for me!" I don't doubt that by this time the young Princess is a warm supporter of woman's suffrage.

Also, we were entertained by a Mr. McNutt who had been in our diplomatic corps at one time in Madrid and Constantinople, at another time had been tutor to the sons of Khedive of Egypt, and was then one of the Papal Chamberlains. He had married a woman of wealth, a Miss Ogden of New York.

Mr. McNutt had one of the most elaborate and beautiful palaces I ever saw. He had studied the customs of Roman society in the picturesque days of the Medicis and the Borgias, had rented the Pamphili Palace and restored it to its pristine glory, and it was here that he entertained us at a dinner, with cards afterward.

I felt like an actor in a medieval pageant whose costume had not been delivered in time for the performance. Cardinals in their gorgeous robes, with gold snuff-boxes, gave to the scene a high colour among the soberer tones of Bishops and Archbishops and uniformed Ambassadors. Then there were Princes and Princesses and other nobilities of Roman society, the men displaying gay ribands and decorations, the women in elaborate costumes, and all in a "stage setting" as far removed from modernity as a magnificent old-world palace could be. To make this reproduction of old customs complete our host made a point of having liveried attendants with flaming torches to light the Cardinals to and from their carriages.

Before I reached Rome, Mr. Taft and his associates had been present at a Papal consistory at which the Pope presided over the College of Cardinals. They were the guests of the Pope and occupied the

Diplomatic Box. I was sorry to miss this exceptional privilege, but we were given ample opportunities for seeing and hearing several noteworthy religious festivals both at St. Peter's and the church of St. John of Lateran. I was educated in the strictest Presbyterianism, while my husband's mother was a Unitarian, and Puritan in her training and in all her instincts. We could not help feeling that we had been led into a prominent position in a strange environment. But, unshaken though we were in our religious affiliations, we appreciated the real beauty of the ceremonies and knew that we should rejoice in the unusual privilege accorded us which would never be ours again.

It was near the end of our stay in Rome that we had our audience with the Pope,—Mrs. Taft, Robert, Helen and I. I wore a black afternoon gown with a black veil on my head, while Mrs. Taft wore her widow's veil as usual. Helen, I dressed in white and, to her very great excitement, she wore a white lace veil. Bishop O'Gorman accompanied us and when we reached the door of the Vatican under the colonnade at the right of St. Peter's, we were met by some members of the Swiss Guard in their curious uniforms, conducted through endless corridors and rich apartments until we came to a small waiting-room where we were left for a few moments by ourselves. We had only time to adjust our veils and compose ourselves when the door on one side opened and we were ceremoniously ushered into the presence of Leo XIII who sat on a low chair under a simple canopy at the far end of the room. He rose to greet us as we entered, and as we were presented one by one he extended his hand over which we each bowed as we received his blessing.

He began speaking to me in French and finding that I could answer him in that language he talked with me for perhaps half an hour with a most charmingly graceful manner of comment and compliment. He spoke of Mr. Roosevelt's present and wished that he knew English so that he might read the books. He referred to Mr. Roosevelt as "President Roomvine" which was as near as he seemed to be able to get to that very un-Latin name; said that he himself, in his youth, had been devoted to the chase and would like very much to read "The Strenuous Life."

Later he called Robert to his side and gave him a special blessing, saying that he hoped the little boy would follow in the footsteps of McKinley and Roosevelt. He asked Bob what he expected to be when he grew up and my self-confident son replied that he intended to be Chief Justice of the Supreme Court. I suppose he had heard the Chief Justiceship talked about by his father until he thought it the only worthy ambition for a self-respecting citizen to entertain.

When we arose to go, His Holiness escorted us to the door and bowed us out with a kindly smile in his fine young eyes that I shall never forget.

Shortly after this I left Rome. It was getting hot and my husband persuaded me to take the children away, promising to join us for a short breath of mountain air before he sailed for Manila. It had been decided that I should remain in Europe for a month or so and I was to choose the place best suited for recuperation. I went first to Florence for a week, then to the Grande Albergo Castello de Aquabella at Vallombrosa. The sonorous name of this hotel should have been a sufficient warning to me of the expense of living there, but I was not in a mood to anticipate any kind of unpleasant experience.

It is a beautiful place reached by a funicular railway from a station about fifteen miles from Florence, and is where Milton wrote parts of Paradise Lost. The hotel was an old castle remodelled, and as we were almost the only guests and were attended by relays of most obsequious servants we managed to feel quite baronial. We spent our time being as lazy as we liked, or driving in the dense black forests of pine which cover the mountains and through vistas of which we could catch fascinating glimpses of the beautiful, town-dotted valley of the Arno some thousands of feet below.

On the 20th of July my husband came up and joined us in this delightful retreat. He had just received his final answer from the Vatican and, while he was disappointed at not being able to settle the matter then, he was hopeful that a way had been found which, though it would entail much future labour, would lead to a satisfactory of the problems. An Apostolic Delegate, representing the Vatican, was to be sent to Manila to continue the negotiations on the ground, and Pope Leo assured Mr. Taft that he would receive instructions to bring about such an adjustment as the United States desired. This assurance was carried out, but only after Leo's long pontificate had come to an end.

The final note was written by Cardinal Rampolla who rendered "homage to the great courtesy and high capacity" with which Mr. Taft had filled "the delicate mission," and closed by declaring his willingness to concede that "the favourable result" must in a large measure be attributed to my husband's "high personal qualities."

I had hoped to have Mr. Taft with us at Vallombrosa for a week or so before he sailed, but the time allotted in our plans for this was taken up by delays in Rome, so that when he did arrive he had only twenty-four hours to stay. His final audience with the Pope was arranged for the following Monday, there were a number of minor details to be attended to, and he was to sail Thursday morning from Naples on the *Princess Irene,* to which he had been obliged to transfer from the *Koenig Albert.*

The last audience with His Holiness consisted chiefly in an exchange of compliments and expressions of thanks for courtesies extended, but it had additional interest in that the Pope chose to make it the occasion for personally presenting to the members of the party certain small gifts, or souvenirs, which he had selected for them. He had previously sent an inquiry through Bishop O'Gorman as to whether or not the Commissioners would accept decorations, but Mr. Taft replied that the American constitution forbids the acceptance of such honours without the consent of Congress, so nothing more was said about it.

The presents he did receive were a handsome Jubilee medal displaying a portrait of His Holiness in bas relief, and a gold pen in the form of a large feather with the papal arms on it. To me the Pope sent a small piece of old German enamel showing a copy of an ancient picture of St. Ursula and her virgins, framed in silver and gold beautifully wrought. Smaller gold medals were given to each of the other Commissioners, while President Roosevelt received a copy in mosaic of a picture of a view of Rome from a corner in the Vatican gardens in which the Pope is seen seated with three or four Cardinals in attendance. This, together with letters from His Holiness and Cardinal Ram-polla to the President and Mr. Hay, the Secretary of State, was given to Bishop O'Gorman to be delivered when he arrived in the United States.

My husband sailed from Naples on the 24th of July, and I, with the three children and their French governess, started north by Venice and Vienna to spend a few weeks in the mountains of Switzerland before returning to Manila.

There were rather terrifying reports of a cholera epidemic raging in the Philippines and I dreaded the prospects of going into it with my children, but I knew that heroic efforts were being made to check it and I felt confident that, in Manila at least, it would have run its course before I should arrive, so I booked passage on the German steamer *Hamburg* and on the 3rd of September sailed for the East and the tropics once more.

LAST DAYS IN THE PHILIPPINES

WHEN Mr. Taft reached Manila he found the city *en fete* and in a state of intense excitement which had prevailed for two days during which the people had expected every hour to hear the great siren on the cold storage plant announce that the little *Alava,* the government coastguard boat which had been sent to Singapore to get him, had been sighted off Corregidor.

When the announcement finally came, everything in the harbour that could manage to do so steamed down the Bay to meet him, and when the launch to which he had transferred from the *Alava* came up to the mouth of the Pasig River and under the walls of old Fort Santiago, seventeen guns boomed out a Governor's salute, while whistles and bells and sirens all over the bay and river and city filled the air with a deafening din.

Wherever his eyes rested he saw people,—crowding windows, roofs, river banks and city walls, all of them cheering wildly and waving hats or handkerchiefs. And the thing which moved him most was the fact that the welcoming throng was not just representative of the wealthy and educated class, but included thousands of the people, barefooted and in calicoes, who had come in from the neighbouring and even the far provinces to greet him.

Mrs. Moses asked Mr. Benito Legarda, one of the Filipino members of the Commission, whether or not there had ever been a like demonstration in honour of the arrival of a Spanish Governor, and his answer was:

"Yes, there were demonstrations always, but the government paid the expenses."

In this case the very opposite was true. The government had no money to waste on celebrations and all government buildings, such as the City Hall, the Post Office and the Ayuntamiento, were conspicuously bare. Their nakedness was positively eloquent of economy in the midst of the riot of gay bunting, the flags, the pennants and the palm leaves in which the rest of the city was smothered. Then there were extraordinary and elaborate arches spanning the streets through which the Governor was to be conducted. One of these, erected by the *Partido Federal*, displayed a huge allegorical picture which had a peculiar significance. Filipina, a lovely lady draped in flowing gauze, was seen, in an attitude which combined appeal with condescension, presenting to Columbia a single star, implying that she desired to be accepted as one of the States of the Union.

I am indebted to the descriptive art of Mrs. Moses, to photographs and to my own knowledge of the Filipino way of doing things for the mental picture I have of this celebration.

At the landing near the Custom House my husband found a great procession in line, ready to escort him to the Ayuntamiento where the speeches of welcome were to be made. There were regiments of cavalry, infantry and artillery, as well as platoon after platoon of native and American police with as many bands as there were divisions of the procession. Picked men from the volunteer regiments acted as a special guard for the Governor's carriage and they must have added much to the impressive array, because I know of my own observation that the volunteers were always as fine a looking body of men as it would be possible to find anywhere.

When Mr. Taft reached the Ayuntamiento he listened to glowing speeches of tribute and welcome in the Marble Hall, then he stood for hours shaking hands with the people who, in orderly file, passed in and out of the building which was large enough to hold only a very small fraction of them. When this was over and his audience had settled down he proceeded to tell them in a clear and simple way all about his experiences in Rome and how far the negotiations with the Vatican had proceeded. This was a matter of paramount importance to the Filipinos and they listened with an intensity of interest which Mr. Taft said seemed to promise serious consequences if the business could not be carried to a successful conclusion.

However, despite the joy and festivity with which he was greeted upon his return, the Governor did not find general conditions in the islands either prosperous or happy.

Everything that could possibly happen to a country had happened or was happening. The cholera epidemic was still raging, and while it had abated to a considerable extent in Manila it was at its worst in Iloilo and other provinces. There had been from seventy to eighty cases a day in Manila for a long time, and the quarantine regulations had incensed the ignorant people to a point where force had to be used to secure obedience. They did not understand sanitary measures and wanted none of them; they clung to their superstitious beliefs, and were easily made to accept as truth wild statements to the effect that the Americans were poisoning the wells and rivers and had stopped transportation and business with the sole purpose of starving or otherwise destroying the entire population. Even the educated ones were not without their time-honoured prejudices in this regard, for while Mr. Taft was in Rome he receive a cabled protest from Filipino members of the Commission with a request that he order the quarantine raised.

When he arrived in Manila the cholera cases had fallen to between ten and twenty a day and business had been resumed to a certain extent, but the situation was still critical and a fresh outbreak on account of polluted water was to be expected at any time. All the sources of water supply were patrolled by American soldiers day and night and every precaution was taken; whole sections of the city were burned in an attempt to stamp out the pestilence, but the disease had to run its course and it was months before it was completely eradicated.

While the people were dying of cholera the carabaos, the only draught and farm animals in the Islands, were dying by thousands of an epidemic of rinderpest. This scourge, too, was fought with all the force of both the civil and military arms of the government, but before it could be checked it had carried off a large majority of the carabaos in the Archipelago with the result that agriculture and all other industries dependent upon this mode of transportation were paralysed. A general drought in China made a rice famine a practical certainty, even if the people should have money to buy rice, so the future looked black indeed.

The cholera and rinderpest had greatly reduced government revenues and many plans for much needed public works had to be modified or abandoned, while the condition of the currency added to the general chaos. There was no gold standard and the fluctuations in the value of silver made it necessary for the Governor to issue a proclamation about once a week fixing a new rate of exchange. In this way it was calculated that the government, with insufficient income at the best, lost a round million dollars gold during a period of ten months.

To cap all and add exasperation to uneasiness the ladrones had become increasingly active with hard times and were harrying the districts around Manila to such an extent that the people were in constant terror. The ravages of the rinderpest had made the carabao a very valuable animal and the chief object of the ladrones was to steal such as were left and drive them off to be sold in distant provinces. Nor were they at all particular about their highwaymen's methods or chary of sacrificing human life. There was a veritable hotbed of ladronism at Caloocan, a suburb of Manila, which was augmented by the roughs and toughs from the crowded and miserable districts in the lower city, while across the Bay in Cavite province, known as the "mother of insurrection," there were several hundred rifles in the hands of marauders who hid away in the hills and jungles and made conditions such that Mr. Taft was asked by the Director of Constabulary to suspend the writ of habeas corpus, thus declaring the province in a practical state of siege. Mr. Taft would not do this, saying that he thought the only course was to "hammer away with the constabulary until the abuse was stamped out by the regular methods of supposedly peaceful times," but the worst feature of the situation was that wherever ladronism showed its head there would be cohorts of "irreconcilables"—posing in every-day life as loyal citizens—ready, within the limits of personal safety, to encourage and assist it. Anything to hamper and harass the government.

Shortly after Mr. Taft's arrival in Manila, the vice-Governor, General Wright, and Mrs. Wright left the Islands for a well-earned vacation and my husband wrote that the amount of work which confronted him was staggering. He took on General Wright's department in addition to his own duties, and if it hadn't been that he had at least half way learned not to try to "hurry the East" he probably would not have lasted long.

Among the first steps to be taken was to provide against the inevitable famine, and to do this it was necessary for the Government to send to China and Saigon for large quantities of rice to be stored in public godowns. They bought and brought to Manila something like forty million pounds of this first of all necessities to an oriental people, and the intention was to sell it at cost when the market supply began to run low and prices began to soar beyond the poor man's reach. A certain degree of paternalism has always been, is now, and probably always will be necessary in the government of the Filipino people.

Mr. Taft besought the United States Congress to appropriate a sum to be used for the importation of work animals, for the purchase of rice and the furnishing of work on public improvements. The animals were not to be given away, but were eventually to be sold at reasonable prices. Three millions were appropriated and spent.

Congress was also petitioned to establish a gold standard of currency, and this too was done, to the inexpressible relief of everybody interested in the Philippine welfare, in the following January. The currency now is as sound as our own, every silver peso, which corresponds to the old "dollar Mex," being worth fifty cents gold.

When I arrived in Manila in early October I found the situation more interesting than it had ever been, even though it was distracting to the men who had to deal with it. My first necessity was, of course, to settle myself once more at Malacarian. During my absence the old Palace had been all done over, painted and patched and cleaned and redecorated until it was quite unlike its quaint, old dilapidated self. Some of the colours were a shade too pronounced and some of the decorations ran a little more to "graceful patterns" than suited my taste, but I was glad of the added comfort and cleanliness.

It was difficult in the beginning to accustom myself to cholera conditions. The disease was communicated to very few Americans or other white foreigners, but safety was secured at the price of eternal vigilance. Water could not be drunk unless it was boiled under one's personal supervision; nothing uncooked could be eaten, not even a piece of imported fruit, unless it had first been washed in a carbolic solution, a process, I may say, which added nothing desirable to its flavour; a good many other precautions were necessary which made us feel as if we were living always in the lowering shadow of some dreadful catastrophe, but, even so, we were surprisingly calm about it—everybody was—and managed to come through the experience without any visible ill-effects.

There was one new thing for me, and that was a live cow. For two long years we had manfully striven to make ourselves believe that we liked canned milk and condensed cream just as much as we liked the fresh milk we had been used to all our lives. In fact, we were fond of declaring that we couldn't tell the difference. But we could. And in our secret hearts we all welcomed as the most delectable treat an occasional gift of skimmed milk from a friend who had been a pioneer in the momentous venture of importing an Australian cow.

The importation of our cow was a real event, and she straightway took up a position of great dignity and importance in our establishment. She roamed at will about the grounds of the Palace and her general conduct was the subject of daily comment in the family circle. A number of people brought in cows about this time, but very few of them lived long enough to prove their dairy worth. Our cow flourished and gave forth large quantities of milk, and this fact became the subject of what was supposed to be a huge joke.

Mr. Worcester, who was the high chief health authority in the Islands, decreed that all animals as they were brought in should be inoculated for rinderpest, tuberculosis, and a number of other things,—"including prickly heat," said General Wright,—but it just so happened that a great majority of these scientifically treated beasts died almost immediately, and General Wright could always arouse the wrath of Mr. Worcester—a thing he loved to do—by suggesting that the only reason our cow lived was because "she had not been inoculated."

The presence of the cow having given me a true farmer spirit—at least, I suppose it was the cow—I decided to a garden. There were very few vegetables that the Filipinos knew how to raise at that time, and our longing for fresh things was constant and intense. I selected a promising looking spot behind the Palace, had it prepared for planting, then I bought a supply of fresh American seeds and carefully buried them in places where I thought they might develop into something. The result was positively astonishing. The soil was rich and the sun was hot, and in an incredibly short time we were having quantities of beans and cauliflower and big red tomatoes and all kinds of things.

My ambition grew with success and I branched out into poultry. The first thing anybody knew I had a big screened yard full of chickens and turkeys little and big, which were a source of great enjoyment to us all both in their noisy feathered state in the chicken yard and done up in a variety of Ah Sing styles on our very well supplied table. I wonder how my cook made up the "squeeze" out of which he was cheated by my industry and thrift.

But, dwelling on these minor details I am getting far ahead of my story. There were many things in the meanwhile engaging my attention, the most important of which, I suppose, was the great church schism.

Gregorio Aglipay, an Ilocano priest of the Roman Catholic Church, joined the original insurrection against Spain, or the Friars rather, at its inception and was excommunicated. He became an insurgent leader with a reputation for great cruelty, and continued in the field against Spain, and subsequently against the United States, until resistance was no longer possible. He was among the last insurrecto chiefs to surrender in northern Luzon. When peace was restored he began immediately to solicit the interest and aid of other Filipino priests, of politicians and influential men in a plan for organising an Independent Filipino Catholic Church, and his temporary success must have surprised even him.

While the people loved catholicism, the failure of the Vatican to accede to their wishes with respect to the Friars, as expressed by the American Commission to Rome, added impetus to the rebellious movement and when the announcement of the new organisation was made it was found to be based on the strongest kind of support. Aglipay constituted himself Obispo Maximo, assumed a fine regalia, and conferred upon fifteen or more of his lieutenants the regular church dignities and titles of a lesser order. He offered the people the same ceremonies, the same relief, the same confessional, and the same faith generally to which they had always been accustomed, so they found it easy enough to transfer their allegiance, and the new church gained adherents with such startling rapidity that it seemed as if a majority of the population would go over to it.

The result may easily be imagined. The Roman Catholic organisation had controlled Philippine affairs, both temporal and spiritual, for so long that the possibility of a rebellion of this character had never been thought of. Every loyal Catholic, and especially every bishop and priest and friar, was horrified, and an almost frantic controversy began to rage about the devoted head of the civil Governor as soon as he arrived in Manila. He was appealed to to take drastic action to suppress the movement and because he could do nothing even to check it the American government was reviled in the Catholic press as it had never been reviled before. Mr. Taft calmly met the storm with an iteration and reiteration of American principles of religious toleration, and declared that he had neither right nor wish to try to direct the religious inclinations of the people, and that all he could do in the matter was to enforce the keeping of the peace.

The people had been taught by Aglipay and his fellow-conspirators, and, indeed, by the whole history of church buildings in the Islands, that church properties belonged to the people and that if they wished to do so it was right for them to oust the regularly constituted priests from the churches and to turn these edifices over to the Independent body. This the government would not allow, holding that any dispute over property rights must be settled by due process of law. A few riots ensued wherein the constabulary and police came in violent contact with the Aglipayanos, but the Filipino is quick to recognise justice, and this decree of the government was very readily given general acceptance.

Mr. Taft was repeatedly warned by the allies of Rome that the movement was nothing but a cloak for the worst insurrection against the government that the Filipinos had yet attempted, and this suspicion was somewhat strengthened by the fact that many of the least tractable insurrecto leaders were among its directors, but in the main the schismatics evinced every desire to obey the injunction laid upon them not to resort to incendiary methods. And it was thought that the treatment they received in return would probably do more than all the preaching in the world to convince them that under American sovereignty they were actually to enjoy complete religious freedom.

Liberty to take possession of property by force was denied them, but liberty to think and worship as they pleased was not only given them, but in the peaceful exercise of this liberty they even enjoyed police protection, and this was a never-before-heard-of thing which gave them food for very serious thought. Under Spanish dominion Aglipay would have been taken to the Luneta and shot as Jose Rizal was shot, and his followers would have met and mourned in secret, but the American authorities held, according to American beliefs, that an Aglipayan, or independent Catholic organisation, had as much right to parade in the streets with candles and images as had the Roman Catholic or any other religious body.

Mr. Taft had vaguely suggested the possibility of some such development as this during his visit to the Vatican, but it made no impression. However, now that it had come, it gave the American Commission some advantage in the Friars and Friars' lands negotiations because it was sure to convince the Vatican that the case of the Friars was hopeless and so inspire speedier action than might otherwise be hoped for.

In the midst of it all the Apostolic Delegate, Archbishop Guidi of Stauropoli, arrived from Rome! He was an Italian, very friendly and tolerant, with neither fanatic nor ascetic tendencies. He was by no means adverse to taking part in any kind of social gaiety and I remember that at one of our first entertainments after his arrival he expressed great regret that he could not join in the *Rigodon*. I came to enjoy association with him exceedingly.

At one of my first receptions that season quite a dramatic scene occurred in the ballroom. A thousand or more people, perhaps, had passed the receiving line. Monsignor Guidi came in all his stately regalia, and shortly afterward Aglipay put in an appearance. The people wandered around all over the place, circulating through the spacious gardens and around the verandahs, so there was a possibility that these two would not meet even though they were both very conspicuous figures. But it was not long before the Papal Delegate hurried up to Mr. Taft and, in a state of visible excitement, inquired who the stranger in the striking religious garb might be.

"That," said Mr. Taft, "is Aglipay."

"But, you know," said the Monsignor, "it is impossible for you to receive him here when I am present!"

Then Mr. Taft once more laboriously explained the standpoint of the American government, saying that Agli-pay was in his house in his private capacity as a citizen, that he had as much right there as any other citizen, and that it would not be possible to ask him to leave as long as he conducted himself as a guest should.

"Then, I shall have to go," said Monsignor Guidi.

"I am very sorry," said Mr. Taft. "I understand your position perfectly and I trust you understand mine as well."

So the highest of insular Church dignitaries got his hat and hastened away while the "renegade and impious impostor" remained—in serene unconsciousness of the disturbance he had created? Perhaps not. At least he was serene.

But our relations with Monsignor Guidi continued most agreeable during our entire stay in the Islands. Mr. Taft thought very highly of him as a man and an ecclesiastical statesman and diplomat and greatly regretted his death which occurred after we left the Islands. Through him, the question of the Friars' lands was settled as Pope Leo had told Mr. Taft it would be, satisfactorily to the United States.

To bring that story, which was distractingly long drawn out in reality, to a close, I will merely add that the government succeeded in purchasing the Friars' lands for the sum of $7,000,000; they were turned into a public domain to be sold under most encouraging conditions, to their tenants and others who wished to acquire homesteads. The Friars were not sent back to the parishes and many left the Islands.

However this was not brought about without the protracted exercise of patience and diplomacy in the very midst of which the long arm of Washington reached out and touched my busy husband on the shoulder. He came home one day with a puzzled air and a cablegram from President Roosevelt. This cablegram read, in part:

Taft, Manila. On January first there will be a vacancy on the Supreme Court to which I earnestly desire to appoint you.... I feel that your duty is on the Court unless you have decided not to adopt a judicial career. I greatly hope you will accept. Would appreciate early answer.

This came before I had been in the Islands a month and when Mr. Taft was so deep in the complications of his work that he was almost a stranger to his friends.

There was an accompanying cablegram from Secretary Root strongly urging acceptance on the score of my husband's impaired health. Mr. Root declared that he was most unwilling to lose his services in the Philippines, but thought it better for him "not to take any serious risk of breaking down and having to leave the Islands an invalid even after a considerable period of further service." As Mr. Taft was feeling particularly well and was taking daily exercise and keeping himself in excellent condition this sounded rather like anticipating a very unlikely calamity, but the last time Mr. Root had seen him he was anything but robust so it was easy to understand the Secretary's friendly concern for him.

What to do? This was not a question which gave Mr. Taft even a shade of hesitation, because he knew immediately what he must do. All his life his first ambition had been to attain the Supreme Bench. To him it meant the crown of the highest career that a man can seek, and he wanted it as strongly as a man can ever want anything. But now that the opportunity had come acceptance was not to be thought of. I had always been opposed to a judicial career for him, but at this point I shall have to admit I weakened just a little. I remembered the year of illness and anxiety we had just been through; and sometimes I yearned to be safe in Washington even though it did mean our settlement in the "fixed groove" that I had talked against for so long.

Mr. Taft's plain and unmistakable duty held him in the Philippine Islands. He knew he could not detach himself completely from the enterprise upon which he was engaged without grave consequences to it. His one cause for uncertainty as to what he should do lay in a suspicion that he might have done something to embarrass the Administration in a political sense, or that his opponents in the monastic orders and Friars' lands controversy might have made representations which caused the President to consider his removal "upstairs" advisable. He discussed the matter confidentially with Mr. Benito Legarda and with the Chief Justice of the Philippines, Mr. Arellano, and the comment of the Chief Justice was: "There, the influence of the Friars has reached even to Washington." Mr. Taft cabled to his brother Henry in New York to make private inquiries in this connection, since he did not wish to remain in the islands if his presence there was in any way undesirable, but at the same time he cabled to the President:

President Roosevelt, Washington. Great honour deeply appreciated but must decline. Situation here most critical from economic standpoint. Change proposed would create much disappointment and lack of confidence among people. Two years now to follow of greater importance to development of islands than previous two years. Cholera, rinderpest, religious excitement, ladrones, monetary crisis, all render most unwise change of Governor. These are sentiments of my colleagues and two or three leading Filipinos consulted confidentially. Nothing would satisfy individual taste more than acceptance. Look forward to the time when I can accept such an offer, but even if it is certain that it can never be repeated I must now decline. Would not assume to answer in such positive terms in view of words of your despatch if gravity of situation here was not necessarily known to me better than it can be known in Washington. TAFT.

He also sent the following cablegram to Secretary Root:

Secwar, Washington. Referring to cablegram from your office of 26th inst. (October, 1902) my health is about as good as when I landed in 1900, but conditions here would make my withdrawal, unless absolutely compulsory, violation of duty. It may be that I shall be ill again, but I am more careful now than before. Chance has thrown every obstacle in the way of our success, but we shall win. I long for a judicial career but if it must turn on my present decision I am willing to lose it. TAFT.

In late November Mr. Taft received this letter from the President:

Dear Will, I am disappointed, of course, that the situation is such as to make you feel it unwise for you to leave, because, exactly as no man can quite do your work in the islands, so no man can quite take your place as the new member of the Court. But, if possible, your refusal on the ground you give makes me admire you and believe in you more than ever. I am quite at a loss whom to appoint to the Bench in the place I meant for you. Everything else must give way to putting in the right man; but I can't make up my mind who *is* the right man.

Always affectionately yours,

THEODORE ROOSEVELT.

So ended that period of wondering what we were to do. At least I thought it was ended, and while I settled down to the continued and continuous round of social "work" and pleasure, Mr. Taft proceeded with his strenuous fight against accumulated and complicated difficulties. We had Major General and Mrs. Miles with us at Malacanan for a time and after they left I went down to Batangas, where General Bell was in command, to "rest" awhile in Mrs. Bell's somewhat less crowded and exciting circle. I accepted with a high degree of pleasure the prospect of perhaps two more years in this very interesting field of work, but President Roosevelt had other views. It was scarcely a month after the Supreme Court incident was supposed to be closed when Mr. Taft received a letter which reopened it with a decisiveness which seemed final. Such parts of the letter as bear directly on the proposal to Mr. Taft I shall quote:

Dear Will, I am awfully sorry, old man, but after faithful effort for a month to try to arrange matters on the basis you wanted I find that I shall have to bring you home and put you on the Supreme Court. I am very sorry. I have the greatest confidence in your judgment, but, after all, old fellow, if you will permit me to say so, I am President and see the whole field. The responsibility for any error must ultimately come upon me, and therefore I cannot shirk the responsibility or in the last resort yield to any one else's decision if my judgment is against it. After the most careful thought; after the most earnest effort as to what you desired and thought best, I have come, irrevocably, to the decision that I shall appoint you to the Supreme Court in the vacancy caused by Judge Shiras' resignation.... I am very sorry if what I am doing displeases you, but as I said, old man, this is one of the cases where the President, if he is fit for his position, must take the responsibility and put the men on whom he most relies in the particular positions in which he himself thinks they can render the greatest public good. I shall therefore about February first nominate you as I have suggested. With affectionate regard,

Ever yours,

THEODORE ROOSEVELT.

This seemed final enough as to be quite unanswerable, so I heaved a sigh of resignation and made some remark about the not unpleasing prospect of our all getting home alive at any rate. General Wright was to succeed to the Governorship, which was a great consolation to my husband, and we began at once to outline a programme of obedience to the President. Mr. Taft announced his impending departure and really considered that further argument was useless, but conditions were such that he could not resist the temptation to hazard one more protest. He cabled to Mr. Roosevelt:

The President, Washington, Recognise soldier's duty to obey orders. Before orders irrevocable by action however I presume on our personal friendship even in the face of your letter to make one more appeal, in which I lay aside wholly my strong personal disinclination to leave work of intense interest half done. No man is indispensable; my death would little interfere with programme, but my withdrawal more serious. Circumstances last three years have convinced these people, controlled largely by personal feeling, that I am their friend and stand for a policy of confidence in them and belief in their future and for extension of self-government as they show themselves worthy. Visit to Rome and proposals urged there assure them of my sympathy in regard to friars in respect to whose far-reaching influence they are morbidly suspicious. Announcement of withdrawal pending settlement of church question, economic crises, and formative political period when opinions of all parties are being slowly moulded for the better, will, I fear, give impression that change of policy is intended because other reasons for action will not be understood. My successor's task is thus made much heavier because any loss of the people's confidence distinctly retards our work here. I feel it is my duty to say this. If your judgment is unshaken I bow to it and shall earnestly and enthusiastically labour to settle question friars' lands before I leave, and to convince the people that no change of policy is at hand; that Wright is their warm friend as sincere as they think me, and that we both are but exponents of the sincere good will toward them of yourself and the American people. TAFT.

After this things began to happen which nobody, least of all my husband, had anticipated. When the announcement was made that we were to leave there was, at first, just a buzz of astonishment and incredulity, but within two days the whole city of Manila was placarded, in all the necessary languages, with the simple and uniform sentiment: "Queremos Taft," "WE WANT TAFT." Mr. Root's rendering of this in English was "I want you, Mah Honey, yes, I do." These announcements were printed in letters of all sizes and all colours, but the wording did not vary in the slightest degree; just, "WE WANT TAFT."

Then on the morning of the loth of January—the letter from Mr. Roosevelt was received on the 6th—we saw marching through the gates of Malacalian a column of citizens, blocks long, with bands playing, flags flying and many transparencies bobbing over their heads. These citizens packed themselves around the entrance of the Palace and proceeded to make a demonstration. It was rather saddening to us in view of our conviction that we must go, but we listened with what composure we could command to the eloquent speeches. The speakers came up into the Palace and addressed the crowd from a great window over the main entrance.

Dr. Dominador Gomez, one of the popular orators and labour agitators, began by saying that Mr. Taft was the "saint" who had "the power to perform the great miracle" of uniting the distinct opinions and contrary motives of the people, and declared that "this is a spontaneous demonstration of affection for our Governor which is to be reduced to expression in a respectful petition to the President."

Dr. Xeres Burgos, an old insurrecto, said he spoke for no political party but in behalf of the mass of people which surrounded us,—"this people who wish to say to you that all those calamities which have weighed and do weigh upon the Filipinos are as nothing compared with the evil effect caused by your impending departure from this government, just at the precise moment when the Filipino people expect, through your honesty and love for them, an end to all economic and governmental disturbances, as well as the solution of the agricultural problem which is so closely interwoven with the Friar question. The Filipino people trust that the home government will not tear from their arms their beloved governor upon whom depends the happy solution of all Philippine questions. In a word: the Filipino people desire the continuation of Governor Taft in these Islands!"

Tomaso G. del Rosario likened Mr. Taft to a ship's rudder adept at "avoiding shallows" and "bringing her safe into port." Then he said the Philippines were "rising from the ashes of a momentous revolution and advancing toward the future with a heart full of enthusiasm and hope," and that "a ruler lacking the qualifications so happily combined in Mr. Taft might faint by the wayside."

There were other speeches, but the climax came when Pedro A. Paterno began by comparing Mr. Taft with Jesus Christ, saying that "as Christ had converted the cross into a symbol of glory and triumph, so had Governor Taft turned a dying people to the light and life of modern liberties."

This sounds quite blasphemous in English, but the Filipinos take strange liberties with holy names which shock us but which to them are mere expressions of piety. Jesus is a favourite name for boy babies, while there is a street of "The Heart of Jesus" in Manila, and many others equally inconsistent with our more reticent taste.

Needless to say the cable between Manila and Washington was crowded that day with protests to the President; protests not only from citizens and committees of citizens, but from all Mr. Taft's colleagues in the government, both Filipino and American. Two days later my husband received a message from Mr. Roosevelt which gave us all a hearty laugh. It read, simply: "Taft, Manila, All right stay where you are. I shall appoint some one else to the Court. ROOSEVELT."

Altogether it was quite an exciting event. After the "smoke of battle" had cleared away Mr. Taft rose up out of his depression and went to work with renewed vigour and strengthened confidence, but I began to think that after all the demonstrations and protestations we should have to remain in the Islands the rest of our lives whether we wanted to or not. Six months later, however, we learned, to our consternation, that Mr. Root was going to resign as Secretary of War in the fall or winter following, and without a moment's hesitation as far as we could judge, the position was offered by Mr. Roosevelt to Mr. Taft. It was urged upon him, in fact. This was much more pleasing to me than the offer of the Supreme Court appointment, because it was in line with the kind of work I wanted my husband to do, the kind of career I wanted for him and expected him to have, so I was glad there were few excuses for refusing to accept it open to him. If it hadn't been that it was merely a case of transferring his services from the necessarily restricted field of work in the Philippines to the broader and more powerful field of general supervision of Philippine affairs in the War Department, he probably would have declined the appointment and begged to be left where he was, but the change was not to take place for a year and he knew that as soon as he had settled the Friars' question and a few other matters of importance in the Islands he could be of more use to the Filipino people in Washington than he could in Manila. General Wright was to succeed him, with Mr. Ide and Judge Smith, both trained men, in line of succession to follow General Wright, so with the promise of a few months in which to close up the affairs in which he was most deeply engrossed, he accepted the Cabinet office.

Shortly before we left Manila to take up our residence in Washington we decided to give a final and memorable entertainment. We wanted it to be something original, so we discussed it and pondered over it at great length. We thought we had given every kind of party that ingenuity could devise during our residence at Malacañan, but one evening, sitting out on the verandah looking across the still, softly-lapping river at the low-hung lights on the opposite bank, it suddenly occurred to me that we had an ideal setting for a Venetian Carnival, and a Venetian Carnival was settled upon without further ado. It was to be a masked ball, the front gates of the Palace grounds were to be closed and everybody was to come by boat to the river landing on the verandah below.

As soon as this plan was noised abroad the town was agog with excitement. The first question, of course, to occur to everybody was: "What shall I go as?" And pretty soon every woman in town, and many men, assumed that labouredly innocent air peculiar to a period of preparation for a masked ball in a community where everybody knows or wants to know all about everybody else.

I knew right away what I should "go as." I would be a Venetian lady of romance days. But the question of Mr. Taft's costume was not so easily settled. If he hadn't interposed so many ideas of his own it would have been much simpler. In writing to his brother Charles he says: "It is a humiliating fact to me that every suggestion of a character for me by me has been summarily rejected by Nellie unless it involved the wearing of a gown of such voluminous proportions as to conceal my Apollo-like form completely. The proposal that I assume the character of an Igorrote chieftain because of the slight drain on capital and our costuming resources did not meet with favour. So it is settled that I must assume the robes and headgear of the husband of the Adriatic, the Doge of Venice. The question is whether the robe can be made historically accurate and at the same time so conceal my nether extremities as to make it unnecessary for me to dye my nether undergarments to a proper colour, for the entire Orient cannot produce tights of a sufficient size. The Council of War, meaning Nellie, has not advised me on the subject, but tights or no tights we shall have a Doge of Venice 'that never was on land or sea.' " And we did.

We called a committee of Filipinos to arrange about illuminations on the river and the decoration of launches, cascoes, bancas, rafts and barges, and this committee took the whole matter out of my hands and went to work with the zeal of children playing at some fascinating new game. They arranged for a number of pavilioned craft decorated with flowers, and offered a prize for the most beautiful and elaborate private launch, or boat of any kind. Then on either bank of the river they stretched lines of coloured electric lights and crossed the river at close with other lines as far as the eye could see in both directions. The whole Palace building was outlined in electric lights, while the great trees and every little bush were wired and strung with a myriad multicoloured globes, hundreds of them covered with Japanese lanterns in fantastic colours and designs. All the garden walks and drives were bordered with tiny coloured lamps burning cocoanut oil, set close in against the well trimmed lawns, and when it was all finished and the light turned on the place was like a fairyland.

The date for the Carnival was set for full moon night, the third of December, and never will I forget the brilliance and beauty of the scene as one gay and picturesque barge or improvised gondola after another, full of laughing, chattering and singing people in masks and all manner of strange costumes, and with mandolins and guitars playing, floated up under the bright canopy of swinging globes, a million times reflected in the ripples of the river, to the ancient-looking, moss-grown landing where Mr. Taft and I, as the Doge of Venice and his Lady, stood receiving our guests with as much mock stateliness as we could command in the midst of such a merry throng. It will linger in my memory always as one of the most entrancing evenings of my life.

Rain was predicted, as usually happens when I give any kind of a garden party, and all day long I had watched the clouds with a feeling of helpless exasperation. I wanted fair weather; I wanted the moonlight; but as night came on the lowering grey canopy seemed to float upward and spread itself out into a mere haze which softened and diffused the brightness and made ten times more effective our myriad swinging lamps and lanterns.

Everybody had done his or her utmost in the matter of costuming, and with a success that I never saw surpassed. All the fine old collections of jewels in the rich Spanish and Filipino families were taken out, and in many cases over into special designs to deck oriental princesses, historic queens and noble ladies of storied fame.

Perhaps the most striking costume of all was worn by Mrs. Rafael Reyes, a tall dark Spanish lady of extraordinary beauty, the wife of a prominent and wealthy Filipino. Senora Reyes came as the Queen of Night, and she was literally ablaze with diamonds. Not brilliants nor rhinestones, but diamonds large and small, sewn all over the long graceful folds of her sweeping black robe to represent stars. On her small shapely head, crowned with a wealth of shining black hair, she wore a large diamond crescent. She caught the light and sparkled, her vivacious personality sparkling with her jewels. On that memorable occasion nobody who saw her could possibly forget her.

Dancing and frolicking continued long into the night, but as the evening wore to a close we began to feel a sense of depression. In a very few days we were to leave the Islands perhaps never to return, and this was our last party at old Malacalian. It is not amiss, I am sure, to say that every laughing face sobered and every voice took on a regretful tone as one by one our guests came up to say good night—and good-bye.

SECRETARY OF WAR

To illustrate what seems to me to be rather widely contrasted views of the position of Secretary of War for the United States, I think I must relate two experiences I had in the beginning of Mr. Taft's career in that office.

Before we left Manila his appointment had been announced and as we passed through Japan en route to Washington we were received with all the ceremony and official dignity that the Japanese naturally would consider proper to the entertainment of the War Minister of a great and friendly foreign power. This was experience number one.

It was just before the outbreak of hostilities between Russia and Japan, and General Kuropotkin, the Russian Minister of War, had very recently been in Tokyo and had been accorded a welcome so elaborate that it became historic. It satisfied the Japanese conception of courtesy to an exalted foreign visitor and we discovered that it was to serve as a model for our own reception, though our time was so short that the programme had to be considerably modified.

Had we remained with our ship to Yokohama there would have been no opportunity to entertain us at all, but a special train was sent to meet us at Nagasaki, the first port of call on the homeward voyage, and nearly the whole length of the Empire from Tokyo, and we were whisked through ahead of everything two or three days in advance of our ship, which had to make two more stops before proceeding to Yokohama.

We were the guests of the nation and were conducted from one function to another with the greatest honour and official formality. Among other arrangements made for our entertainment was a luncheon at the Palace with the Emperor and Empress, and Mr. Taft was permitted, in his capacity of a war secretary, to witness the evolutions of a crack Japanese regiment, of 3,000 troops ready for the field massed on a single great parade ground.

The Japanese Minister of War, General Terauchi, was a soldier—which seems fitting, and which is usual in most countries I believe—and he assumed at once, in common with all the other Army officers whom he encountered, that Mr. Taft was a soldier, too. This has nothing to do with my immediate story, but I remember it as one of the most amusing circumstances of that visit to Japan. Whatever Mr. Taft may be he is not martial, but these Japanese warriors proceeded to credit him with all manner of special knowledge which he had never had an opportunity to acquire and to speak to him in technical terms which, it must be admitted, strained his ability for concealing his ignorance. He finally said that if anybody asked him again about the muzzle velocity of a Krag-Jorgensen, or any like question, he intended to reply: "Sh! It's a secret!"

General Kodama, who afterward made himself world-famous as Chief of Staff during the Russo-Japanese War, had been Military Governor of Formosa and he was especially interested in Mr. Taft because he conceived that in the Philippines we had a parallel for their Formosan problem. He grew quite confidential, telling Mr. Taft many things about the Japanese administration of Formosan affairs and drawing comparisons between his difficulties and those that we had encountered under similar circumstances. He ended by saying:

"We had to kill a good many thousands of those people before they would be good. But then, of course, you under-stand,—you know,—you know!"

This story could not have been told at that time because there were groups of active anti-Imperialists in the United States who would have pounced upon it as something to be made the most of as an argument for their cause, but in the light of history that has been made I think it is safe to tell it now. Mr. Taft had to admit that he was a man of peace, that so far as he personally was concerned he had never killed nor ordered killed a single Filipino in his life, and that his whole endeavour had been to form a friendly alliance with the Philippine people and to dissuade them from indulgence in the personal danger involved in their useless opposition to temporary American control.

We made something of a triumphal progress through Japan during our short stay and were escorted to our ship by numerous dignitaries who were extremely gracious and who cheered us on our way with such "banzais!" and such a waving of flags as made me feel that we were quite important personages. Later on I had my sense of the importance of my position rudely shaken. There is one thing to be said for the American Republic and that is that no public official is permitted to retain for very long a too exalted opinion of himself.

One day shortly after my arrival in Washington, I was at tea at the house of a friend and found myself in conversation with a lady, the wife of an Army officer, whom I had known in Manila. We talked around and about various subjects, after the manner of ladies at a tea, when she finally said to me:

"You know, Mrs. Taft, I have thought about you so often and wondered how you liked it here in Washington after your life in Manila. Why, out there you were really a queen, and you come back here and are *just nobody!*"

There was another lady who sat next to my husband at a dinner one night. It was a place of honour, next to a Cabinet officer, and she no doubt considered it necessary to "make conversation" while the candle-lights shone. She went along quite successfully for awhile, but eventually blundered into this:

"Do you know, Mr. Secretary, I really think you ought go out and see the Philippine Islands. They say they are so interesting!"

Poor man, most of his reputation, such as it then was, had been made in the Philippine service, but he replied to her:

"That's right, I should go. And I'm going, too, just as soon as I can possibly get away."

He meant that. He had promised the Filipinos that he would return to open their first Assembly, and even then he had a fixed desire to lead a party of American Congressmen to the country whose affairs they were endeavouring to settle by long-distance legislation founded upon very mixed and, in some cases, greatly distorted, second-hand information.

Mr. Taft became Secretary of War at the beginning of 1904, but I spent the remainder of the winter after our arrival in the United States in Santa Barbara and did not join him until May, when I met him at St. Louis, where he went to open the Louisiana Purchase Exposition.

President Roosevelt was to have done this, but urgent affairs kept him in Washington, so the Secretary of War was asked to represent him and to make the speech which announced to the world the inauguration of this great Fair. I remember the occasion especially because I had been so long out of touch with the kind of buoyant Americanism which made itself felt in St. Louis that I had almost lost my own identity with it, and I began then to think that it was really good to be back in my own country.

I knew fairly well what it would mean to settle down in Washington as the wife of a Cabinet officer because I had lived in Washington before. While I didn't expect to be and didn't expect anybody to consider me "just nobody" I knew that it would not be at all like entering upon the duties and privileges of the wife of the Governor of the Philippine Islands. I thought what a curious and peculiarly American sort of promotion it was which carried with it such diminished advantages.

My first necessity in my generally considered enviable position was to find a house in Washington large enough to contain my family, to permit such participation in social life as would be expected of us, and the rent for which would not wholly exhaust the stipend then allowed to a Cabinet officer.

Eight thousand dollars a year, sufficient income though it may be when it is expected to accommodate itself to an ordinary eight-thousand-dollars-a-year standard of living, shrinks alarmingly when its recipient is expected to maintain on it the dignity of a Cabinet position. If we had not had some private resources I don't quite see how we could have managed. Fortunately for my husband, and more so for his successors in office, this figure was raised to twelve thousand before he left the War Department, and still there are complaints which I am amply able to appreciate.

We finally settled, on the first of October after my arrival at Washington, in a pleasant, old-fashioned house on K Street near 16th. It was not the most elegantly equipped house available, but we preferred a little extra space to the more elaborate modern conveniences, so we took it.

We were spared one item of expense by having the use of the War Department carriage and its big Irish coachman, Quade. Quade was quite a character. He had been at one time in the artillery service and had occupied the position in which we found him through several administrations. He was never able to lose the habits and manners of an artillery man, and Mr. Roosevelt used to say he never drove behind him without feeling as if he were on the caisson of a gun wagon going into action. He kept his horses in fine condition, though a trifle too fat perhaps, and he took great pride in the speed he could get out of them. He would swing around corners and dash past street cars and other vehicles in a way that was anything but soothing to nerves, but there was no use protesting. Quade's character was fully formed.

He used to feed Mr. Taft's private riding horse at the public expense, and Mr. Taft didn't approve of this. He thought he ought to include the pay for its keep in his personal accounts, and he told Quade so, asking him at the same time to have a bill made out so that he might settle it. Quade regarded him in utter disgust for a moment, then said:

"Well, Misther Sicretary, what with the good an' plinty o' fodder we got in the stables, I guess ye can go on a-feedin' your horse here without the Government's a-worryin' anny."

I remember going one day to a reception at the house of Justice Harlan on the occasion of his twenty-fifth anniversary on the bench. President Roosevelt was already there and as we drove up we found the bicycle policemen surrounding the entrance waiting for him. Quade, with great friendliness but with an absolute lack of decorum, leaned over on the box and shouted to them as we passed:

"Ah, Begorra! Ye'll be a-waitin' around fer my boss one o' these days!"

248

Faithful Quade lived to see his prophecy fulfilled, but not long afterward he lost his life at his post of duty in a shocking accident. He was driving the Department carriage for Secretary of War Dickinson's family; the pole broke, the horses became frightened and bolted. There were young children and a nurse in the carriage, so Quade bravely held on to the reins and finally succeeded in turning the horses into a fence. He saved the occupants of the carriage from injury, but he himself was thrown forward violently, falling in such a way as to break his neck.

Another War department employe whom we valued highly was Arthur Brooks, a coloured department messenger, and a major of militia. Arthur was the most useful individual I ever knew anything about, combining absolute loyalty with an efficiency and accuracy that were most comforting to his employers. He went into the War Department during President Arthur's administration and gradually won for himself a position of especial trust. Mr. Root, as Secretary of War, found Arthur most valuable and reposed the utmost confidence in him.

For me he did all kinds of things which without him would probably have been done very badly. He "managed" all my larger entertainments, being present, after I had done all I could by way of preparation, to see that everybody was properly received, that the service ran smoothly and that nothing went amiss. When Mr. Taft became President he had Arthur transferred to the position of custodian of the White House and I shall have occasion to speak of him in that capacity later on.

Taking things all in all, I think we managed to get on very well indeed, though I did sometimes sigh for the luxurious simplicity and the entire freedom from petty household details that I had left behind me in Manila. I did not find that my very large and very black cook was so capable as to make me forget the excellencies and the almost soundless orderliness of Ah Sing; nor did my coloured butler and one housemaid quite manage to take the places of Ah King and Chang, my two upstairs "Chinaboys" at Malacarian. As for the six or eight barefoot *muchachos* who "skated" my Philippine hardwood floors to a state of mirror gloss and kept everything speckless without ever seeming to do any work at all, they could have no substitute in a Washington establishment.

The life of a "Cabinet lady" newly arrived in the Capital is one of rather monotonous stress. In the first place she is expected to call on nearly everybody who calls on her, and, of course, nearly everybody does that. This custom in my time was especially insisted upon with regard to the wives of all the Congressmen and of all the men connected with the various departments. Then there were the wives of the members of the Supreme Court, women whose husbands were connected with the many different bureaus and a large and most attractive civilian society which contributes so much to the gaiety of the city. And besides all these there were the Army women, any number of them.

Every afternoon throughout the winter when I was not "at home" myself I started out on certain rounds of calls, and I think I made as many calls as any one I knew. Irksome to me as this duty sometimes was, in the formal discharge of it I made some of the pleasantest friends I ever had. I have always found Army women particularly delightful, and it is easy to understand why they are so. In the course of their wanderings and their many changes of habitation, and in consequence of the happy-go-lucky attitude toward life that they are bound to assume, they acquire a cordiality of manner and an all-round generous tone which make them very attractive.

One morning each week Mrs. Roosevelt held a meeting of the Cabinet ladies at the White House, but this was not a social affair. We met to discuss various matters supposed to be of interest to us all, and would gather in the library from eleven to twelve for this purpose.

After calling, the most important social duty devolving upon a Cabinet officer's wife is dining out. We always dined out when we were not giving a dinner party at our own house, so that from the time Mr. Taft became Secretary of War we almost ceased to know what it was to have "a quiet evening at home." Of course such a life gave us an opportunity for meeting many interesting men and women who contributed much to the sum total of what the world seemed to have in store for us.

It has been the custom through a good many administrations for the President, sometime during the season between December first and Lent, to dine with each member of the Cabinet, and all other members of the Cabinet, with only a few outside guests, were usually invited to these parties. It can easily be imagined that they did not offer much variation, especially in view of the fact that hard and fast rules of precedence settled for the hostess just where each of her guests should sit. Mr. Roosevelt did not care for this custom, so during his last Administration it became usual to ask to such dinners only people outside the "official family," as it is called. The dinner to Mr. and Mrs. Roosevelt which we gave each year was our most ambitious social function and it was my desire always to invite as many persons as possible who would themselves prove entertaining and who would not be likely to meet the President in the ordinary course of events. I often asked friends from different parts of the country to visit us for the occasion.

Every Wednesday afternoon all the ladies of the Cabinet were "at home" and nearly all Washington called on each of them. Then, too, the casual visitors to the Capital were free to attend these informal receptions and I used to be surprised at the number of curious strangers who found their way into my drawing room.

However, this is only a glimpse in general of the life of a Cabinet lady during the regular social season. Fortunately for me my husband was, from the very beginning, a travelling Secretary. I remember most of the cartoons of those days pictured him either as "sitting on the lid," wreathed in cherubic smiles, while President Roosevelt rushed off on some flying trip, or as himself making a frantic dash for the rear platform of a moving train. The rush of Mr. Roosevelt was always expressed by the backward sweep of the ribbon attached to his eyeglasses, while Mr. Taft was usually pictured with a perspiring look, his hat lifted off his head by the wind and a busy looking suitcase, labelled in large letters: "Taft," swinging wildly along behind him.

And these cartoons were rather accurately descriptive of real conditions.

I had hardly got my house on K Street in order before something happened in Panama which made it imperative for the Secretary of War to go down to the Isthmus and give the situation his personal attention. There was a state of popular discontent among the Panamanians complicated by question of zone boundaries, jurisdiction, postal regulations, tariff inequalities and a few other matters, and by that time we had too much at stake in the Canal Zone to risk long distance or dilatory regulation.

The building of the Panama Canal was not included in the business of the War Department until after Mr. Taft became Secretary, nor was there at that time any definite idea of having it done by the Army Engineer Corps, but it has long been recognised that in the War Portfolio accommodation can be found for any and every kind of governmental problem, and Mr. Taft had not been Secretary long before Mr. Roosevelt transferred the administration of Canal Zone affairs to his already well-laden shoulders.

I was very glad to have an opportunity to see the beginning of what I knew was to be the greatest enterprise ever undertaken by the United States, so I fully approved of my husband's suggestion that I accompany him to Panama. Senor Obaldia, the Panamanian Minister to Washington, went also, and among others in the very interesting party were Rear Admiral J. G. Walker, President of the Canal Commission, Judge Charles G. Magoon, law officer of the Commission, and Mr. Nelson W. Cromwell, counsel for the Republic of Panama.

On this trip Mr. Taft went to Panama as a representative of the President of the United States for the purpose of presenting to the President of Panama a message of friendship, and to make, if possible, an amicable adjustment of the differences between American and Panamanian interests.

It was in November, 1904. We went from Washington to New Orleans and were greeted in a kindly manner all along the way. When we arrived we were met by a most imposing committee of citizens who escorted us to our hotel. No sooner were we installed, in the midst of all the luxury that could be prepared for us, than Governor Blanchard, with due ceremony and accompanied by members of his staff in uniform, called to pay his official respects. We hadn't very long to stay, but every hour was filled with entertainments made memorable by the courteous and highbred lavishness for which New Orleans is famed, the only private event of our visit being a dinner with Archbishop Chapelle, now dead, who was Archbishop of Manila when Mr. Taft first went to the Philippines and with whom he good-naturedly, but persistently, disagreed on the important problems connected with the necessary disentanglement of the affairs of Church and State in the Islands.

We sailed on the little *Dolphin* from New Orleans to Pensacola, where the cruiser *Columbia* lay waiting to take us down to Panama, and it was to the boom of saluting guns, the cheers of hospitable Pensacola citizens and the strains of "The Star Spangled Banner" that we got under way on this first memorable trip to the Canal Zone.

We arrived at Colon on a Sunday morning, and I remember distinctly that it seemed more like "getting home" than like getting to a strange place. The whole atmosphere and surroundings, the people, the language they spoke, the houses and streets, the rank earth odours and the very feel of the air reminded me so strongly of the Philippines as to give me immediately a delightful sense of friendly familiarity with everything and everybody.

We were met at Colon by the vice-President of Panama, Senor Arosemana, and a number of other Panamanian officials, by General Davis, then Governor of the Canal Zone, and by Mr. John Barrett, the American Minister to Panama. A private train was waiting to take us across the Isthmus and we lost no time in getting started. Our visit had been "programmed" almost to the last hour of our time, and the first event was to be an exchange of formalities between the Secretary of War and the President of Panama that very afternoon.

When we got to the city of Panama just before luncheon we went to the home of Mr. Wallace, the Chief Engineer, whose guests we were to be during our stay, and early in the afternoon Mr. Taft, accompanied by uniformed aides and other Army officers, with enough ceremony to satisfy even the most formal, went to call on

President Amador. The call was promptly returned with due formality, and the decks were then considered "cleared for action."

Negotiations began at once, but the conferences were private, and in our daily round of sight-seeing and social diversions it did not seem that the delicate machinery of diplomatic transaction was in motion at all.

Our Minister, Mr. Barrett, had a charming house in the old tropic city and on the Monday evening after our arrival he gave a dinner at which were gathered many high officials of the Panama Republic as well as all the interesting Americans who were then directing our great Canal building enterprise. Mr. Barrett, being a bachelor, placed President Amador opposite himself; he took Madame Amador at his right; Mr. Taft sat next to her, while I occupied the place at the right of the President and had on my other side Senor Arias, the Minister of Foreign Affairs. General Davis, Mr. Wallace, Colonel Gorgas—"the man of the hour" during that cleaning-up period,—many Army officers and Cabinet Ministers in full regalia and many decorations, with their wives, were seated in order of rank along the sides of the great table, which, laden with flowers and gleaming glass and candles, made a picture long to be remembered even by one whose memory is overcrowded with dinner-party scenes.

The formality of this occasion, however, began and ended with its costuming and its beautiful tropic "setting." Nearly everybody, including the President and Madame Amador, spoke English as well as Spanish, and the evening was gay from the outset. There is a wonderful fish caught in Panama waters; I wish I could remember its name; it is delicious and rare beyond description, and our pleasantries began with the President's demand for a second helping which the embarrassed host and the more than flustered servants were unable to supply. The persiflage then turned upon the unenviable position of a bachelor diplomat and we all advised Mr. Barrett to get married. He parried our jibes as best he could until President Amador volunteered the information that the American Minister was honorary President of the Iris Club, an association of

254

some three hundred-odd of the choicest girls in Panama. "And he can't get one out of the lot," said the President.

After dinner a large reception was held in the salon which, as in all Spanish houses in the tropics, was on what might be called the second floor, the first floor being only a sort of plastered and stone-paved street-level basement. The highly-polished floor of the big room didn't look to me to be particularly safe and I suppose Mr. Barrett observed my worried looks as it "gave" under the weight of my husband. He hastened to reassure me by telling me that he had taken the precaution to have it shored up with heavy timbers under the spot where Mr. Taft was to stand to receive the long line of guests. He seemed to consider this a fine joke, but I thought it a most commendable measure.

When we arrived in Panama we were not at all certain that we should find the country in a state of tranquility; nor did we exactly; though by prompt action the President had nipped a budding revolution only a short time before. Hostilities had been averted, but the people were in a bad temper and it was thought best to keep them "merely guessing" while the negotiations between the Secretary of War and the Panamanian government were in progress, and much of Mr. Taft's time, therefore, was spent behind the closed doors of President Amador's council chamber.

In the meantime I made myself familiar with the wonderful American project which brought the Panama Republic into existence. The Canal then was a sorry sight. The public clamour in the. United States was for "making the dirt fly," but it did not look to a mere layman as if we could ever make it fly fast enough or in sufficient quantities to really bring the two oceans together. All along the line of operations the old French machinery lay buried in pathetic ruin in a tropic jungle which had all but effaced the evidences of the French enterprise, and such conditions of general unhealthiness prevailed as made it seem almost too much to expect that any kind of clean-up programme could be made effectual.

But all that story has been told; told in actual accomplishment with which all the world is familiar. I am only glad that I saw Colonel

Gorgas and his men in that initial and contagious enthusiasm which, being sustained, resulted in a record of which we are all so proud.

The Panamanians are nothing if not expansively hospitable. On the 4th of December, after we had been on the Isthmus a couple of weeks and while the results of the official negotiations were still, as far as any one knew, "in the lap of the gods," an ocean steamship was chartered by a company of hosts, and about three hundred guests, the elite of the whole republic, were invited for a picnic party to the Pearl Islands in the Bay of Panama, and a sail out into the Pacific Ocean. It was an all-day expedition and included the exploration of the beautiful little group, some pearl-diving for our especial benefit, a most amazing luncheon, and a dance on deck, to the music of a stringed band in gay most decorative uniforms, at which Mr. Taft made a tremendous "hit." The tiny Panamanian woman who first danced with him was thought to be very courageous, but as one after another followed suit his reputation grew and it finally was conceded, in the midst of great merriment, that he was as light of foot as the slimmest Panamanian of them all.

Having always been used to my husband's dancing, and knowing how much he likes it, I never thought of it as anything unusual, but during the days when he was being "boomed" for the Presidency and was therefore much in the public prints, it was made the subject of frequent jest. I have one bit of doggerel in my scrap-book which appeared in the Baltimore *American* after the reception we gave on the occasion of General Kuroki's visit to this country, and the last verse of which runs:

> That Taft is just a wonder
> Is a thing which we all know;
> That as Presidential thunder
> His big boom is like to go.
> But as butterfly, blooms sipping,
> And as waltzer, simply ripping! '
> Tis a sight to see Taft tripping
> On the light fantastic toe!

As a matter of fact he dances exceedingly well, if his wife who has been dancing with him for the past thirty years may say so.

256

When we returned from the Pearl Islands to Panama City that evening we were met by a pleasing surprise. The text of the agreement which had been reached by Mr. Taft and the government of Panama, and which had not been mentioned by anybody all day, had been made public during our absence and newsboys were crying "extras" in all the streets, while excited groups stood about here and there wreathed in smiles and talking with great animation. Everybody seemed wholly satisfied and wherever we went we were met with cheers and cries of "Viva!"

The keynote sounded in this agreement was that justice should be done at Panama. Mr. Taft interpreted the treaty between our country and the infant republic; he adjusted the differences with regard to postal regulations and the tariff; he defined the harbour boundaries; and, much to the satisfaction of the Panamanians, he kept within the hands of the American authorities all matters pertaining to the public health. The people realised the necessity for a pure water supply, for sewer systems, clean and well-paved streets, and the elimination of the dread diseases which made the Isthmus a death trap for white men, and all these things America offered to Panama as a free gift that the great work of building the Canal might go on. If vociferous cheers are an expression of gratitude the people were grateful.

The next day a great demonstration took place in Cathedral Plaza. We stood on a balcony of the Grand Central Hotel, on one side of the square and opposite the Cathedral, and looked out across a veritable sea of moving, swaying, white-clad humanity. As far as one could see in every direction there were people, and when Mr. Taft stepped to the balcony rail to address them they gave voice to a cheer which made it seem certain that all cause for quarrel between us had happily been removed.

There had been vague rumours that the deposed War Minister of the Panama government who had attempted to start the rebellion would, with his followers, take this occasion to make a hostile demonstration, but he was evidently sensible enough to realise that his was an unpopular cause. Moreover, his original army of two hundred and fifty men had been reduced to twenty-five, and if that were not discouraging enough he had only to contemplate the natty American Marine corps in the Canal Zone and the Pacific squadron, including the *New York,* the *Boston,* the *Bennington* and the *Marblehead,* lying out in Panama harbour unobtrusively but very positively guaranteeing peace.

Mr. Taft in his speech to the Panamanians was earnest. He was imbued with the spirit of conquest as represented in our Panama Canal enterprise. It was to be a conquest of nature's own forces in their most formidable aspects and he expressed a determination to enforce, during his term of administration, the laws necessary to make that conquest possible, and capping all his promises of fair treatment to the people of Panama, he emphasised an insistence upon orderly government in the little republic which brought forth round after round of applause.

He was destined to have almost endless difficulties of various sorts in the Canal Zone, but he had the great privilege of occupying an administrative office, first as Secretary of War and then as President, until the end of the work was in sight and all the problems had been fully solved. During those eight years, wherever he might be or whatever business happened to be temporarily paramount, Canal questions were with him always and were always given first consideration.

The history of the Panama Canal is divided into two great periods. The first covers the full discussion and final settlement of the question as to which route should be adopted, the Nicaraguan or the Panama; the negotiation of the Hay-Herran Treaty with Colombia, by which we were given the right to complete the Panama Canal, and under which we secured all the rights of the French Panama Canal Company; the rejection of the Hay-Herran Treaty with Colombia; the revolution of Panama; the establishment of the Panamanian Republic and its recognition by President Roosevelt, the negotiation of the Hay-Varilla Treaty with Panama, by which we acquired dominion over the Canal Zone, and the right to build the Canal from the Republic of Panama, guaranteeing at the same time the integrity of that Republic. During all this period Mr. Taft was in the Philippines. In February, 1904, when he became Secretary of

War, the Hay-Varilla Treaty was pending in the Senate. In a few weeks thereafter, it was consented to by the Senate, the Panama Commission was appointed, and early that spring the second period of the construction of the Canal began. The work was placed by the President under Mr. Taft as Secretary of War. From that time until his retirement from the office of President, March 4, 1913, the construction was constantly under his supervision. Sometime this history must be written. The chief crises in this work as he has recited them were the organisation of the force under the Commission, the adjustment of the relations of Panama to the work under the treaty, the change of engineers from Mr. Wallace to Mr. Stevens, the consideration by an International Commission, with a divided report, as to the proper type of the Canal, whether sea level or lock, the very close fight in Congress to sustain the Administration view in favor of the lock type, the settlement of the issue whether the Canal should be built by contract or by Government agency, the selection of a successor to Mr. Stevens when he resigned, and the placing of the work under Army engineers and the selection of Colonel Goethals as the man to take the responsibility, the adjustment of critical labour troubles, and the confirmation by a Commission of the security of the foundation of the Gatun Dam. These were the points of critical importance in Mr. Taft's Administration. In deciding the questions which came to him, it was necessary for him to visit the Canal seven times in as many years, and I went with him on three of his visits. The contrast between the Canal when we first visited it and were the guests of Mr. Wallace, the first engineer, and as it was when we were the guests of Colonel Goethals in 1912, when the Gatun Lake was more than half filled and nothing but the slides in the Culebra remained for excavation, it is most interesting to look back upon. I was twice the guest of Colonel and Mrs. Goethals, and the beautiful view of the Canal Valley from the windows of their house in the town of Culebra, which has now disappeared, will long remain in my mind.

It was not long after our return to Washington from the first trip to Panama before arrangements were completed for the tour of the big Congressional party which Mr. Taft "personally conducted" to the Philippines and back, and which was destined to be slightly overshadowed as a Congressional party by the personality of Miss Alice Roosevelt who, under the chaperonage of Mr. Taft and Mrs. New-lands, made the trip just, as Kipling sings, "for to be old and for to see."

Knowing that I should have an opportunity to go again to the Far East in two years to be present at the inauguration of the first Philippine Assembly, I decided to remain behind this time. I did not think I would much enjoy this brief busy trip to the Orient with three children and decided that a quiet summer in England would be better for us all. So I took a cottage in Oxford for the summer and with my two younger children and one of my Cincinnati friends and her two children made various trips here and there and found myself most pleasantly entertained.' It was an exceedingly quiet summer, unbroken save by the somewhat lurid accounts which we gathered from the British and European press of the progress of the Congressional party with Mr. Taft and Miss Alice Roosevelt in the East. One German paper went so far as to announce that Miss Roosevelt was undoubtedly engaged to be married to her father's War Secretary.

It was my intention to sail from Southampton and meet Mr. Taft in New York on his arrival from the East. We had been inveighing all summer against the British system of handling luggage and when we went to look after our trunks in the Oxford station we were charmed to find a new method of labelling had been introduced and that our luggage would travel down to London and across London to the station for Southampton without any assistance from us. We pocketed our British substitutes for American baggage checks with considerable satisfaction and started on our way.

When we arrived in London I sent the boys over to the station from which we were to leave for our steamer to make sure that our baggage had really been delivered as promised. Unfortunately the boys got to the station just as King Edward arrived, and they were so excited about getting a glimpse of the monarch that they gave up trying to look after baggage. We, having nothing else to do, drove to the station a full hour before the steamer train was to leave, and had occasion to congratulate ourselves for being so early. Our trunks were not in the station. My friend jumped in a hansom and rushed to the station where we had come in. I spent the time ransacking every corner and looking over piles of all kinds of luggage and three-quarters of an hour passed before a telephone message came to say the trunks were found and that they had started across town.

But the train would leave in five minutes! I was frantic. Otherwise I should never have played my last card and exposed myself to the jibes of my family forever after. I rushed into the office of the station-master determined to overawe him by revealing to him my official position.

"I am Mrs. William Howard Taft of Washington," I cried. "I must get my trunks on that boat train. They'll be here in a few minutes. Can't you hold it for me!"

He looked at me blankly.

"My husband is the Secretary of War of the United States," I went on desperately.

"I am very sorry, Madam," he began, then I made my last effort.

"You must have heard of him. He's travelling now with Miss Alice Roosevelt."

At last I had produced the effect I desired. Immediately the station was my castle. The station-master was my humble servant. He accompanied me out, ordered the train held, and superintended a whole obsequious force which hustled our baggage aboard as soon as it arrived. Since we made the boat, which we would not otherwise have done, I was able to bear the chaffing of my children and friends when they continued to refer to me as *The* Mrs. Taft whose husband was travelling with Miss Alice Roosevelt.

Early in the autumn of 1906 the American Consul General at Havana began cabling to the government at Washington that the Cuban republic under President Palma was rapidly going to pieces. What was described as "devastating and paralysing civil strife" was rampant, and a serious insurrection was threatened.

The Constitution of the Cuban republic and the Cuban Treaty with the United States contains a "self-acting" clause, known as the Platt Amendment, which was introduced by the United States Congress, and which provides for American intervention in Cuban affairs whenever such intervention is deemed requisite to a continuance of peace and good government in the island.

Sometime during the first week in September the situation became acute and President Palma, fearing that it would become formidable and knowing that he had no adequate force to protect life and property, urgently, though secretly begged our government to send warships to his assistance. On September 12 he despatched a cablegram imploring that an American Army be landed in Havana at once to prevent a threatened massacre of citizens; on September 13 he decided to resign the Presidency and compel the United States to assume the responsibility of government; on September 14 President Roosevelt called a conference at Oyster Bay where it was decided that Mr. Taft should undertake the task of Cuban pacification, peaceful if possible—and on September 20 Mr. Taft, accompanied by Mr. Robert Bacon, Assistant Secretary of State, as a fellow Peace Commissioner, landed at Havana. They didn't lose much time.

Then began what Mr. Taft always refers to as "those awful twenty days." The people were divided into various warring factions, the result, largely, of political habits inherited from the old Spanish regime wherein a new party arose on the slightest provocation, basing its antagonism to the others on nothing finer nor more patriotic than individual desire for political patronage.

President Palma still held the reins of government, but camped just outside Havana were twenty thousand men under arms ready at any moment to open hostilities. These insurgents, as well as the party in power, had appealed to the United States for intervention, but neither faction had any intention of accepting any form of compromise which did not include all their demands.

For about a week the fiercest storm that Mr. Taft had ever encountered raged about his head. His one immediate de-sire was to avoid bloodshed. His investigations proved that no real obstacle to tranquillity, or to compromise, existed and he made every effort to induce the Cubans to settle their differences on high non-partisan grounds, each yielding some-thing to the other for the sake of the general good. But he found very little interest in the "general good." Indeed, all through his despatches during those days there runs a complaint that except with President Palma and a few others patriotism was not very apparent, that petty jealousies and personal ambitions, often of a brazen or a sordid nature, constituted the chief secret of all the dissension and strife.

Events must have moved with feverish rapidity. The insurrectos demanded the annulment of the election which continued the Palma government in power, and the situation developed new complications with every argument and piece of testimony presented by either side. Finally when it was decided to begin an investigation of election returns with the hope of arriving at a just conclusion, President Palma, who had certainly been elected by irregular methods, though with no connivance on his own part, promptly resigned; his Congress failed to meet and elect his successor. To forestall a state of absolute anarchy, with the approval of President Roosevelt, Mr. Taft issued a manifesto proclaiming an American provisional government with himself as the provisional governor of the republic. This happened on the eighth day after his arrival in Havana.

American marines had already been landed to guard the Treasury and a large force of United States troops, under General Frederick Funston, was in readiness to sail at once for Havana.

There was a strong sentiment among the better elements of Cubans, and an almost unanimous expression on the part of foreign residents, in favour of annexation to the United States. Indeed, feeling ran so high on this point, and especially among those, of whatever nationality, with financial interests at stake in Cuba, that it was thought for a time that an effort would be made to stampede or force the United States government into such action. But Mr. Taft's Philippine experience proved of value to him in this crisis, and his proclamation provided only for a provisional government "to last long enough to restore order and peace and public confidence." The

Cuban flag was not hauled down; no Cuban official was to be disturbed in the discharge of his regular duties; and the American flag was to fly over nothing but American troops. In other words, the Cuban Republic was not to cease for an instant to exist. It was a curious situation.

Shortly after the provisional government was instituted, Mr. Magoon was appointed to relieve Mr. Taft in the office of governor, and was instructed to proceed at once to Havana. Mr. Taft cabled me and Mr. Bacon cabled to Mrs. Bacon, asking if we did not want to accompany Mr. Magoon, and, of course, we immediately decided to do so. We sailed on the *Mascotte* with the battleship *Texas* in our wake, carrying three hundred marines from Norfolk, and for the first time in my life I felt as if I were actually "going to war." There was such a sense of rush throughout the whole performance that it seemed tremendously serious. As a matter of fact, intervention was accomplished without the firing of a single gun, and when we landed at Havana, on the afternoon of the loth of October, just twenty days after Mr. Taft's arrival on the scene, the principal enterprise in progress was the disarmament of insurgent troops which was by that time almost completed.

When we landed in Cuba I found myself once again, although only for the moment "the first lady of the land," and we were received with much ceremony. It reminded me of Manila days.

As we passed the Cabanas fortress at the entrance of Havana harbour the *Texas* fired a salute and the echo of the answering guns cracked and rattled from piers and surrounding sea-walls. Everything in the harbour dipped its flag as we came in, while from out of the maze of battleships and cruisers, transports, merchant vessels and shore boats we saw a launch approaching in the bow of which I could easily make out my husband's generous proportions. With him were his colleague, Mr. Bacon, his aide, Captain McCoy, and a second aide, Captain Jose Marti, an artilleryman and son of an old Cuban patriot whom he had appointed to this position, to the intense gratification of the Cuban people.

A second launch followed, bearing General Funston and his aide, Captain Cloman, while a third full of Cuban newspaper men brought up the rear. These men were the most engaging reporters I ever encountered. They didn't approach Mrs. Bacon and me with pads and pencils and a few ill-considered questions. No, indeed. They came bearing flowers, great, gorgeous bouquets for each of us, and we were permitted to receive these without having to say anything more compromising than: "It was a very pleasant voyage, thank you," and, "Yes, indeed, we are very glad to get to Havana."

When we reached the wharf of the Captain of the Port we found a large gathering of American naval officers and Cuban citizens, and we were formally welcomed by Senor Julio de Cardenas, the Mayor of Havana, who was continuing to exercise his official authority exactly as if nothing unusual had occurred. He was accompanied by the members of the City Council and with them later escorted us to the Palace.

As Mrs. Bacon and I stepped into our carriage the commander of the rebel army and his wife came up to welcome us with what the paper that evening described as "a floral offering," but we saw nothing of the deposed President or his followers. Upon his resignation he had gone down into the country, where he was said to have been received with marked enthusiasm and sympathy. Nobody ever accused President Palma of being anything but an honest man and a sincere patriot, the victim of political chicanery on the part of his supporters. It was afterward shown that he could easily have been re-elected without trickery, but dishonest politics were the only kind of politics that his people had yet learned how to play.

When we arrived at the Palace, Mr. Taft, Mr. Bacon and Mr. Magoon went into a long conference in the governor's office, while I wandered around the imposing building. It was about as cheerful as a mortuary chapel. It seemed to be admirably adapted for the display of gold lace, gorgeous decorations and lofty martial manners. After a brief inspection I sought the spacious discomfort of my own room and an hour's repose under a betasseled canopy.

Mr. Magoon was not to assume the office of governor until disarmament was completed and an amnesty proclamation had been issued. Mr. Taft intended to leave him with no insurgents except those who refused to give up their arms, and these were no longer to be known as insurgents. They were to be called bandits and were to be hunted down and treated as such.

I was mistress of the Palace at Havana for just three over-crowded days. Before our arrival Mr. Taft and Mr. Bacon had been the guests of the American Minister, Mr. E. V. Morgan, at his beautiful home about nine miles outside the city. This house stood between two insurgent camps and the mediators had to pass by automobile through rebel lines every morning and evening while the uncertain negotiations were in progress, but the strange part of this intervention was that it was welcomed by all the parties concerned except the intervening party, so the mediators were shown every courtesy.

Mr. Taft did not take possession of the Palace immediately after the President's abdication, but when Mr. Magoon was arriving he thought it wise to do so in order that he might induct him into the office and all its dignities with due form, and so it happened that we found him living there.

On the afternoon after our arrival Mrs. Bacon and I gave a reception which I remember as a most notable affair. It was attended by hundreds of Cubans, by all the members of the different foreign colonies and by every American Army and Navy officer who was not at the moment on active duty. Everybody seemed to be especially happy and festive after the month of gloom, and the pretty white gowns, the gay Cuban colours and the crisp smartness of American uniforms mingled together in the great rooms with quite brilliant effect. While we stood shaking hands with the throng passing by in single file, the Municipal Band in the Park before the Palace played American music, from the latest ragtime back to "Swanee River," interspersed with well-rendered classics and a few gay, lilting airs peculiarly Spanish.

On the following afternoon Mr. Morgan tried to outdo the affair at the Palace with a reception in our honour at his house, and succeeded admirably. Mr. Taft had written of Mr. Morgan: "He is something of a sybarite. He has a very fine house, a French cook and all the luxuries, and we are being exceedingly well taken care of;— though I do think we eat too much!" In fact, Mr. Morgan is a true host, combining imagination and great ability with the wish to entertain. His house at Havana was like a scene from some tropical grand opera. Standing in the midst of fine gardens heavy with groups of big drooping palms and ferns, and bright with wide spaces of green lawn, it seemed like a veritable story-book house. It had wide corridors and a quaint, moss-softened patio, in the middle of which a fountain played over a mass of brilliant tropic plants. The spacious rooms were filled with curios and art treasures from all parts of the world, and I was especially interested in a splendid collection of brass-bound and inlaid Korean chests. Mr. Morgan was America's last Minister to Korea, being transferred from Seoul to Havana when Japan established her Korean protectorate.

Although it was nine miles out to Mr. Morgan's house, everybody came, and it was said to be the most representative gathering of the city's leading families that had been seen in many a day. Of course there was music and dancing and refreshments and all the elements which go to make up an enjoyable entertainment, and even though there was a general celebration going on in the city, the crowds took their departure reluctantly.

The general celebration was in commemoration of the anniversary of the outbreak of the Ten Years' War in 1858, and it was strange to see all parties uniting in a demonstration of what seemed to be real patriotism. Havana was decorated in regular old-fashioned Fourth of July style, and there were parades and speeches, bands, banners and fireworks, just as if Cuba were the solidest little Republic in the world. One really couldn't take the situation very seriously after all,—except that it was costing the country a great deal of money and certainly would have cost many foolish lives had it not been taken in hand so promptly.

The next morning we inaugurated Governoon Magoon and took our departure, leaving him to his uncomfortable fate. I remember later a cartoon depicting him as sitting in agony on a sizzling stove labelled "Cuba," while Mr. Taft appeared in the distance in a fireman's garb carrying a long and helpful-looking line of hose. But that illustrated subsequent history.

We sailed from Havana on the battleship *Louisiana,* escorted by the *Virginia* and the *North Carolina,* Mr. and Mrs. Bacon, General Funston, Mr. Taft and I, on the 13th of October, just twenty-nine days from the day on which Mr. Roosevelt had called the momentous conference at Oyster Bay to decide what should be done about Cuba, and we escaped by only a few hours the terrible storm which swept east from the Gulf of Mexico that same evening. It was one of the worst storms the locality had ever known. It did untold damage to property, killed a number of people and by cutting the island off from outside communication gave the United States a short period of acute uneasiness on account of the thousands of American soldiers quartered in Cuba and the big fleet of American battleships lying in Havana harbour. The waters of Hampton Roads were so rough that after boarding the *Dolphin* for the trip up the Chesapeake and the Potomac to Washington we went ashore at Fort Monroe and took the train.

BUSY YEARS

THESE were the days when Mr. Roosevelt, Mr. Root and Mr. Taft were known and very aptly caricatured as "The Three Musketeers," a thing which both pleased and amused them. Mr. Roosevelt was, of course, D'Artagnan, Mr. Root was Athos and Mr. Taft was Porthos, and they worked together in such harmony and with such high mutual regard as one remembers now with singular satisfaction.

Mr. Hearst was running against Mr. Hughes for Governor of New York, and the situation in Idaho, complicated by the murder of Governor Steunenberg and the activities of the anarchistic element in the Western Federation of Miners, seemed also to demand special attention from the Administration, so Mr. Root was delegated to "hurl the spear of civilisation and right thinking" in New York, while Mr. Taft was sent into the West with Idaho as the climax of his itinerary.

All this had been arranged for him while he was away on the mission of averting disaster in Cuba, and when he returned to Washington he had just time, as he expressed it, "to pack the War Department into a suitcase" before he was off on a speech-making trip which took him from Baltimore through Ohio, Illinois, Nebraska, Wyoming and Idaho and back through Kansas, Oklahoma, Texas and New Orleans to Washington, with only such time for preparation of speeches as he could get on the trains between stops.

His letters to me were dictated to his stenographer, and in re-reading them I get the impression that I was made the victim of his thinking processes since he poured into them all the politics and the turmoil of the hour, together with lengthy comments which kept me very much alive with interest in the campaign in which he was engaged.

About this time there appeared in the New York *Sun* an editorial which pleased me and which expressed the rush of our lives with singular vividness. It said in part:

Merely to record the movements and missions of the Secretary of War requires a nimble mind. He journeys from Washington to

Manila to reassure ten millions of natives restive under an experimental scheme of civil government and turns up in Panama to speed the digging of the Isthmian Canal. To give a fillip to a campaign for reform in some western State, or direct the southern Republicans in the way they should go, or enlighten the people Down East as to the President's home policy, or illuminate the recesses of a problem in jurisdiction for the benefit of a bar association, is only a matter of grabbing a time table and throwing a change of clothing into a travelling bag. Such are mere relaxations and holiday jaunts for the Hon. William H. Taft.

A Cuban revolution would be a poser to most statesmen, and to an ordinary Secretary of War a labour of Hercules; but to the business of bringing peace with honour to a distracted land, deposing one government and setting up another, meanwhile gratifying everybody and winning the esteem of the fiercest warrior, Mr. Taft devotes only one page of the Calendar and takes ship for the States to resume his routine duties as if he had done nothing out of the common.

But routine duties in Washington do not hold him long. An itinerary is made up for him and he plunges into the stress and turmoil of a political campaign. He is to make speeches in Ohio and Illinois, and Idaho claims him too. From Havana to Pocatello is something of a change and a far cry, but it is all in the day's work for William H. Taft... all nice problems look alike to the Secretary of War who should be called the Secretary of Peace, so uniform is his success in smoothing the wrinkled front of conflict and making two laughs echo where one groan was heard before.

No emergency, no exigency can put the Hon. William H. Taft down. With a heart for any fate, buoyant as hope, versatile as the kaleidoscope, indefatigable as fate and indomitable as victory, he is a most amazing and effective Secretary of War. "Cabinet help" when William H. Taft is the instrument and medium, is tantamount to the energy and force of a whole Administration. Yet there are those who would circumscribe his activities by investing him with the robes and immobile dignity of judicial office.

This subject of my husband's appointment to the Supreme Bench cropped up with what seemed to me to be rather annoying

270

frequency. While we were in Cuba it was rumoured that he would be asked to fill the vacancy created by the retirement of Justice Brown, but the report correctly stated that he would be likely to refuse the appointment because of the rapidly developing possibility that he would be the Republican nominee for the Presidency the following year.

At this time Mr. Taft was all but impervious to any friendly advice which, being followed, would have tended to enhance his own political advantage. He was not playing politics for himself; he was attending strictly to business, fully imbued with the conviction that the public desired a continuation of the Administration as it stood. Mr. Roosevelt's personal popularity could not be denied nor in any way belittled, but he had already announced that he was not a candidate for a third term, and all over the country the party was organising to support Mr. Taft, while a number of other names were prominently mentioned as "possibilities." Mr. Roosevelt had assured my husband that he could count on his support, and he also urged him to lose no opportunity to give personal encouragement and impetus to the campaign that was being started in his behalf. But Mr. Taft paid very little attention, and never did he cease to regard a Supreme Court appointment as vastly more desirable than the Presidency. If his letters of that period could be read it would readily be seen that he was a most difficult candidate for his loyal and eager supporters to manage.

About this time, in conversation with Mr. Roosevelt in respect to Mr. Taft's candidacy, I got the impression that he was discouraged over my husband as a candidate because he had avoided co-operation with certain political organisations in the West, and, further, that Mr. thought he might have to join with other Republicans in supporting Governor Hughes, because Mr. Taft was such a poor politician.

I reported this to Mr. Taft and urged him to display a little more enthusiasm on his own account, but in reply I got a good-natured reminder that there was "plenty of time," together with an analysis of the public feeling which, he decided, was not running in his favour at all. He wrote to Mr. Roosevelt:

Mrs. Taft writes me that you are disposed to lecture me for not being more cordial in co-operation with some of my... friends who want to organise a campaign for me for the presidential nomination. I told them just exactly what the fact was and nothing more, and I don't find myself equal to becoming part of any organisation of that sort. The truth is in... and some of the other States, if a man does not join in a way as to imply a kind of obligation to look after these people, should success follow, there is no particular enthusiasm in his favour, and in my state of indifference about it the organisation is not likely to follow me.

Mrs. Taft said that you said you might have to support Hughes for the presidency. If you do you may be sure that you will awaken no feeling of disappointment on my part. While I very much appreciate your anxiety that I shall be nominated, and regard it as the highest compliment possible to me, and as a most gratifying evidence of your good will, you know what my feeling has been in respect to the presidency, and can understand that it will not leave the slightest trace of disappointment should you change your views and think it wise to make a start in any other direction.

In Mr. Roosevelt's reply to Mr. Taft, he said I had misunderstood him, that what he had said was that Mr. Taft must not be too entirely aloof because if he were it might dishearten his supporters and put all Republicans in such shape that some man like Governor Hughes, or more probably some man from the West, would turn up with so much popular sentiment behind him that there would be no course open but to support him.

The 1905 campaign was a hotly contested one. The Republicans won in New York and Idaho, and generally, I believe, though I remember those two States especially, and I find Mr. Taft writing to Mr. Root from Ft. Leavenworth, Kansas, on his way back from Boise City:

Dear Athos:

I saw a copy of your speech when I was in the "wilds" of Idaho, and I cannot tell you the comfort it gave me to read it, and how it intensified the affection and admiration I have always had for the speaker. I can just think of your making up your mind to say the thing and do the thing that the occasion demanded.... You selected the psychological moment, and I have no doubt that you did a great deal to prevent Hearst's election, and I do not doubt also that you are receiving the commendations of your grateful fellow citizens of New York, and all over the country, as you ought to, for hurling your spear full and fair at this "knight of evil."...

From everything I have seen in the west my judgment is that the President cannot avoid running again.... There is no real second choice where I have been. Of course there are complimentary allusions to others.... So far as you and I are concerned I think we are well out of it, and whatever may be our ambitions for honourable service, there is a compensation in not having to be exposed to the horrors of a campaign with this product of yellow journalism whom you have had so much satisfaction in sending down to defeat for a time.

Apropos of this victory, Mr. Roosevelt wrote to Mr. Taft:

Upon my word I do not know which to be the more proud of, what Root did in New York or what you did in Idaho.

When Mr. Taft got back to Washington he found the following letter from Mr. Root, which completes the triangle of this mutual admiration society of the Three Musketeers:

Dear Porthos:

I have been disappointed that your most important and admirable speech in Idaho has not been more freely published and commented on in the East. I have just suggested to the Editor of *The Outlook* that he ought to print it *in extenso* and call attention to it. He will apply to you directly for it and I hope you will let him have it.

I am going to start Saturday afternoon to be away for a week, and if you see any gaping lids about my Department in the meantime, please sit on them gently.

Faithfully yours,

ELIHU ROOT.

"Sitting on the lid" was not in any sense the stationary and reposeful performance the expression seems to suggest. Before Mr. Taft returned to Washington from a tour of inspection of brigade posts, which followed immediately upon his trip to Idaho, Mr. Roosevelt had gone to Panama, leaving behind him various questions, including the one which resulted from the discharge without honour of the three companies of coloured troops at Brownsville, Texas, for the Secretary of War to keep within bounds until his return. Then there were many matters of a purely executive nature which, as long as they did not require the signature of the President himself, Mr. Taft was authorised and expected to dispose of. And with the Secretary of State also absent, his office became government headquarters, practically, where foreign Ambassadors, Senators and officials of other Departments had to take their chances of an interview along with visitors or representatives from the Philippines, Hawaii, Cuba, Porto Rico, Alaska and the Canal Zone, and with Army officers and War Department clerks.

I finally gave up all idea of ever getting him home to luncheon, but we nearly always had a dinner engagement, so along about the hour when I knew he would have just time to rush home and dress I would call him on the telephone. And then, if I were fortunate enough to get him without a disgraceful delay, he almost invariably came in, followed by an extra private secretary bearing a large portfolio of papers to be disposed of before such hour as he chose to consider bedtime.

The winter of 1906-7 was too busy to remember as anything except a sort of hazy nightmare lightened in spots by contemplation of the delightful possibilities contained in a rapidly growing Presidential "boom," but it came to an end, and early in the summer I gathered up my family and a few necessary belongings and went to Murray Bay. We were to leave some time in August for the Philippines and the trip around the world via the Trans-Siberian Railway, and I wanted very much to have my husband get away for a few weeks of absolute detachment from public affairs, feeling sure that it would be his last opportunity for rest and relaxation for many a day. But no man can be a candidate for President of the United States and indulge at the same time in even a short period of complete tranquillity.

Before Mr. Taft joined me he, in deference to the wishes of the men who were conducting his "boom," made another speech-making trip through the West on the method so aptly described as "whirlwind," and did not arrive in Murray Bay until the first week in July.

It just occurs to me that I have covered all these different periods of our lives without even mentioning Murray Bay, although a large part of the Taft family has been spending the summers there for twenty years or more. We went there before the place became in any sense "fashionable," when the only kind of hotel accommodation was in quaint old inns of the real French-Canadian type in which no English was spoken, but where service of such delightfully simple and satisfactory quality as can no longer be obtained was smilingly offered at rates which would now be considered absurdly low. After our first year in 1892 we always had a cottage,—and on going to Murray Bay we prepared to enjoy ourselves in the luxury of complete simplicity.

The cottage which we have occupied for a number of years is perched on a rocky headland overlooking the sixteen miles wide stretch of the St. Lawrence river and almost entirely hidden in a dense grove of fragrant pine trees. It is roomy and comfortable, but simple as a camp in the woods, being finished in unpainted pine and furnished with only such things as may be locked up and left year in and year out. There is nothing to tempt any possible robber, the only distinctive things in the house being some Philippine curios, wall decorations and floor mats, called "petates," which we have brought with us at different times from Manila.

Mr. Taft stayed at Murray Bay about five weeks, but during that time our cottage in the woods was the United States War Department and headquarters of a very probable Presidential candidate. Then, too, Mr. Taft was beset with the nagging necessity for preparing speeches which were really to launch his campaign for the nomination before he left for the trip around the world. The campaign in Ohio became centred and active during the summer, with Mr. Taft far in the lead among possible candidates, and all over the country organisations

275

were forming which demanded whole-hearted and unremitting attention.

The busy man wrote to Mr. Roosevelt: "I am enjoying my vacation," but his vacation consisted in a release from constant social formalities and a daily round of golf on the links of the Murray Bay Club which he liked so much and over which he had played for so many years,—nothing more.

Early in August he left for Washington with the understanding that I should complete arrangements, and taking Charlie with me, should meet him at the entrance of Yellowstone Park at the end of the month. In the meantime he had one more long speech-making trip to begin at Columbus on the 19th of August and to take him through Ohio, Kentucky, Missouri, Oklahoma and to Denver.

His mother, to whom the whole family was strongly devoted, was at this time very ill. It did not seem possible that she could be with us for long, and all of her sons wished sincerely to be able to remain near her. One of them, Horace, was able to do so, but when my husband declared to her his desire to give up the trip to the Philippines and stay in the United States until she recovered she said to him:

"No Taft, to my knowledge, has ever yet neglected a public duty for the sake of gratifying a private desire. You promised the Filipinos that you would be present at the opening of their first Assembly, and if you should break that promise and neglect your plain duty on my account, it would give me no pleasure."

This was the last serious thing she ever said to him, and it gave him great comfort throughout the long trip as the reports of her failing strength came to him. He never saw her again.

With my son Charlie, who was then nearly ten years old, I met my husband and his party at Livingston Junction, on the Northern Pacific Railroad in Montana, and we proceeded together to Gardiner at the entrance to Yellowstone Park. There we were met by General Young, the Superintendent of the Park, and Colonel Henry T. Allen, and by the head of the Park transportation company and began at once a wonderful three days' trip, which included, among other

276

things, the business of inspecting the Army post with the purpose of making recommendations for changes in the Park patrolling system.

As our time was very short we had to drive about fifty miles every day, which meant hurrying on at top speed, with relays of Army mules, and not much more than a how-d'ye-do and good-bye at every place we stopped. In consequence we completely lost track of the days of the week and made what I then thought would prove to be a fatal error.

We got back to the Mammoth Springs Hotel one evening and found the place quite gay with crowds of tourists. There being nothing else to do, I suggested that after dinner we play bridge in the lobby where all the people were and where everything seemed so lively and entertaining.

We did. Mr. Taft and I, General Clarence Edwards and another member of our party sat there and played until quite late, enjoying ourselves immensely. Everybody looked at us, and I noticed a few persons taking special pains to pass close enough for a really satisfactory inspection, but we were used to being gazed at and paid no attention to it. It was not until the next morning that every look that was cast upon us assumed for me a special meaning. The next morning was Monday!

Under any circumstances it would have shocked us somewhat to find that through forgetfulness we had played bridge during a whole Sunday evening, but with Mr. Taft generally recognised as a probable candidate for President, our shock was merged into serious concern with regard to the effect the story might have on the millions of good Sabbatarians throughout the country. And there was no possible explanation that we could make. Playing cards was bad enough, but to have forgotten Sunday altogether was a great deal worse, so we were perfectly helpless. Up to the day Mr. Taft was elected I looked for the story to rise up and smite us. I had visions of glaring headlines: "Taft Plays Cards on the Sabbath Day." Having been brought up on strictly Sabbatarian principles myself, I knew what good use could be made of the incident in the hands of our political enemies. But we never heard a word from it, and I have a warm regard for all those good people who failed to avail themselves of such an opportunity for a bit of valuable gossip. Or had they all forgotten it was Sunday, too'?

On the way from Yellowstone Park to Seattle I had a taste of real campaign work and always thereafter enjoyed a full realisation of its difficulties. I got completely worn out as a mere onlooker, and as I saw Mr. Taft encountering the throngs at every stopping place, speaking until his voice was reduced to a hoarse whisper, and shaking hands he groaned with the ache of his muscles, my political enthusiasm waned slightly, though temporarily, and I could think of nothing to be more thankful for at the moment than the fact that we were about to set out on a two weeks' ocean voyage, beginning a three months' trip around the world.

A HURRIED TRIP AROUND THE WORLD

I HAVE not the space to give a detailed account of this trip around the world. After a pleasant voyage on the steamship *Minnesota* we were given in Japan the same warm welcome that we had always had there, and Mr. Taft and I were entertained at the Shiba Detached Palace, one of the Imperial residences. We lunched with the Emperor and also with Prince Fushimi, and we met the admirals and the generals who had won such distinction in the Russo-Japanese War. These included Admiral Togo and Field Marshal Prince Oyama. It was explained to Mr. Taft by the Court Chamberlain that we were regarded as personal guests of the Emperor. Marquis Saionji was then Premier, but Prince Katsura, whom he had succeeded and who was our old friend, was still powerful in the councils. Mr. Taft held a number of interesting and useful interviews with these statesmen of Japan, and also with the Minister of Foreign Affairs, Count Hayashi, and with Marquis Terauchi, the Minister of War, who has now become Governor of Korea. He was able, from what they told him, to understand the attitude of Japan toward the United States, and to feel confident of her wish to remain in bonds of amity with us. At a dinner in Tokyo, given by the Minister of Foreign Affairs, Mr. Taft made a speech in which he pointed out the absurdity of a war between Japan and the United States, and showed how the true interests of both nations required a strengthening of the bonds of friendship between them. This speech attracted much attention throughout the Orient and was cabled back to the United States as an expression of the Administration on the subject. The Japanese residents of Yokohama presented to Mr. Taft and me on this visit a very hansdome silver tea set.

Our course took us by way of Shanghai and we stopped there for just one busy day. In the morning Mr. Taft dedicated a Young Men's Christian Association building which had just been constructed and to the cost of which a number of Chinese Mandarins, though not Christians, had made substantial contribution. The afternoon was devoted to shopping and to a most elaborate and picturesque reception and tea which was given for us by the Chinese guilds of the city. At this tea I was presented with a very curious and interesting bowl of Chinese silver which is among my most valued possessions. In the evening a great banquet was given by the leading citizens of Shanghai at the Astor Hotel, where provision was made for the ladies to hear the speaking from a platform erected at one end of the room. Mr. Taft made a speech on the subject of the relations of the United States to the development of China, which was long remembered as a succinct and forcible presentation of the policy of the United States toward that country, then in an interesting stage of its awakening from a long lethargy.

In Manila, at the formal opening of the first Assembly, Mr. Taft laid down the purposes of the Administration in the passage of the Philippine Act, plainly saying to the Philippine people that independence was not near at hand, and that it could only come after a period of earnest effort on their part to fit themselves for complete self-government. His candour and frankness did not please many of the Assembly, but his view has always been that the only way in which to deal with the Filipino people is to tell them the exact truth, unpalatable though it may be, and to fulfil promises with the greatest care. Filipinos may be very lax in discharging the full measure of their own assurances, but the way to maintain influence over them is to pursue a policy of clear and candid statement, full performance and exact justice. They are prone to accept every declaration in the same sense in which they would like to construe it, and the utmost care must be taken to prevent their being misled.

Demagoguery with them is likely to be most pernicious in its ultimate results.

During this visit we were the guests of Governor General Smith at Malacañan Palace and I experienced a pleasant renewal of old impressions and sensations. Mr. W. Cameron Forbes, who succeeded Governor Smith, was then Secretary of Commerce and Police and, in this capacity, was in charge of Public Works. He had built for himself at Baguio a fine country residence which he called "Topside," a name which fits it exactly, since it stands, literally, at the "topside" of the island of Luzon, at an elevation of more than five thousand feet, and overlooks the broadest and most colourful stretch of mountain scenery imaginable. We visited Mr. Forbes at "Topside" and were able to see for the first time the splendid achievements in the development of the summer capital which I anticipated in Chapter IX. Mr. Taft assured an enthusiastic enquirer that he was not surprised at the magnificence of the Benguet Road because he had authorised the expenditure of a sufficient amount to produce something unusual, and that he would, indeed, have been surprised if it hadn't been done. But he had to confess to a little surprise at the improvement of the town of Baguio. The difference was so great that it was almost impossible to recognise the place as the site of the ragged little Igorrote village where I had spent such pleasant and "uncivilised" days just before my husband's inauguration as the first governor of the Philippines.

It would be useless for me to attempt to detail the thousand and one events of this visit to Manila. Upon our arrival we were handed a printed schedule of dinners, luncheons, teas, receptions, balls, meetings, celebrations, trips of inspection, and business conferences which we had to do our best to carry out. Fortunately provision was made for a few hours of rest which could be used for other things when we got behind with the programme.

On a day in November, when blue Manila Bay lay sparkling in the sun, we set sail for Vladivostok on the U. S. S. *Rainbow,* flying the flag of Admiral Hemphill, and convoyed by two other naval vessels. The most amusing incident of this trip, which was quite a tempestuous one, was the gradual freezing up of our Filipino orchestra. They left Manila clad in natty white uniforms, responding with enthusiasm to the strains of the many bands on shore and on the fleet of harbor launches which accompanied us down the bay. They played for us at dinner that night and gave a concert on deck the next day, but then began the rapid descent of the mercury in the thermometers and the consequent undoing of our tropical musicians. They first changed into heavy blue uniforms and tried their best to look comfortable. Then they put on their overcoats and kept them on. Finally they deserted the deck altogether and their rather disconnected strains came up to us through a partly open hatch just over the engine room. When we reached the forbidding harbour of Vladivostok, where the temperature stood below zero, the poor bugler was so thoroughly cold that he couldn't adjust his lips to his bugle to pipe distinguished visitors aboard. Our party on this trip around the world was small, including only my son Charlie, Mr. Taft's secretary, Mr. Fred C. Carpenter, General Clarence R. Edwards, Mr. and Mrs. Martin Egan and two other newspaper correspondents.

Shortly before we reached Vladivostok there had been a mutiny on one of the torpedo boats in the harbour, and a woman anarchist had induced the crew to take the boat out into the stream and raise the red flag. This outbreak was suppressed with a heavy hand, and a number of those suspected of complicity in the plot were arrested. As the Governor had power of life and death over them it was assumed that the extreme penalty was visited on some of them at least, but no publicity was given to the proceedings. The effect of the tragedy upon our arrival, however, was marked. The town was in a most unquiet state and there were vague rumours of danger to be met on every hand. We were not permitted to go ashore without a heavy guard of bristling Cossacks, and everywhere we went we were under the closest and most careful protection. It was most exciting, though in the midst of the cordial hospitality of our Russian hosts we could not feel that there was the slightest cause for apprehension. As soon as we dropped anchor in the harbour we were welcomed to Vladivostok by the Governor and General Commanding. He assigned Prince Bariatinski, Colonel of a regiment stationed at Vladivostok, to act as Mr. Taft's aide during our stay, and from Saturday until Tuesday he and the Princess, both of whom spoke English, were with us constantly, adding much to our enjoyment. Our visit concluded with a dinner and ball given by the Governor, and the next morning we bade good-bye to the *Rainbow* and Admiral Hemphill and made our way, surrounded by Cossack guards, to the railway station where the train waited to start on its twelve days' trip across Siberia. The government provided us with a large private car of the armoured variety which contained a number of compartments that were fully as spacious and comfortable as an average steamship cabin and we settled ourselves in them quite as we would have done on a trans-Pacific liner.

The trip across Siberia is exceedingly interesting. One anticipates endless monotony, but only the landscape lacks variety. For days together the train runs along through a country which looks exactly like South Dakota or Nebraska and which is interesting only in its wonderful possibilities. It is one of the world's open spaces, undeveloped but capable of producing anything. I had always imagined Siberia as a country filled with sadness and I expected it to depress me, but it arouses no such feeling. We met trainload after trainload of happy Russian colonists on their way to new settlements, and at all the well-built stations along the way we saw a great number of sturdy peasant farmers and their families who looked thoroughly comfortable and contented. We whiled away the hours with bridge and books, and, though the train never made more than two or three stops a day, the time passed quickly. Throughout the journey our car was guarded by stalwart Russian soldiers in most picturesque uniforms, stationed on both platforms, and each time the train stopped this guard was changed with considerable ceremony. Also at every station near an army post Mr. Taft was greeted by the Commander of the District with strict military form, all of which added colour and interest to the journey.

Mr. Willard D. Straight, then United States Consul at Mukden, met us at Vladivostok with plans for our reception at Mukden. When we arrived there we were welcomed by a company of Chinese soldiers dressed in the old Mongolian custom, and by a squadron of Cossacks. We were hurried in a carriage behind two fast trotting Orloff horses to a hotel where all the consuls assembled greeted us with cakes, champagne and very short speeches. There was considerable excitement among the consuls with regard to the toasts to be drunk and the order of precedence in which the rulers of the different countries were to be named, but Mr. Straight was diplomatic enough to mention every proper name in right order and the result was a round of congratulation and merriment. In the meantime the leisurely and accommodating train was waiting, so we hurried back to the station at the terrific pace usual to the Russian with his beautiful horses. No people not inherently fine could ever produce the kind of horses one sees in Russia. And the Russians love them. I can think of nothing more pleasing than the picture of a great, shaggy, gruff-voiced Russian coachman on the box of his carriage or droshky, gently urging his well- kept horse on to his best speed in terms of endearment. "On, Little Brother!" says he.

At Moscow we were right royally entertained by the Governor-General of the city who did everything possible to make our visit memorable. We arrived late Saturday night and on Sunday the Kremlin was opened for our especial benefit and we were given full opportunity to see every part of that ancient and interesting home of Russian autocracy with all its collections of priceless treasures. A hurried round of entertainments, which included a special ballet performance at the Opera, ended with a dinner given by the Governor-General, and we left on the midnight train for St. Petersburg. We had not been there more than an hour or so the next morning when we received a telegram announcing that a woman Nihilist had thrown a bomb at the Governor's sleigh which had exploded under the horses, killing them and the coachman and throwing the Governor and his aide backward into the snow unharmed. As these gentlemen had both been very kind to us it brought home in a startling way the danger that attends high position in Russia.

In St. Petersburg we dined with the Minister of Foreign Affairs, M. Iswolski and Madame Iswolski, and with them received the Diplomatic Corps. Mr. Taft and General Edwards had an audience with the Czar and attended the annual Saint's day celebration of a famous regiment numbering about 3,200, no man of which measures less than six feet two. They were also present at a luncheon which the Czar gave to the officers of this regiment at the Czar-Koe-Selo Palace. In the Czar's suite there were two or three gentlemen who remembered Mr. Taft's father as Minister to Russia, so he very greatly enjoyed the experience of meeting them.

Our visit was a hurried one, and after a stay of three days we left for Berlin. Mr. Roosevelt and Mr. Root were not disposed to have Mr. Taft visit any of the courts of Europe except at St. Petersburg and that only for the purpose of conveying his grateful acknowledgment of the courtesies shown us in our long trip across Siberia. Nor in the state of his mother's health, which we knew to be precarious, was he disposed to accept the invitations which he received from the German Emperor, the King of Belgium, the President of France and others, to visit their countries and become their guest. At Berlin we had just time to dine with the American Ambassador and Mrs. Tower, and to meet a few American friends whom they had invited in, then Mr. Taft and the other members of the party went to Hamburg to take the Steamship *General Grant* at that port, while I, with Mrs. Post Wheeler, rushed down to Paris to do a few hours' shopping, planning to join the *Grant* at Boulogne the next evening. In the meantime a terrible storm began to rage along the coast, and when we reached Boulogne there was some question about our being able to get to the *Grant* which lay at anchor just outside the breakwater. However, we boarded the little tender and she started for the very wild looking open channel. She had no sooner struck the heavy seas before she had broken her rudder and was being buffeted about in a really terrifying manner. We managed in some way to get back inside the breakwater where some repairs were made, then we started out again. We repeated this performance several times, listening meanwhile to generally voiced predictions that nothing on earth could save us from going to the bottom, and, although it was only nine o'clock in the evening when we boarded the little vessel, it was four o'clock in the morning before she came alongside the *Grant* and discharged her dilapidated and exhausted passengers.

Mr. Taft had waited up for us and had seen the tender come out of the harbour and go back, and, assuming from what was told him that no attempt would be made to transfer the passengers before morning, he went to bed. When I got aboard the steamer, filled with excitement over the dangers through which I had passed, and found him peacefully sleeping in his cabin, I declined to accept any explanation. A French sub-prefect, who had been sent out by the Minister of the Interior of France with greetings and compliments, and who had come in his full regimentals with a cocked hat, was waiting to see Mr. Taft and I was cruel enough to insist that he should get up and receive him. Throwing a long fur coat over his pajamas the Secretary of War of the United States walked out into the salon to meet the polite representative of the politest of peoples, but after a grave exchange of formal salutations the situation proved too much for their gravity. They burst out laughing at each other, to the immense enjoyment of the bystanders, and the gloom of the wee sma' hour was lifted.

When we touched at Plymouth that afternoon we received a despatch announcing the death of Mr. Taft's mother. The funeral took place in Cincinnati, at the home of Mr. Charles Taft, several days before we could reach New York.

On our return to the United States we found that my husband's rivals for the Republican nomination had been making great headway. Mr. Roosevelt was quite impatient at the loss of ground that Mr. Taft's candidacy had suffered and he urged him to take a more active interest in the situation. He insisted that Mr. Taft should change the subject of a speech which he had agreed to deliver in Boston from the Philippine problem to a discussion of the financial situation which was then acute after the depression which had taken place during our absence. Mr. Roosevelt's forcible expression was that the business and political public had no more interest in the Philippines than in the subject of "nature faking."

I cannot go into the details of the preliminary fight. My husband's brother Charles devoted a full year to it, established headquarters in Ohio and Washington, and bore the brunt of the contest. The afternoon of the convention when the voting came, we all assembled at my husband's office in the War Department and received the news over the telephone as it came in. I have a series of photographs, taken by a friend, of the expressions on my husband's face as the results of the voting were being announced. Soon after the nomination was made, on the first of July Mr. Taft resigned from the Cabinet, and we established ourselves at Hot Springs, Virginia, where he spent some weeks preparing his address of acceptance. This he submitted to Mr. Roosevelt and Mr. Root before he went to Cincinnati to deliver it. Mr. Charles Taft made elaborate preparations to receive and entertain the Committee of Announcement, and on a platform in front of his fine old house, in

Pike Street, on one of the hottest days of the summer, my husband delivered his acceptance. We then returned to Hot Springs and spent another month in preparation for the campaign. From Hot Springs we went to Middle Bass Island on Lake Erie to spend a week or more there. We then went to Cincinnati. Upon this latter trip Mr. Taft made a good many speeches from the platform of our car. In September Mr. Bryan's campaign looked very hopeful. The opposition of Mr. Gompers and organised labour seemed formidable. Mr. Taft determined to meet this issue fully and frankly. He was attacked because he had delivered a number of labour decisions supposed to be against the interest of labour. He had sent to jail, for six months, the chief lieutenant of Debs in the Debs railway rebellion of 1894, breaking it up in Cincinnati and the vicinity. He did not apologise in any way for the action he had taken. A meeting of the railway trade organisations was called in Chicago at Orchestra Hall, and there he explained his action, defended it, and that were the same questions presented to him again, he would do the same thing he had done, and that he had no excuses to offer. From that point he made a long trip in the West, upon which I did-not accompany him. I remained in Cincinnati with Mrs. Charles Taft and my sister Mrs. Anderson. It was the first political campaign in which Mr. Taft was a candidate before the people. The reports that came indicated that he had lost his voice, and I was greatly concerned lest he might break down in his strenuous labours and new experience. The ups and downs of such a campaign, the prophecies, the hopes, the fears aroused by favourable and opposing newspapers were all new and trying to me, and in a way I think I was under as great a nervous strain as my husband was, without the steadying help of the hardest kind of work. However as the campaign drew near to a close, the Republican confidence grew stronger and stronger, so when we were assembled finally under the hospitable roof of Mr. and Mrs. Charles Taft, with a company of friends to receive the dispatches on election night, the news of the great success that came did not surprise us.

PRESIDENT OF THE UNITED STATES

SHORTLY after my husband's election, having spent a couple of restful weeks at Hot Springs, Virginia, we went to Augusta, Georgia, and took the old house known as the Terrett Cottage, near the Bon Air Hotel. To me the weeks we spent there were exceptionally happy ones and I should like to mention each friend—friends then and friends still—who contributed to our constant enjoyment, but there were too many of them and their kindnesses too numerous.

Mr. Taft, of course, immediately became engrossed in the difficulties of securing a Cabinet which would satisfy everybody and disappoint none,—an impossibility,—as well as a thousand and one other matters not connected in any way with the daily games of golf on Augusta's sandy links which attracted such wide attention. But even then my own problems became to me paramount and I began to give them my almost undivided attention and to neglect the political affairs which had for many years interested me so intensely. Perhaps with my husband safely elected I considered all important affairs satisfactorily settled. At any rate I found little time or inclination at the moment to worry about who should have the high offices in the new President's gift, or what policies should be pursued during his administration.

At my request Captain Archibald Butt came down to Augusta to consult with me as to changes I wished to make in the White House service, and together we went over the whole situation. As President Roosevelt's aide he knew the whole lexicon of customary White House social formalities.

I had been a member of Washington's official family for five years and knew as well as need be the various phases of the position I was about to assume, so my plans not so difficult to put into form, however difficult I may have found them to put into execution.

We made a trip to Panama in February before the Inauguration and did not reach Washington until the end of the month when we went to stay with our friends, Mr. and Mrs. William J. Boardman, and their daughter, Miss Mabel Boardman, at their residence on Dupont

Circle. We spent with them a busy week as the recipients of varied and delightful hospitality, which was terminated by a splendid reception in our honour on the evening of the second of March.

Captain Butt, who was to be continued as aide to President Taft, called on me at once upon my arrival in Washington to assure me that my instructions had been carried out and that the new regime, fully organised, would go into effect at the White House on the morning of March fifth.

Some time before the Inauguration, indeed shortly after Mr. Taft's election, President Roosevelt expressed a desire that we should dine with him and Mrs. Roosevelt on the evening of the third of March and spend that night in the White House as their guests. This was breaking a precedent, but it was Mr. Roosevelt's plan for bidding us a warm welcome to the post which he was about to vacate, and my husband accepted with grateful appreciation. My impression is that neither Mrs. Roosevelt nor I would have suggested such an arrangement for this particular evening, but, it having been made for us, we naturally acquiesced.

The third of March, a stormy day, was filled with innumerable minor engagements and small incidents, with instructions and counter-instructions and, especially, with weather predictions and counter-predictions, so it was not until shortly before eight o'clock that Mr. Taft and I, having dressed for dinner, arrived at the White House. The other guests at the dinner were Senator and Mrs. Lodge, Senator and Mrs. Root, Admiral and Mrs. Cowles, Mr. and Mrs. Nicholas Longworth and Miss Mabel Boardman.

Now there is always bound to be a sadness about the end of an administration, no matter how voluntarily the retiring President may leave office, no matter how welcome the new President and his family may be. Mrs. Roosevelt seemed depressed, not, I am sure, over the prospect of leaving the White House,—Presidents' wives are always given plenty of time to prepare themselves for that event,— but for other reasons which one easily could surmise. Her husband and son were about to start for a long and, possibly, dangerous trip into the jungles of Africa, and she was looking forward to a year of anxiety. She was leaving a full and busy life; she had occupied her high position for nearly eight years, during which she had made a host of friends, and a great number of them had called during the afternoon to say farewell and to express their deep regret at her departure. I knew all of these things, realised their depressing effect and sympathised with her deeply. The President and Mr. Taft, seconded by other guests, did their best with stories and conversation, made as general as possible, to lighten the occasion, but their efforts was not entirely successful.

As my husband had an engagement to attend a "smoker" which was being given to him at the New Willard Hotel by a large gathering of Yale men, the party broke up very early and, as soon as the last of the guests had gone, I went immediately to my rooms. We had been assigned to the suite in the southeast corner, known in the White House as the Blue Bedroom.

This Blue Bedroom gave me food for interesting reflection. Conspicuous, under the mantel against the side wall, I found, on a bronze plate, the following inscription (which I read as I struggled with my hooks): "In this room Abraham Lincoln signed the Emancipation Proclamation of January 1, 1863, whereby four million slaves were given their freedom and slavery forever prohibited in these United States." It is only a state bedroom now, having been made so by the plans of the McKim restoration which was accomplished during the Roosevelt administration, but it was once Lincoln's Cabinet room, a room in which he lived through many terrible days during the Civil War. It seemed strange to spend my first night in the White House surrounded by such ghosts.

[During the Roosevelt administration, the White House was found to be dangerously unsound. An extensive restoration was accomplished and you can read about it in _Restoration of the White House_.]

I went to bed reasonably early, hoping that I might have a good, long sleep and get up refreshed and ready for an eventful day. But the press of circumstances was against me. My mind was never more wide awake. In spite of my determination to rest, I went carefully over the whole Inaugural programme. I wondered if this had been done, if that had been attended to. I worried over many petty details with which I had no reason to be concerned. I suppose I must have been excited, a condition quite rare with me, but then, too, the weather had something to do with it. Never was seen such a night in Washington. It will be remembered that Mr. Moore, the Chief of the Weather Bureau, had prophesied that the storm of the third would pass and that the Fourth of March would dawn as clear and bright as any Inaugural Committee could wish. He made himself very popular with the anxious officials, who were expending their energies in the preparation of a fair weather programme, but his popularity was short lived. He afterward learnedly explained that some wholly unprecedented thing had happened in the wind currents, causing a "flareback"—what-ever that may be. It was a memorable "flareback" in any event, not to be forgotten by those who were so seriously inconvenienced by its results.

After I had fallen asleep in the early morning hours, thinking—with faith in the prophet—to wake up and find a smiling world, I was roused by loud, crackling reports which seemed to be in the immediate vicinity of my windows. I got up and looked out. It was light enough for me to see that the world was ice-bound and that the storm, instead of abating, had increased in violence. The crackling I had heard was the noise of twigs and tree limbs breaking with the weight of the ice which encased them. It didn't look hopeful for the Inaugural Ceremonies, and I had a ludicrous vision of a haughty, gold-laced parade sliding, rather than marching with measured precision, down Pennsylvania Avenue, striving to maintain its dignity while it spasmodically lost its footing. But mine was rueful mirth.

In the morning Mr. Taft found President Roosevelt in the great hall below, genially alert.

"Well, Will," he exclaimed, "the storm will soon be over. It isn't a regular storm. It's nature's echo of Senator Rainer's denunciations of me. As soon as I am out where I can do no further harm to the Constitution it will cease."

"You're wrong," said Will; "it is my storm. I always said it would be a cold day when I got to be President of the United States."

It was really very serious. Railroad and telegraphic communications were paralysed all along the Atlantic Coast. Wires were down in every direction and traffic of all kinds was at a practical standstill. Thousands of people, on their way to Washington for the Inauguration, were tied up at points outside the city and it was impossible for awhile even to get a telegram in or out. However, Inaugurations do not wait for fair weather and the programme had to proceed.

About half past ten I saw the President and the President-elect, in a closed carriage, accompanied by Senators Knox and Bacon of the Inaugural Committee, and a brilliant mounted escort, start on their slippery way toward the Capitol. The Inauguration ceremonies would not take place until twelve o'clock, but there were a number of bills waiting for the signature of Mr. Roosevelt, and it was for him to go early to the office of the President at the Capitol to attend to this and other final business details.

Before they left the 'White House it had not yet been decided whether or not the Inauguration would take place out of doors. Mr. Taft regretted exceedingly the necessity for disappointing thousands of people, but at the same time he recognised the danger of exposing the crowds to the wet and penetrating cold, and he considered, especially, the impossibility of asking Chief Justice Fuller, who was then over seventy years old and very frail, to brave a blizzard, even for the purpose of administering a Presidential oath. However, he decided to wait until the weather had given its ultimate indication before changing the programme. He said afterward that as he drove to the Capitol there were many brave citizens in the streets who gave voice to as hearty cheers as could possibly be expected under the circumstances.

I was being taken care of by Captain Archibald Butt, so I had nothing except the weather to worry about. With a last hopeless look out of doors I proceeded to don my Inauguration finery, feeling duly thankful that it was not too spring-like in its character. The newspapers say I wore a purple satin suit, and a small hat trimmed with gold lace and a high white aigrette. This is as good a description as any, though it might have been more flattering, considering the importance I attached to the subject. I remember the hat perfectly. The aigrette was not quite as high as it started out to be. It had nearly met an untimely end at a reception the day before where it collided with a lighted gas-jet. Fortunately it was put out before it was greatly damaged, but it had to be trimmed down some, and I imagined that it exuded a faint odour of burning feathers.

At least two years before the election, when no one could anticipate who would be the next President, President Roosevelt had announced at a Cabinet meeting that he did not intend to ride back to the White House with his successor. It was a precedent which he did not like and which he desired to break. Mrs. Roosevelt went, with her family and friends, directly from the White House to the station to wait for her husband to join her after the Inauguration. It was about half past eleven when Captain Butt and I started in a limousine for the Capitol where we arrived to find the "scene set" for the ceremonies in the Senate Chamber.

Our children were already in the gallery, waiting eagerly. It was an event in their young lives never to be forgotten, and I believe that Robert and Helen were in properly receptive moods. My son Charlie, however, seems not to have been so confident. Charlie is a great lover of adventure stories and it is a favourite tradition in the family now that he carried with him to the Senate Chamber a copy of "Treasure Island" with which to while away the time in case the Inaugural address should prove too long. Charlie was only eleven years old and I consider it a great tribute to his father's eloquence that "Treasure Island" was not opened that day.

This Inauguration was said to be, by persons who had seen many, one of the most impressive ceremonies that ever opened the administration of a President. The oath of office is usually administered and the Inaugural address delivered from a large platform erected in front of the Capitol before which ten thousand people can assemble. But the ten thousand people are sure to have been waiting in a massed crowd for an hour or more; they are always tired and uncomfortable, so when they finally discover that few of them can really hear anything, and that they have seen all there is to be seen, they begin to move about and talk, the noise and agitation greatly detracting from the impressiveness of the ceremony. Because my husband's Inauguration took place in the Senate Chamber it was no less "in the sight of all the people." There was room on the floor of the Chamber for the whole official personnel of the Government of the United States, resident in Washington. There were the retiring President and his Cabinet, the Justices of the Supreme Court in their robes of office, the Senate and the House of Representatives, besides the foreign Ambassadors and the whole Diplomatic Corps in their brilliant uniforms, while the galleries were crowded with official families and a substantial number of unofficial auditors.

It was a great presence; and the taking of the oath and the delivering of the Inaugural address before assembled national authority and the world's representatives, in a solemn silence in which every word could be heard, left a deep impression.

As soon as Mr. Taft had finished speaking Mr. Roosevelt walked rapidly up, and giving his hand a mighty grasp, said something which sounded like "Bully speech, old man!" and hurried out of the Chamber accompanied by members of his Cabinet who were to see him off at the station. My husband told me afterward that what he really said was: "God bless you, old man. It is a great state document."

Since the ex-President was not going to ride back to the White House with his successor, I decided that I would. No President's wife had ever done it before, but as long as precedents were being disregarded I thought it might not be too great a risk for me to disregard this one. Of course, there was objection. Some of the Inaugural Committee expressed their disapproval, but I had my way and in spite of protests took my place at my husband's side.

By the time the Inauguration ceremonies were concluded the skies had cleared and the sun had come out. Mr. Taft left the Senate Chamber with the Committee, followed by the assembled dignitaries in the order of precedence. With Captain Butt I hurried from the gallery and him in the great hall under the Dome, on his way to the platform on the North Side where the Inauguration would have taken place but for the weather. In front of the temporary structure many people had gathered, and as we descended to the front they called for the new President. In response he stepped to the platform where the Inaugural oath was to have been administered, and bowed repeatedly.

A platoon of mounted Police and our escort, the Cleveland City Troop, with their elaborate and beautiful uniforms somewhat bedraggled by the morning's sleet and mud, met us at the steps leading down from the platform. We entered the official coach and four and were slowly driven down through the Capitol grounds to Pennsylvania Avenue, and thence to the White House. As I have said, the clouds had rolled by; the day was cold but bright; the expected and expectant crowds were thronging the sidewalks and filling the stands, and our greeting from them was all that my fancy had pictured it.

For me that drive was the proudest and happiest 'event of Inauguration Day. Perhaps I had a little secret elation in thinking that I was doing something which no woman had ever done before. I forgot the anxieties of the preceding night; the consternation caused by the fearful weather; and every trouble seemed swept aside. My responsibilities had not yet begun to worry me, and I was able to enjoy, almost to the full, the realisation that my husband was actually President of the United States and that it was this fact which the cheering crowds were acclaiming.

There was nobody at the White House to bid us welcome except the official staff and some of our own guests. But it didn't matter. There is never any ceremony about moving into the White House. You just drive up and walk in,—and there you are. The aides and ushers who greeted us at the entrance, treated our occupation of our new residence so much as a matter of course that I could help but feel something as Cinderella must have felt when her mice footmen bowed her into her coach and four and behaved just as if they had conducted her to a Court Ball every night of her life. I stood for a moment over the great brass seal, bearing the national coat-of-arms, which is sunk in the floor in the middle of the entrance hall. "The Seal of the President of the United States," I read around the border, and now—that meant my husband!

But I could not linger long because my duties as a hostess began at once. I was not unused to the accepted regulations of official life, so, in spite of a slight feeling that the whole thing was unreal, I was not embarrassed as I walked into the great dining-room and took my place by the door to receive guests for the first time as mistress of the White House.

I had left to the efficient management of Captain Archibald Butt as many of the details of the day's programme as was possible. Some time before I had carefully gone over the plans with him, we had provided for any reasonable emergency, and I knew my instructions would be carried out. Captain Butt—later Major Butt—had been military aide to President Roosevelt; we had known him well, both in the Philippines and in Washington, and we were glad to have the opportunity of continuing him in that capacity. Whatever Major Butt did was done faultlessly—always. During the three years he was with us—day in and day out, upon every possible occasion, in the closest intimacy—I never ceased to wonder at his genius for work, his comprehensive grasp of important matters and of small details, his extraordinary accuracy. His very presence inspired the utmost confidence. Archie Butt, as everybody called him, became our close and dearly loved friend. Indeed, we felt that he belonged to us, and nothing in all our experience ever touched us as deeply as the tragedy of his death. Returning from a short vacation abroad, he went down on the *Titanic,* facing death like a soldier, after the lives of nearly all the women and children had been saved.

We had invited a large number of people to the usual Inaugural luncheon. The cook and several of the staff of servants were to accompany Mrs. Roosevelt to Oyster Bay, but they remained until the afternoon of the Fourth when the staff I had engaged were installed. There are a few old, official servants who remain in the house from one administration to another, keeping in operation an uninterrupted household routine, so there was no reason why the Inaugural luncheon should not be carried through with the same smoothness and despatch to be expected on ordinary occasions. But again we reckoned without the weather. The difficulties of traffic, added to the crush on the avenues, made it impossible for our guests to arrive on time and they continued to straggle in throughout the whole afternoon, each one wishing to apologise in person and make special explanation. This, of course, made anything like systematic reception out of the question and the result was that the luncheon really ran into and became a part of the tea for my husband's classmates of Yale, which was scheduled for five o'clock. There was some confusion, but much goodwill and frank enjoyment and the fact that the President was not there to receive his classmates caused nothing more than a few repetitions of, by that time, familiar comments on the elements.

Mr. Taft was reviewing the Inaugural Parade and the last of it did not pass the reviewing stand until after nightfall. He came in, however, in time to exchange greetings with old-time, enthusiastic friends, the members of the Yale class of '78, and to hold them longer than they had intended to remain. When the last of them had wished us Godspeed and said good-bye, we stood, the five of us,— my husband, my three children and I,—alone in the big state dining-room, and tried to realise that, for the first time, the White House was really our Home. The great walnut-panelled room, with its silvered chandeliers and big moose heads, seemed very empty with only the Taft family in it, after all the clatter and chatter that had been sounding there all day. We gazed at each other for a moment, with slightly lost expressions on our faces, and then nature asserted herself in the new President.

"Let's go up stairs, my dears, and *sit down!*" said he.

Poor man, he had not experienced the blissful sensation of sitting down since early that morning; so we proceeded out to the elevator, which Charlie, true to his boy nature, had, of course, already learned to operate. For once, I am glad to say, it did not stick between floors. This was a habit to which it became addicted in later days, a habit it was sure to indulge on occasions when the President proudly used it for taking a large party of men upstairs after dinner. But this time he was able, without delay, to reach the best easy-chair in the sitting-room where he remained until I prodded him once more into activity by reminding him that he must get into evening clothes else the Inaugural Ball could not take place.

Not having been taxed so greatly, I was not yet ready to succumb to fatigue; besides I was now eager to roam around the house, to familiarise myself with the mysteries of my new home and to plan the assignment of rooms among various members of the family who were to come to us that very night.

The second story of the White House, where all the family living rooms are, corresponds in spaciousness with the floor below, which, with its broad hall, its great East Room, its large reception rooms and state dining room, is familiar to the public. Upstairs there is a very wide hall running the entire length of the building. The rooms occupied by the President and his wife are in the south-west corner and at that end of the house the hall is partially partitioned and screened off and pleasantly furnished with desks, sofas and easy-chairs to make a fairly large and very private family sitting-room. It was here that I left my tired husband while I went on my first tour of exploration.

At each of the four corners of the house there is a suite; all arranged on the same plan, exactly alike, except as to decoration. Each consists of an exceedingly large bedroom with a spacious bath, and a smaller room adjoining which may be used as a bedroom or dressing-room. I went first into the large bedroom which my husband and I expected to occupy. The windows of this room look out on the White House gardens where the large fountain plays, and, beyond, on the Washington Monument, the Potomac River and the distant Virginia hills. This, I think, is the most glorious vista in Washington, which is a city of splendid vistas, and seeing it that March night by the long line of lights which stretch across the Potomac bridge and meet the lights of Arlington, it was, indeed, inspiring.

The room was the room where Lincoln slept, indeed, where every President since Jackson has slept. A tablet under the mantel states this fact. It is the room which must necessarily have more intimate and personal association with the men who have occupied the White House than any other. Other parts of the house have been the scenes of great historic events and of magnificent hospitality, but here, one after another, the Presidents of the United States have really lived and been at home.

Its furnishings have, undoubtedly, been changed many times and yet I found it to contain many old and interesting pieces. The most striking object in the room was an enormous four-poster bed with a great curved canopy of wood, decorated with carved and gilded eagles and upholding heavy draperies of blue and white brocade. In this bed, we had been told, the Prince of Wales slept when he visited this country in 1860, but on the first night I discovered that, whatever its historic interest, I did not like it as a bed to sleep in. I soon replaced it with two smaller mahogany beds and I dispensed altogether with the draperies. There were canopies of the same gilded eagles over the windows, and the curtains suspended from them, as well as the upholstery of the sofa and chairs, were of the same blue and white brocade. Some of the furniture was colonial, some Victorian. The colonial furniture in the White House is very good and there is quite a lot of it in all the bedrooms, but many of the bureaus and wardrobes are of the scarcely-to-be-called beautiful style of the Victorian era. I secured for our room, later on, the beds, a dressing-table and some chairs, all colonial. These were about the only pieces of furniture I bought for the White House. I also substituted heavy chintz for the brocade draperies and upholstery, and did away with the canopies entirely, as they seemed to me to be too heavy for a sleeping room. The small room in the corner of our suite Mr. Taft used for a dressing-room.

The corresponding suite across the hall I gave to Helen, my daughter. It had been occupied by both of the Misses Roosevelt and before them, I believe, by Mrs. McKinley. It had been fitted up in pretty flowered chintz for Miss Ethel Roosevelt, after Miss Alice had married, and we left it unchanged.

I strolled down the hall, which contains only a large table and a few portraits of Presidents for which there is no wall space down stairs, and looked into the Library which is exactly in the center of the house on the south side. It is oval like the Blue Drawing Room beneath it and it is a little dark in the daytime, being shaded by the roof of the south portico. This was Mrs. Roosevelt's favourite room and it had been fitted most charmingly with many of her own belongings, but as they were now gone and my own had not yet been moved in, it looked rather bare. The furniture had not been upholstered for many years and it was a little shabby. Later on I had it all recovered and the walls of the room retinted, and when I had put in some of the Oriental tapestries and handsome pieces of furniture which I had brought with me from the Far East it made a very beautiful and livable room. We used it a great deal, especially when there were guests, but for the family the sitting-room at the end of the hall was always the favourite gathering place.

Opposite the Library a short corridor extends to the window under the roof of the front portico and on each side of this doors open into smaller bedrooms; smaller, that is, in comparison with the four large ones. Even these would be considered large in an ordinary house. One of them I assigned to the housekeeper and the other to my two sons. The boys' room was rather dark, with its windows directly under the roof of the portico; and it was furnished, moreover, in dark red, a colour which does not add light to gloominess, but the boys got it because they were the members of the family who would care the least and who would be the most away.

The great staircase descends from the central hall just beyond these rooms and facing the staircase is the President's Study. The eastern end of the building was all used as offices until the new offices were built and the house restored in accordance with the original plan. The Presidents with large families must, indeed, have been in an uncomfortable situation when they had to confine themselves to the rooms in the west end, the only rooms then available for living purposes. The facts are that such families found the house to be less commodious than a "five-room flat," as the wife of one President expressed it. I believe the Roosevelts, until the house was remodelled, were unable to accommodate one guest.

There is a story that when Prince Henry of Prussia was in Washington, President Roosevelt invited him to ride. The Prince accepted and just before the appointed hour appeared at the White House in his street clothes, accompanied by a valet bearing his riding clothes. He had very naturally expected to change at the White House, but it happened that on that day there was not one room that could even be prepared for a Royal dressing-room, so the President was compelled to request His Highness to return to the German Embassy to change. I believe this incident had the effect of hastening the deliberations of the members of the Appropriations Committee of the House who were then leisurely figuring on the amount necessary for the restoration.

Senator McMillan, who was at the head of the District Committee in the Senate, and who, in his lifetime was the leading spirit in the improvement of Washington, in the revival of the L'Enfant plan, and in the creation of a Commission of Fine Arts to pass upon contemplated structures and changes, conferred with Mr. and Mrs. Roosevelt and with Senator Allison of the Appropriations Committee, and by an amendment in the Senate, in the spring of 1902, to which Speaker Cannon and the House Appropriations Committee assented, the necessary funds for this restoration were eventually provided and, most fortunately, the whole work was committed to Mr. James McKim, of McKim, Meade and White, who, among all the architectural monuments to his genius which he left, left no greater evidence of his mastery of his art than this. He added the gracefully beautiful terraces on either side, equipped with electric light standards, and in accord, really, with the original plan of the house, and utilised them in a most ingenious way. He made of the one on the west a very dignified and convenient approach, through the basement, for large companies attending state entertainments. Cloak stands for the accommodation of thousands were fitted into each side of this passageway and guests now are able to dispose of their wraps and proceed to the staircase leading up to the main hall on the first floor without the slightest interruption or discomfort.

The ample and airy space beneath the high portico on the south side was used for domestic offices and servants' quarters, thus greatly increasing the capacity of the house, and the construction of the very convenient executive office building, reached by a covered, or cloistered passage from the White House basement, was carried out on lines so like in style and appearance to the north portico, so low and classically simple, that it detracts nothing from the general effect and interferes in no way with the dignified outlines of the home of the Nation's Chief Magistrate.

During the reconstruction the President and Mrs. Roosevelt lived either at Oyster Bay or in a house a few steps from the White House on Lafayette Square. Mr. McKim frequently consulted Mrs. Roosevelt as to interior changes and many of her views were adopted, so that the woman's side of the new White House was well looked after.

The work took longer and cost more than was expected and this elicited much criticism of the architect as well as of the architectural result. His aim had been to make as little outward change in the main lines as possible and yet to make as great a change as space would permit in interior accommodation. Considering what he had to accomplish his success was remarkable. But the Philistines among the Congressmen and Senators, who don't like architects anyway, found much to complain of. In their daily visits to the President they did not, by Mr. McKim's plan, reach him through the historic front entrance, supported by the great, white pillars, but they were relegated to a business office, simply and conveniently equipped, and it offended the sense of due proportion of some of them as to who were the real power in the government, the legislative representatives calling on business or the social guests of the President.

But now, after all the ignorance, ill-feeling and prejudice displayed in the most unjust attacks upon Mr. McKim, those whose judgment is worth anything, and that includes the whole body of the people of the United States, rejoice in their hearts that the greatest of American architects was given a free hand to adapt to modern needs, but also to preserve in its dignity and beauty, this most appropriate official home of the Head of the Republic.

These observations may not be in place just here, but they occurred to me on the first evening of my occupancy of the White House, and I congratulated myself that I was to enjoy the results of that successful reconstruction of what had been a most uncomfortable mansion.

The President's Study, as it is now called, is the only room of the old Executive offices which has not been changed into a sleeping room. It is now the President's more personal office where he can receive callers more privately than in the new office building. A small bronze tablet under the mantel tells, in simple words, the history of the room. Here all the Presidents since Johnson held their Cabinet meetings, and here the Protocol suspending hostilities with Spain was signed in McKinley's administration. A picture of that event, painted by Chartran, hangs in the room and conveys a remarkably vivid impression of the men who had a part in it. The faces of President McKinley, of Justice Day, who was then Secretary of State, and of M. Cambon, the French Ambassador, are especially striking. This room, in which there had been a great many personal mementos gathered by Mr. Roosevelt in his interesting career, also looked, after their removal, rather bare on that evening of my first inspection and, save for the pictures and the tablet, had little in its character to make real in one's mind the great events that it had witnessed. Yet, as I roamed around that evening, the whole house was haunted for me by memories of the great men and the charming women whose most thrilling moments, perhaps, had been spent under its roof, and I was unable to feel that such a commonplace person as I had any real place there. This feeling passed, however, for though I was always conscious of the character which a century of history had impressed upon the White House, it came, nevertheless, to feel as much like home as any house I have ever occupied. That Study, which seemed at the moment so much a part of American history and so little even a temporary possession of the Taft family, was later hung with amusing cartoons illustrative of events in Mr. Taft's career, with photographs of his friends, and with what are called at Yale *"memorabilia"* of his varied experiences, and it became, in time, for us all, peculiarly *his* room.

The Blue Bedroom, where we had slept the night before as guests of the Roosevelts, belongs to one of the four corner suites and I planned to give it to my sister Eleanor, Mrs. Louis More, and her husband, while the smaller room in the same suite I assigned to Miss Torrey, our Aunt Delia—and during our administration apparently the country's "Aunt Delia." She had been staying with us at the Boardmans' and was probably enjoying the Inauguration of her nephew more than anyone in Washington. The last of the suites, which was exactly like the blue suite except that it was hung in pink brocade, I gave to my husband's sister and brother-in-law, Dr and Mrs. Edwards of San Diego.

When I had finished my explorations and arrangements I glanced at the clock in the Pink Room and discovered that I had no time to lose before beginning that important toilet which would make me ready for the Inaugural Ball, the last, but not the least of the Inaugural functions.

I hurried to my room and found the hairdresser waiting for me. I sat down with a feeling of great comfort and submitted myself with hopeful patience to her ministrations. But she was so overcome by the greatness of the occasion that, although she was quite accustomed to the idiosyncrasies of my hair, she was not able to make it "go right" until she had put it up and taken it down twice, and even then it was not as perfectly done as I had fondly hoped it would be. I believe this hairdressing process made me more nervous than anything else in the whole course of the day.

While it was going on, my new gown lay glittering on the bed, where the maid had placed it, and I was very anxious to get into it. It had given me several days of awful worry. It was made in New York and the dressmaker had promised that I should have it at least a week before it was needed so that any necessary changes could easily be made. But day after day went by and no dress,—the third of March arrived and then I began, frantically, to telegraph. I finally received the reassuring advice that the dress was on its way in the hands of a special messenger, but the special messenger was, with many other people, held up for hours by the blizzard and did not arrive at the Boardmans' until after I had left for the White House, wondering, disconsolately, what on earth I should wear to the Inaugural Ball if it happened that the messenger couldn't get there at all. The suspense had been fearful and it was a comfortable relief to see the gown all spread out and waiting for me.

It was made of heavy white satin which I had sent to Tokyo to have embroidered, and the people who did the work surely knew their art. A pattern of golden-rod was outlined by a silver thread and cleverly fitted into the long lines of the gown, and no other trimming had been used except some lace with which the low-cut bodice was finished. It fitted me admirably and I hoped that, in spite of all the mishaps in my preparations, I looked my best as I descended from the White House automobile at the entrance of the Pension Office.

The Pension Office was not built for balls, Inaugural or otherwise, and on the evening of March Fourth, 1909, after a day of melting sleet and snow, the entrance was not especially inviting. Neither was the dressing-room which had been assigned to me. I suppose that for years it had rung with the ceaseless click of scores of typewriters and that its walls had beheld no more elaborate costume than a business blouse and skirt since the occasion of the last Inaugural Ball which had marked the beginning of the second Roosevelt administration four years before. But as I needed to do very little "prinking" it really didn't matter and I quickly rejoined the President and proceeded, on his arm, to the Presidential Box, this being a small round gallery above the main entrance of the great ballroom which is itself, in everyday life, the principal workroom of the Pension Office.

A brilliant, an almost kaleidoscopic scene spread before us. The hall is of tremendous proportions, pillared with red marble and with walls tinted in the same colour. Every inch of floor space seemed to be occupied. The bright colours and the gleam of women's gowns met and clashed, or harmonised with the brighter colours of diplomatic uniforms. Officers of the Army and Navy, in full regalia, mingled with the hundreds of men in the plain black of formal evening dress. It was a wonderful glittering throng, more magnificent than any I have ever seen. It was not possible to distinguish individuals except in the space directly below the box, but there, as I looked down, I saw a great semi-circle of faces— thousands, it seemed to me—smilingly upturned toward us. The din of human voices was terrific; even the loudest band procurable had difficulty in making itself heard. But the scene was so gay in colour, and the faces that gazed up at us were so friendly and happy that I felt elated and not at all overwhelmed.

The first person whom my eyes rested upon in the box was Aunt Delia, already installed in a chair near the back and drinking in the scene with visible pleasure. Aunt Delia, at that time, was eighty-three years old, but not for anything would she have missed one feature of this crowning day of her life. Having no children of her own, she had for many years given the greater part of her thought and interest to her nephews and nieces, and she followed every step in my husband's career with an absorption, not to say an excitement, as great as my own. All day long she had travelled from ceremony to ceremony, conducted by Lieutenant Reed, one of the Naval aides. She would arrive, leaning on his arm, among the first at each appointed place, ready and eager for any new event. She didn't miss even the late supper of birds, salads and ices which was served to us later that night, before we left the Ball. And now she sat in the President's Box, her soft, white hair arranged by the best hairdresser, gowned in rich, old-fashioned, black velvet, adorned with all the good old lace which she had been treasuring for years for an occasion justifying its display.

The Vice-President and Mrs. Sherman arrived shortly after we did and shared the box with us. They also had with them a large family party and were both so jolly and so much in the festive spirit that formality disappeared. Many friends and officials of distinction came, in the course of the evening, to pay their respects; and members of our own family came and went at intervals as they were inclined.

I may as well say here that my husband and I both came from such large families that all Washington, at the time of the Inauguration, seemed filled with our near and dear relatives. Mr. and Mrs. Charles P. Taft took a comfortable house for ten days, while Mr. and Mrs. Henry Taft and Mr. Horace Taft were at the New Willard.

About eleven o'clock the President and I descended to the ballroom floor, followed by Vice-President and Mrs. Sherman and, as is the custom, proceeded slowly down the length of the hall and back between the closely packed rows of people who stood aside to make room for our promenade. This ceremonious parade was not as trying for me as it may sound, for not only did I have the reassurance of my husband's arm, but the crowd was too large to seem very personal. So I was quite serene, except for frequent spasms of anxiety lest my gorgeous length of train be stepped on.

Except for this ceremony, and for a short supper which was served to us and a few invited guests in a private room, the President and I remained in the box until shortly after one o'clock when we once more descended and made our way to a waiting automobile which very quickly whisked us away to much needed rest.

However, I must still have had energy enough left to worry over domestic arrangements since the last thing I remember of that eventful day was a hearty laugh from my husband when I exclaimed in sleepy tones: "I wonder where we had all better have breakfast in the morning!"

THE WHITE HOUSE

THE members of my family, and especially my children, are prone to indulgence in good-natured personalities and they like to make the most of my serious attitude toward my domestic responsibilities, saying that I make them three times as difficult as they need be by a too positive insistence on my own methods.

Perhaps I did make the process of adjusting the 'White House routine to my own conceptions a shade too strenuous, but I could not feel that I was mistress of any house if I did not take an active interest in all the details of running it.

The management of the White House is, of course, a larger task than many women are ever called upon to perform, and, incidentally, the same "white light that beats upon a throne" sheds its sometimes uncomfortable radiance upon the usually unprepared heads of America's Chief Executive and his family. Accustomed as I had been for years to publicity, yet it came as a sort of shock to me that nearly everything I did, and especially my slightest innovation, had what the reporters call "news value."

I have lived too much in other countries ever to underestimate the importance of outward form, yet I think I may claim a wholesome regard for and a constant acquiescence in the principles of democratic simplicity, though not the kind of "democratic simplicity" which is usually written in quotation marks.

I made very few changes, really. As a matter of fact no President's wife ever needs to unless she so desires, because the White House is a governmental institution thoroughly equipped and always in good running order. Each new mistress of the house has absolute authority, of course, and can do exactly as she pleases, just as she would in any other home, but in the beginning I confined my efforts largely to minor matters connected with the house service itself. I wished to install certain members of the house personnel of my own choosing, and this I did. Later I made some changes in a few important social usages.

There are certain duties connected with the White House routine which have been performed by the same employes throughout one Administration after another and each new President's wife finds these men invaluable and wonders, I am sure, how the White House could ever be run without them. For instance, there are Mr. Warren S. Young, who has been for thirty years the Social Executive Officer, and Colonel W. H. Crook, who became Chief Custodian under Lincoln in 1865 and is holding the same office to-day. The duties of each of these men are delicate in the extreme, but they know their work down to the minutest detail and it would be difficult to measure their value to the woman who, in public opinion, is wholly responsible for the White House.

As to my own innovations, I decided in the first place to have, at all hours, footmen in livery at the White House door to receive visitors and give instructions to sightseers. Before my time there had been only "gentlemen ushers" who were in no way distinguishable from any other citizen and many a time I have seen strangers wander up to the door looking in vain for someone to whom it seemed right and proper to address a question or to hand a visiting card. The gentlemen ushers I retained, the head usher, Mr. Hoover, having become invaluable through similar service under every Administration since Cleveland's first, but I put six coloured men in blue livery at the door, two at a time, relieving each other at intervals, and I think many a timid visitor has had reason to be thankful for the change. Incidentally they lend a certain air of formal dignity to the entrance which, in my opinion, it has always lacked..

These footmen received everybody who sought to enter the White House. If it happened to be a party of tourists they were directed to such parts of the building as are open to the public at stated hours; if it were a caller, either social or official, he or she was conducted to one of the drawing-rooms. But sensible as this innovation seemed to me, it met a varied criticism from the adherents, sincere and otherwise, of our too widely vaunted "democratic simplicity."

Another change I made was the substitution of a house- keeper for a steward. I wanted a woman who could relieve me of the supervision of such details as no man, expert steward though he might be, would ever recognise. The White House requires such ordinary attention as is given by a good housekeeper to any house, except, perhaps, that it has to be more vigilantly watched. Dust accumulates in corners; mirrors and picture glasses get dim with dampness; curtains sag or lose their crispness; floors lose their gloss; rugs turn up at corners or fray at the ends; chair covers get crumpled; cushions get crushed and untidy; things get out of order generally; and it is a very large house. Kitchen helpers grow careless and neglect their shining copper pots and pans and kettles; pantry boys forget and send in plates or glasses not polished to perfection; maids forget to be immaculate and linen is not properly handled; they are just like employes in other homes and they need a woman's guidance and control. I engaged my housekeeper before my husband's Inauguration and she reported for duty on the morning of March fifth.

If I could remember how many turkeys the President gives away every Christmas I could tell just how many persons there are in the White House service. I know it is something like one hundred, but they go to employes of all kinds, to important house officials, to minor officials, to servants of high and low degree, to gardeners, stable boys, chauffeurs and all.

The staff of the White House proper is not so numerous, eighteen or twenty perhaps, including cooks, kitchen maids, butlers, boys, housemaids and laundresses. There was one coloured cook, Alice, who prepared the meals for the servants' dining-room and who had been in the White House twenty years.

My head cook, whom I engaged, was Swedish. She was a miracle of a cook, but she displayed a romantic tendency as well. She must have been about forty, apparently quite staid, when she acquired a husband, a policeman on duty at the White House, and, in due course, a baby. She had been married only a little over a year when her husband contracted tuberculosis. We had always been very much interested in her, deploring the home-making tendency which took her away from us, so when we learned of her misfortune Mr. Taft immediately took steps to have her husband sent to Ft. Bayard, the Military Tuberculosis Sanatorium in New Mexico. The cook, who earned seventy-five dollars a month, put her baby out to nurse and returned to the White House, where we got regular reports as to the progress of the invalid and the infant, each of whom proceeded to do as well as could be expected.

The other servants in the White House are paid the usual wages, from twenty-five to fifty dollars, and are no more and no less efficient than other good houseworkers in other homes. The entire White House staff is paid by the Government, the only private servants in our employ being a Filipino valet who had been with Mr. Taft for a number of years, and my personal maid.

In fact, all White House expenses are paid by the Government except actual table supply bills, and Mr. Taft is fond of insisting upon his conviction that the country treats its President exceedingly well. He was the first President to receive a salary of $75,000.00 a year, and when the subject of his nomination was uppermost in political discussions he did not hesitate to say that he thought this increase from $50,000.00 was an absolute necessity. He did not expect to spend $75,000.00 a year, but he knew by careful calculation and by a knowledge of President Roosevelt's expenditures that he would have to spend at least $50,000.00 a year and he thought he had a citizen's right, even as President, to provide a small competence for his family, a thing which in his twenty years of poorly paid official service he had never had an opportunity to do. He was fifty years old with two sons and a daughter in school and college and, as Secretary of War at least, he had long been working for a wage which was insufficient. But the country really is good to its President. It does not make him rich by any means, but it enables him to banish the wolf a fair distance from his door if he is sensible enough to assist its generosity by the exercise of a mild form of prudence.

My first inspection of the White House on the evening of my husband's Inauguration was casual, but the next day I assumed the management of the establishment in earnest and proceeded upon a thorough investigation which resulted in some rather disquieting revelations.

Mrs. Roosevelt, as the retiring Mistress of the White House, naturally would make no changes or purchases which might not meet with the approval of her successor, so I found the linen supply depleted, the table service inadequate through breakages, and other refurnishing necessary. There is a government appropriation to meet the expense of such replenishments and repairs, and every President's wife is supposed to avail herself of any part of it she requires to fit the mansion for her own occupancy.

Perhaps nothing in the house is so expressive of the various personalities of its Mistresses as the dinner services which each has contributed. For my part I was entirely satisfied with the quiet taste displayed by Mrs. Roosevelt and contented myself with filling up the different broken sets in her service to the number necessary for one hundred covers.

I always enjoyed, however, using some of the old historic plates and platters at small luncheons and dinners. There are enough plates left of the Lincoln set to serve a course to a party of thirty. Though I speak of the different designs as expressive of personalities they represent, perhaps, various periods of popular taste rather than individual preference. Samples of all the different services, displayed in cabinets in the long eastern corridor, are among the most interesting exhibits in the White House.

From the day my husband became President I never knew for certain until I entered the dining-room just how many persons there would be at luncheon. He always did credit me with a miraculous ability to produce food for any number of persons at a moment's notice and when he was Governor of the Philippines and Secretary of War I always had to keep an emergency supply cupboard, but I did not feel that I could carry with me into the White House the happy-go-lucky attitude toward the formalities which I had enjoyed in those days, so meeting his sudden demands became a slightly more serious matter. His haphazard hospitality was of more concern to the servants than to me, however, and I think it is only his own gift for inspiring respectful devotion on the part of his household staff that ever enables me to keep a cook more than a week at a time.

During our first spring in the White House Congress was in extra session for the purpose of revising the tariff and Mr. Taft was in constant conference with the different Senators and Representatives. We had members of Congress at luncheon and dinner daily, and at breakfast quite frequently.

Always, in consultation with my housekeeper and the head cook, I made out the daily menus.

"How many for luncheon, Madame?" was the cook's invariable question.

"I haven't any idea," was my invariable reply.

If no guests had, to my knowledge, been invited I would give instructions to have luncheon prepared for the family only, emergency provision being a thing understood. My day's plans would then be sent over to Mr. Young, the Executive Social Officer, who had his office in the Executive wing of the building, and I would go on about my accustomed duties and pleasures knowing that no surprise would find us quite surprised.

Along about eleven o'clock the house telephone would ring, or a note would be sent over, and announcement would be made that Mr. So and So would lunch with the President and Mrs. Taft. The table would be laid while the kitchen staff stood calmly by awaiting final orders. In another half hour might come the announcement of a second guest, or group of guests, whereupon the amiable butler would have to make a complete change in table arrangements. Only about a half hour before the stated luncheon hour did the cook ever consider it safe to begin final preparations, but too often for the maintenance of entire smoothness in domestic routine Mr. Taft would come across from the Executive offices anywhere from a half hour to an hour late, bringing with him an extra guest, or even a number of extra guests whose coming had not been announced at all.

This system, or this lack of system, obtained throughout my four years in the White House, but I and my capable and willing staff, all of whom were devoted to the President, eventually adjusted ourselves to it and I began to take great delight in the informal meeting of so many interesting and distinguished, men at our open luncheon table.

I tried to insist that the dinner hour should always be properly respected, and it usually was. While we gave many informal, small dinners,---nearly every night as a matter of fact,—there were crowded into my first season from March until I became ill in May most of the big official functions which are a part of White House life always, as well as a number of entertainments which were a part of my own scheme of innovations.

Our first official entertainment was the Diplomatic Tea on the 12th of March, just eight days after the Inauguration, and before I had time to settle myself in the midst of my own belongings which were to fill the empty spaces left by the removal of Mrs. Roosevelt's personal effects. At this tea we received the entire Diplomatic Corps, including all heads of Missions, and all Secretaries and Attaches, with their wives.

Nothing could be more statelily important. It was the first presentation of the Diplomatic Corps to the new President and though, having been for several years in Washington society, we knew many of them quite well, the method of procedure was as formal as the State Department could make it. Explicit directions as to the manner in which they were to present themselves were sent in printed form to every diplomatic representative in Washington, but while an almost oppressive dignity marked the proceedings, our wide acquaintance made it possible for us to depart somewhat from the rigid form decreed and to lend to the occasion an air of general friendliness it could not otherwise have had.

It might be interesting to those not familiar with Washington life to know just what the prescribed ceremonies are for such an event. I confess that at first they seemed to me to be rather formidable, accustomed as I was to the dignities of government.

The guests are not received by the President and his wife as they arrive. They are requested to "present themselves (in uniform) at the East entrance and to assemble in the East Room at a sufficient interval before five o'clock to enable them by that hour to place themselves in the order of precedence, each Chief of Mission being immediately followed by his staff and ladies of his Embassy or Legation."

They are met in the East Room by the Secretary of State and other State Department officials, and by some of the aides-de-camp on duty at the White House.

In the meantime the President and his wife take their positions in the Blue Room and exactly at five o'clock the doors are thrown open and announcement is made in the East Room that they are ready to receive.

The Dean of the Diplomatic Corps then steps forward, past the military aides stationed at the door leading into the Blue Room and is presented by the senior military aide to the President. He in turn presents each member of his suite, all of whom pass promptly on and are presented by another aide to the President's wife, the head of the Mission being presented to her at the end of these ceremonies. Each Ambassador or Minister, in strict order of precedence, passes by with his staff, and they all proceed through the Red Room and into the state Dining Room where tea and other refreshments are served.

At the conclusion of the presentations the President and his wife usually retire and leave their guests to be entertained for a few formal moments by whomever has been invited to preside at the tea-table, but Mr. Taft and I followed them into the dining-room to have tea with them. I knew this was a departure from established custom, but it seemed a perfectly natural thing for us to do. I forgot to take into consideration the attitude of our guests, however. Our unaccustomed presence rather bewildered the diplomats for a moment. There were no rules to guide them in such an emergency and they didn't know exactly what was expected of them. I had finally to instruct one of the aides to announce unofficially to the wives of some of the more important of them that nothing at all was expected, and that they should retire without making any adieus whenever they so desired. I was told afterward that nearly everybody was pleased with the innovation, and in the official White House Diary—kept for the purpose of establishing precedents, I suppose—it was recommended that it be followed on all future occasions of a similar nature.

At our first state dinner, given to the Vice-President and Mrs. Sherman, there were thirty-two guests, all Cabinet Officers, Senators and Representatives. To prove my claim to a natural tendency toward simple and everyday methods I need only say that even as the President's wife it seemed strange to me to have our guests arrive without immediate greetings from their host and hostess. Many a time at Malacañan Palace and in other homes I have gone through the not unusual experience of a hostess who spends the last possible moments in putting "finishing touches" to preparations for a dinner, then hurries off to dress in record time that she may be able to meet her first arriving guest with an air of having been ready and waiting for ever so long.

But at the White House the guests assemble in whatever room may be designated and there, grouped in order of rank, await the entrance of the President and his wife. At this first formal dinner of ours the guests assembled in the Blue Room, the Vice-President and Mrs. Sherman being first, of course, and nearest the door leading into the corridor, while beyond them were the Cabinet officers, then the Senators and Representatives in order of seniority.

Upon our appearance the band began to play "The Star Spangled Banner"—which, let me say parenthetically, is almost as difficult a tune to walk by as Mendelssohn's Wedding March—and played just enough of it to bring us to the door of the Blue Room. After we had shaken hands with everybody the senior aide approached Mr. Taft with Mrs. Sherman on his arm and announced that dinner was served, whereupon Mr. Taft offered his arm to Mrs. Sherman and started for the dining-room.

For my first dinner I chose pink Killarney roses for table decorations and it would be difficult to express the pleasure I felt in having just as many of them as I needed by merely issuing instructions to have them delivered. The White House greenhouses and nurseries were a source of constant joy to me. I had lived so long where plants are luxuriant and plentiful that a house without them seemed to me to be empty of a very special charm and the head horticulturist remarked at once that during my regime his gems of palms and ferns and pots of brilliant foliage were to be given their due importance among White House perquisites. I filled the windows of the great East Room with them, banked the fireplaces with them and used them on every possible occasion.

The state Dining Room is one of the many splendid results of the McKim restoration and, next to the East Room, is the handsomest room in the White House. It is not so tremendously large, its utmost capacity being less than one hundred, but it is magnificently proportioned and beautifully finished in walnut panelling with a fireplace and carved mantel on one side which would do honour to an ancient baronial hall. A few fine moose and elk heads are its only wall decorations.

We had table-tops of all sizes and shapes, but the one we had to use for very large dinners was in the form of a crescent which stretched around three sides of the room. For any dinner under sixty I was able to use a large oval top which could be extended by the carpenters to almost any size. Indeed, I have seen it so large that it quite filled the room leaving only enough space behind the chairs for the waiters to squeeze their way around with considerable discomfort. On this table I used the massive silver-gilt ornaments which President Monroe imported from France along with his interesting collection of French porcelains, clocks and statuettes which still occupy many cabinets and mantels here and there in the house.

These table ornaments remind one of the Cellini period when silversmiths vied with each other in elaborations. Based on oblong plate glass mirrors, each about three feet in length, they stretch down the middle of the table, end to end, a perfect riot of festooned railing and graceful figures upholding crystal vases. Then there are large gilded candelabra, centre vases and fruit dishes to match. In their way they are exceedingly handsome, and they certainly are appropriate to the ceremony with which a state dinner at the White House is usually conducted.

The White House silver is all very fine and there are quantities of it. It is all marked, in accordance with the simple form introduced at the beginning of our history, "The President's House," and some of it is old enough to be guarded among our historic treasures.

When I went to live at the White House I found, much to my surprise, that this silver had always been kept in a rather haphazard fashion in chests, or boxes, in the storeroom. I decided to remedy this even though in doing so I was compelled to encroach somewhat upon the White House custodian's already limited quarters. These quarters are a good-sized office with the house supply rooms opening off it, and a smaller room adjoining. They are on the ground floor just across the wide corridor from the kitchen. At one end of the smaller room I had built a closet with regular vault doors and combination locks. I had the space divided into compartments, with a special receptacle for each important article, and velvet-lined trays in drawers for flat silver, each one of which could be slipped out separately. This silver closet became the joy of Arthur Brooks' life, he being the War Department Messenger who was my right hand man all the time my husband was Secretary of War and who was appointed White House Custodian at our request a short time before Mr. Taft was inaugurated.

I was "at home" informally at the White House about three afternoons a week when my friends came to see me and when I received many ladies who wrote and asked for an opportunity to call. I always received in the Red Room which, with fire and candles lighted, is pleasant enough to be almost cosy, large and imposing though it be. I usually had twenty or more callers and I found this a delightful way of meeting and getting close to people as I could not hope to do at the great formal receptions.

As an example of one of these, I might cite my first afternoon reception to the Congressional ladies for which something like four hundred invitations were issued. I intended to carry this off without assistance, other than that rendered by the ladies I had asked to preside over the refreshment tables, but in the end I asked Mr. Taft to receive with me, a task never very difficult for him. There were no men invited, so he had the pleasure of shaking hands and exchanging pleasantries with several hundred women, and he did it without a single protest. I made the mistake on this occasion of receiving in the East Room as the guests arrived, thinking that by so doing I could make the party somewhat less formal. But I only succeeded in having the stairway leading up from the east entrance overcrowded and in making the affair much more formal than it would have been had I followed the usual course of permitting the people to assemble in the East Room and to be received in the Blue Room on their way through to the Dining Room. It amuses me to find that Captain Butt in the Official Diary has carefully recorded all my mistakes as well as my successes for the supposed benefit of other Mistresses of the White House.

I do not wish to convey an impression that life in the White House is all a public entertainment, but there are a certain number of set functions during every season which are as much a part of Washington life as is a Congressional session. But even with teas, luncheons, musicals, small dinners, garden parties and dances coming at short intervals between the more official entertainments, we still had many evenings when there were so few guests as to make us feel quite like a family party. Indeed, once in a while we dined alone.

We began immediately, as our first spring advanced, to make almost constant use of the porches and terraces which are among the most attractive features of the White House. The long terrace extending from the East Room I found to be a most delightful promenade for guests on warm spring evenings, while the corresponding terrace leading out from the Dining Room proved most useful for large dinner parties at times when dining indoors would have been rather unpleasant.

With Congress in session nearly all summer Mr. Taft gave a series of Congressional dinners and the last one he had served on this terrace. A curious incident marked the occasion for special remembrance. It was known that one of the Senators invited had never crossed the White House threshold because of his unfriendly feeling toward the administration. He paid no attention whatever to his invitation—a formal one, of course, requiring a formal answer— until the day before the dinner. He then called the White House on the telephone and asked if he would be expected to wear a dress suit.

Mr. Hoover, who received the inquiry, replied that evening dress was customary at White House dinners, whereupon the Senator mumbled something at the other end of the line. Mr. Hoover asked him whether or not he intended to come. He replied that he guessed he would, and abruptly rang off.

The next evening the party waited for him for a full half hour before they decided to sit down without him, and even then his vacant place was kept open for him. He did not come nor did he ever offer any kind of apology or excuse for his extraordinary conduct. There are certain manifestations of so-called Jeffersonian simplicity in this country of ours that I am sure Jefferson would deplore if he lived in this day and generation.

The north verandah of the White House is pleasant enough, but it lacks the charm of seclusion peculiar to the south portico which runs around the oval Blue Room and looks out upon the broad south garden with its great fountain, and with Potomac Park, the River and Washington's Monument in the background. This soon became our favourite retreat and we used to sit there in the ever lengthening spring evenings, breathing the perfume of magnolia blossoms, watching the play of lights on the tree-dotted lawns and on the Monument—which is never so majestic as in the night—and realising to the full the pleasant privilege of living in this beautiful home of Presidents.

Mr. Taft had a Victrola in the Blue Room and he never failed, when opportunity offered, to lay out a few favourite records for his evening's entertainment. Melba and Caruso, the Lucia Sextette, some old English melodies, a few lively ragtime tunes; in those delightful surroundings we found a Victrola concert as pleasant a diversion as one could desire. With no applause, no fixed attention, no conversation, no effort of any kind required, my husband found on such quiet evenings a relaxation he was fully able to appreciate during that first trying summer.

That Manila could lend anything to Washington may be an idea that would surprise some persons, but the Luneta is an institution whose usefulness to society in the Philippine capital is not to be overestimated. At least it was so in my day; and for a long time before Mr. Taft became President I had looked with ambitious designs upon the similar possibilities presented in the drives, the river-cooled air and the green swards of Potomac Park. I determined, if possible, to convert Potomac Park into a glorified Luneta where all Washington could meet, either on foot or in vehicles, at five o'clock on certain evenings, listen to band concerts and enjoy such recreation as no other spot in Washington could possibly afford.

The Army officer in charge of Public Buildings and Grounds had a bandstand erected in an admirable location at the end of an ellipse, and we decided that the long drive theretofore known as "The Speedway" should be renamed Potomac Drive. Arrangements were made to have band concerts every Wednesday and Saturday afternoon from five to seven o'clock.

Saturday, the 17th of April, the concert began, and at five o'clock Mr. Taft and I, in a small landaulette motor-car, went down to the driveway and took our places in the throng. The Park was full of people. As many as ten thousand crowded the lawns and footways, while the drive was completely packed with automobiles and vehicles of every description. Everybody saw everybody that he or she knew and there was the same exchange of friendly greetings that had always made the Luneta such a pleasant meeting place. I felt quite sure that the venture was going to succeed and that Potomac Drive was going to acquire the special character I so much wished it to have.

I also thought we might have a Japanese Cherry Blossom season in Potomac Park. Both the soil and climate encouraged such an ambition, so I suggested that all the blooming cherry trees obtainable in the nurseries of this country be secured and planted. They were able to find about one hundred only. Then the Mayor of Tokyo, having learned of our attempt to bestow the high flattery of imitation upon his country, offered to send us two thousand young trees. We accepted them with grateful pleasure, but one consignment was found to be afflicted with some contagious disease and had to be destroyed. I watched those that were planted later with great interest and they seem to be doing very well. I wonder if any of them will ever attain the growth of the ancient and dearly loved cherry trees of Japan.

One of the delights of living in the White House is in being able to entertain one's friends from a distance with a confidence that they are being given a real pleasure and an experience of an unusual kind. More often than not we had house guests, old friends from Cincinnati, from New Haven, from the Philippines, from here, there and everywhere; friends with whom we had been closely associated through the years and who felt whole-hearted satisfaction in my husband's attainment of the Presidency.

To be stared at is not pleasant because it keeps one self-conscious all the time, but one gets more or less used to it. And anyhow, I enjoyed a sort of freedom which Mr. Taft did not share in any way\,would probably have been recognised instantly in any crowd anywhere, I found that in most places I could wander about unobserved like any inconspicuous citizen. It was a valued privilege.

My daughter Helen likes to tell about an experience she had one day in Philadelphia. She was a student at Bryn Mawr College and she went in to Philadelphia to do some shopping. Among other things she had to get herself some shoes. At the shoe store she was waited on by a girl who was anything but intelligently attentive. She had tried Helen's patience considerably by suggesting in a certain nagging way that her superior knowledge of what was "being worn" deserved respect, and that Helen didn't know what she wanted anyhow.

Helen selected some shoes and decided to have them charged to me, and she thought what a satisfaction it was going to be to reveal her identity to the patronising and offensive young person. The young person produced pad and pencil to make out the check.

"Please have them charged to Mrs. William Howard Taft," said Helen with what I am sure was her loftiest air. "Address'?"

"Washington."

The salesgirl held her pencil poised over the pad and with the familiar expression of satisfaction over a sale accomplished said pleasantly:

"D.C?"

SOME WHITE HOUSE FORMALITIES

MY very active participation in my husband's career came to an end when he became President. I had always had the satisfaction of knowing almost as much as he about the politics and the intricacies of any situation in which he found himself, and my life was filled with interests of a most unusual kind. But in the White House I found my own duties too engrossing to permit me to follow him long or very far into the governmental maze which soon enveloped him.

I was permitted fully to enjoy only about the first two and a half months of my sojourn in the White House. In May I suffered a serious attack of illness and was practically out of society through an entire season, having for a much longer time than that to take very excellent care of myself. During this period my sisters, Mrs. Louis More, Mrs. Charles Anderson, Mrs. Laughlin and Miss Maria Herron, came from time to time to visit us and to represent me as hostess whenever it was necessary for me to be represented.

But even in my temporary retirement, as soon as I was strong enough to do anything at all, I always took a very lively interest in everything that was going on in the house, and from my apartments on the second floor directed arrangements for social activities almost as if I had been well.

I didn't even have the privilege of presiding at all my first year garden parties, though this was a form of hospitality in which I was especially interested and which, I believe, I was able to make a notable feature of our administration. Garden parties are very popular in the Far East and I think, perhaps, I acquired my very strong liking for them out there, together with a few sumptuous notions as to what a garden party should be like.

The Emperor and Empress of Japan give two each year; one in the spring under the cherry blossoms to celebrate the Cherry Blossom season, and one in the autumn in the midst of chrysanthemums and brilliant autumn foliage. These are the events of the year in Tokyo, marking the opening and the close of the social season, and society sometimes prepares for them weeks ahead, never knowing when the

Imperial invitations will be issued. The time depends entirely on the blossoming of the cherry trees or the chrysanthemums in the Imperial Gardens. When the blooms are at their best the invitations are sent out, sometimes not more than two days in advance, and society, in its loveliest garments, drops everything else and goes. It would be very nice, of course, to have always some such special reason for giving a garden party, but it is only in the "Flowery Kingdom" that the seasons are marked by flowers.

Nothing could be finer than the south garden of the White House. With its wide lawns, its great fountain, its shading trees, and the two long terraces looking down upon it all, it is ideally fitted for entertaining out of doors. And I must mention one other thing about it which appealed to me especially, and that is the wholesomeness of its clean American earth. This is lacking in the tropics. There one may not sit or lie on the ground, breathing health as we do here; the tropic soil is not wholesome. Not that one sits or lies on the ground at garden parties, but the very feel of the earth underfoot is delightfully different.

I determined to give my first garden party at the White House as soon as spring was sufficiently far advanced to make it possible. I issued invitations, 750 of them, for Friday, the 7th of May, planning at the same time three others to complete the season, one each Friday during the month.

In order to put possible bad weather off its guard, I made the invitations simply for an "At Home from 5 to 7 o'clock," because all my life the elements have been unfriendly to me. Whenever I plan an outdoor fete I begin to consult the weather man with the hopeful faith of a Catherine de Medici appealing to her astrologer, but for all my humble spirit I very frequently get a downpour, or else a long-drawn-out and nerve-trying threat. Quite often the lowering clouds have passed and my prayers for sunshine have been rewarded, but quite often, too, I have had to move indoors with an outdoor throng for whom no indoor diversions had been arranged.

By way of preparation for my first garden party I had a large refreshment tent put up in the northwest corner of the garden where it would be handy to the kitchen and serving rooms, while under the trees here and there I had tables spread at which a corps of waiters were to serve tea during the reception. The Marine Band I stationed behind the iron railing just under the Green Room. For any kind of outdoor entertainment at the White House the band had always been placed in the middle of the lawn between the south portico and the fountain, but I thought, and correctly, that the house wall would serve as a sounding board and make the music audible throughout the grounds. I arranged to receive under one of the large trees in a beautiful vista looking south.

No sooner were my plans completed, however, than the weather man predicted rain. It was coming, sure. Of course, I knew it would, but I had had too much experience to think of coming in out of the rain before it began to come down. I always sustain my hopeful attitude until the deluge descends.

About half past three it began to rain in torrents and I saw all of my festive-looking preparations reduced to sopping wrecks before there was even time to rush them indoors. By five o'clock, when it was time for the people to begin to arrive, it had stopped raining, but the lawns were soaked and the trees were dripping dismally, so I directed the band to move into the upper corridor, as usual for afternoon affairs, had the refreshment tables spread in the state Dining Room and took my by that time accustomed position to receive the long line of guests in the East Room.

A week later I had better luck. I sent out the same kind of invitations, made the same kind of preparations, slightly elaborated, and was rewarded with a perfect mid-May day.

The guests arrived at the East Entrance, came down the Long Corridor, out through one of the special guest dressing-rooms, and down the long slope of the lawn to the tree where Mr. Taft and I stood to receive them, with Captain Archibald Butt to make the presentations. At the next garden party I requested the gentlemen to come in white clothes, in thin summer suits, or in anything they chose to wear, instead of in frock coats. Some young people played tennis on the courts throughout the reception; it was warm enough for bright coloured parasols and white gowns; the fountain made rainbows and diamond showers in the sun, and altogether it was a most pleasing picture of informal outdoor enjoyment. Each year after that the four May garden parties were among the most popular entertainments of our social season.

The question of a "Summer Capital," as the President's summer home is called, was quite a serious one for us to settle. We had been going to Murray Bay for so many years that we had few affiliations with any other place, and we were most uncertain as to what we might be able to do.

We finally selected a number of likely places and made our choice by the process of elimination. One location was too hot, another had a reputation for mosquitoes, another was too far away, another hadn't first-class railway, postal and telegraph facilities, and another, worst drawback of all, had no good golf links. It wouldn't have been a livable place for Mr. Taft without golf links because golf was his principal form of exercise and recreation. Also the whole family agreed that we must be near the sea, so our search finally narrowed to the Massachusetts coast. I decided on the North Shore, as the coast from Beverly to Gloucester is called, because it had every qualification for which we were seeking, including excellent golf at the Myopia and Essex County clubs. Then, too, it had a further attraction in that the summer homes of a number of our friends were located there, or in the near vicinity.

I went up in the spring to Beverly Farms, with my friend Miss Boardman, and inspected houses for three days, finally selecting one, principally for its location. It stood near the sea and its velvety green lawns sloped all the way down to the sea wall. From its verandah one could see out across Salem Harbour to Marblehead.

The house itself was a modern frame cottage, as simple as anything well could be, with a fine verandah and a dormer windowed third story. It was large enough for the family and for such visitors as we inevitably would have to accommodate, but besides the Taft family, which was numerous enough at that time, there were Captain Butt and a large corps of secretaries and stenographers, to say nothing of the Commander of the *Sylph*, the President's smaller yacht, who all had to be within call when they were wanted. Then, too, there was the necessity for Executive Offices and I didn't think it would seem

327

like having a vacation at all if the Executive Offices could not be somewhere out of sight so that they might sometimes be out of mind. The President didn't expect to be able to spend much of his time away from Washington the first summer but when he did come to Beverly I wanted him to feel that he was at least partially detaching himself from business. So another house was found in the town, yet on the seashore, and was fitted up for Executive Offices and as a home for the office staff and Captain Butt. The secret service men, like the poor, we had with us always, but it never seemed to me that they "lived" anywhere. They were merely around all the time. They were never members of the Cabinet and their wives and a few especially distinguished outsiders are invited.

The hostess doesn't have to worry about seating the Cab-inet officers because it is all a matter of precedence and is attended to by the Social Executive Secretary. The rank of a Cabinet officer is determined by the date on which his office was created and not, as one might think, by the relative importance of his official status.

The only time when a friendly democracy presents itself to the President *en masse* is on New Year's Day. At the New Year's Reception he receives just as many persons as he can shake hands with between the hours of eleven in the morning and half past two or three in the afternoon. His wife, the wife of the Vice-President and the ladies of the Cabinet receive with him as long as it is physically possible for them to do so. While writing in the third person I am thinking in the first, of course. These were our customs.

Yet if anybody unfamiliar with Washington life imagines that a New Year's Reception means throwing open the White House doors and admitting the public without consideration of rank or the rules of precedence he is mistaken. The Reception, up to a stated hour, is as carefully regulated as any other function, and I consider the list of the especially favoured most interesting as a revelation of the complexity of Washington's social life.

Announcement is made that the President will receive at 11:00 A.M.—the Vice-President, the members of the Cabinet and the Diplomatic Corps; at 11:20 A.M.—the Supreme Court, members of the Judiciary of the District of Columbia, former Cabinet officers

328

and former diplomatic representatives of the United States; at 11:30—Senators, Representatives and Delegates in Congress; at 11:45—Officers of the Army, the Navy, the Marine Corps and the Militia of the District of Columbia; at 12:15 P.M.—Regents and Secre-tary of the Smithsonian Institution, all the various Commissions, Assistant Secretaries of Departments, the Solicitor General, Assistant Attorneys-General, Assistant Postmasters-General, the Treasurer of the United States, the Librarian of Congress, the Public Printer, heads of all Bureaus and the President of the Columbia Institution for the Deaf and Dumb; at 12:30 P.M.—The Secretary, of the Cincinnati, the Aztec Club of 1847, the Associated Veterans of the War of 1846-47, the Military Order of the Loyal Legion of the United States, the Grand Army of the Republic, the Medal of Honor Legion, the Union Veteran Legion, the Union Veterans' Union, the Society of the Army of Santiago, the Spanish Minute Men, the Sons of the American Revolution and the members of the Oldest Inhabitants' Association of the District of Columbia; at 1:00 P.M.—Citizens.

As all the men present themselves in the dress uniform of their various services or orders, or wearing the decorations they have won in epoch-marking events, one gets a most illuminating view of organised American patriotism.

There is an old system obtaining at the White House known as inviting guests "behind the line." This means that a chosen few are permitted as special guests to be present in the Blue Room while a reception is in progress. It is a system which has at times been so carelessly regulated as to engender jealousies and dissatisfactions, and we determined if possible to avoid on all occasions any appearance of favouritism. So at our first New Year's Reception we decided to limit special privileges to the Diplomatic Corps, the wives of Assistant Secretaries and our own house guests. This made the distinction a mere matter of official rank and did away with all possibility of unpleasant comment from distinguished members of civilian society.

For instance, there has always been a delicate question in connection with the Judicial Reception as to whether or not on this occasion the Justices of the Supreme Court take precedence over the members of the Diplomatic Corps.

The Justices have always contended that at their own Reception they do, but the unwritten code has it that no person under the rank of President or Vice-President ever takes precedence over an Ambassador who is the direct representative of his sovereign.

We settled this question by inviting the heads of all Missions to the Blue Room where they were greeted by the President before he took his place in the receiving line, and where they were permitted to remain as long as they desired, being, as it were, a part of the receiving party. This was a solution which satisfied everybody and pleased the Diplomats particularly.

A great many special arrangements are necessary for a New Year's Reception at the White House. For every state occasion or any large function there are always many extra footmen, policemen, guards, waiters, cloak room attendants and ushers on hand, but on New Year's Day the array of them would be most imposing if they were not almost lost in the midst of a thronging populace. All the people who come to these receptions do not pass the receiving line. Many of them find points of vantage in the vicinity merely to look on, and yet the President shakes hands with from six to eight thousand of them before the gates are closed. I have seen the line of waiting people stretching out through the spacious grounds, down the street, around a corner and out of sight at a time when I had already given up in utter exhaustion. And the way the carriages come and go in perfect order, without a hitch, each coachman with his card of a particular colour telling him just where to make his exit, was a thing I never could understand.

The corps of aides arrange all these details and each department, including the police and the secret service, has its printed and explicit orders for the day a long time ahead. Some of the police orders are interesting. For instance: "No person under the influence of liquor, disorderly in his behaviour or bearing any advertisement will be allowed in line. Conspicuously dirty persons will not be admitted." Also: "Except in the most aggravated case a coachman will not be taken from his box and put under arrest. It will be sufficient to take his name and address and arrest him on the following morning."

After a New Year's Reception the White House is a sorry sight, even though by using extra strips of carpet to protect the polished floors and by removing fine rugs and breakable bric-a-brac every possible precaution is taken to make the damage as slight as possible. But it doesn't take long to restore the house to its normal condition. The way the crowd of workmen used to go about putting the place in order after an invasion of this kind always reminded me of the well-drilled stage hands at a hippodrome who manage to set different scenes and keep things spic-and-span without even interfering with a continuous performance.

Very shortly after the New Year's Reception, three days later in fact, we gave the next big event of the season, the Diplomatic Reception. It is understood, of course, that one of the chief occupations of the President of the United States is shaking hands. I am moved to this observation by memories of uncounted hours by my husband's side in a receiving line at the White House when thousands of guests passed by, each separately introduced to both the President and to me and each extending an untired hand to give and to receive the hearty grasp which all good Americans so highly regard. And there is no conceivable form of work or exercise more fatiguing. If it were not for the mental stimulus afforded by the friendliness of a gay throng, by music and lights and a general festive atmosphere, it could hardly be borne.

For Mr. Taft it was never so hard because in his long public career, and especially through a political campaign, he had had considerable training for it. But for me it was somewhat more difficult. My friends used to wonder how I could stand it, but when I was well I never found it so much of a strain that I could not very quickly recover from it. When I was not feeling particularly strong I would resort to all manner of innocent pretexts to give myself short intervals of rest. I would turn around and engage in important conversation with someone behind me; I would consume minutes in taking a drink of water; or I would get into serious difficulty with my flowers or something. Then, too, I sometimes would sit frankly down and let the crowds pass by.

To me the long standing was the real strain and I soon came to a point where I was willing to sacrifice appearance to approximate comfort by wearing wide flat slippers with low heels.

The Diplomatic Reception is undoubtedly the most brilliant of the set state functions which are given at the White House each year, but to me it was never as interesting as the Diplomatic Dinner which follows it. There are thirty-nine foreign Embassies and Legations in Washington. Each Ambassador and Minister has his own distinctive and sometimes very elaborate regalia; each attache, military and naval, wears the uniform of his service, in many cases very picturesque and often positively flamboyant; the foreign women, gowned exquisitely, are many of them crowned with tiaras and laden with jewels, and when they are all gathered around one great, glittering and gorgeously decorated table they present such a picture of varied colour and magnificence as is not to be seen on any other occasion in Washington.

I used always to wonder how they managed to get along with each other. There is an impression quite general among us that we are the only nation on earth that sends abroad diplomatic representatives without any knowledge of the French language. This is not quite true. There are a good many diplomats in Washington who do not speak

French, and there are more diplomats' wives. But as both men and women are seated at the Diplomatic Dinner in strict order of rank, there is no chance to take into consideration the seemingly important question as to whether or not dinner partners will be able to communicate with each other very freely. They do speak English, of course, but many of them imperfectly, and, taking them all, with exactly thirty-nine different accents. Imagine the wife of the Chinese Minister sitting between the Minister of Salvador and the Minister of Cuba, or the wife of the Japanese Ambassador having on one hand the German Ambassador and on the other the Minister of Costa Rica!

It all depends on how long they have been in Washington. When I first went to the White House the Italian Ambassador was the Dean of the Diplomatic Corps, with the Austrian Ambassador next, while among the Ministers those from Siam and from Costa Rica, I think, had precedence over all others. If the Minister of Haiti remained in Washington long enough he could outrank the Minister of Spain. The Minister of Haiti is the only negro diplomat in the Corps and his place at table in my time was with a group of envoys of almost equal rank who sat together near one outer end of the great crescent.

It was not possible to invite many outsiders to the Diplomatic Dinner because there were enough of the Diplomats themselves with their wives and attaches to tax the capacity of the State Dining Room. But Mr. Taft never did take space limits into consideration. For both Receptions and Dinners I used always to go over the invitation lists and do my best to keep them within bounds. Regretfully enough would I cut them wherever I found it possible, but my husband, according to his fixed habit, invariably added more names than I took off, so, thanks to him, we have to our credit the largest dinner parties ever given in the new Executive Mansion. Mr. McKim in his report on the restoration of the White House says the Dining Room will hold one hundred, but strained to its utmost capacity ninety-two was as many as I could ever crowd into it, and then everybody was aghast at the number. We might have put a star in the hollow of the crescent so as to accommodate a few more, but I never thought of it until this moment. I'm glad it never occurred to Mr. Taft. With his expansive disposition he certainly would have had it tried.

The Reception crowds I did manage to cut down. It simply had to be done. When more than two thousand people get into the White House it is a literal "crush" and nobody has a good time. We not only introduced dancing in the East Room at Receptions, a feature which delighted everybody and especially the young people, but we always served refreshments to every guest within our gates.

This was, I suppose, the most generally approved departure from established custom that was made during my administration. It was made possible by cutting down the list of guests one half and inviting one half to one reception and the other half to the next. As a matter of fact, preparing a buffet supper for a company of 2,000 people is not much more of a strain on ordinary household resources than serving a nine or ten course formal dinner to eighty or ninety guests. Neither undertaking is particularly simple, but the White House kitchen and pantries are large and adequate, we had an efficient staff and we never had any mishaps or embarrassments that I remember.

Several days before a large reception my cooks would begin to turn out piles upon piles of small pastries and to do all the things that could be done in advance. Then on the day of the reception, with plenty of extra assistants, it was found easily possible to prepare all the salads and sandwiches, the ices and sweets, the lemonades and the punches that were necessary. Nor did we find that it interfered in the least with the usual household routine. We took our meals in the small family dining room adjoining the State Dining Room, and even gave small and successful dinner parties while the State Dining Room was in the hands of the carpenters and decorators.

Referring to the serving of refreshments reminds me of an incident which gave us some uneasiness shortly after Mr. Taft's election. It was during that phase of his career which all Presidents pass through, when his most casual remark was likely to be construed into an "utterance," and his most ordinary act was likely to become a widely heralded "example." It was while he was still being held up as a model of all the excellencies—framed in a question mark: "What will he do?" In other words it was before his Inauguration.

He was at a dinner at Hot Springs, Virginia. As the wine was being served one of the diners turned down his glass with the remark that he had not taken a drink for eighteen years. Mr. Taft, in the most usual and commonplace manner, followed suit, saying that he had been a total abstainer for nearly two years and expected to continue so. The incident was made the basis of a sensational newspaper story which created the impression that he had acted with great dramatic effect and that his remark amounted to a declaration of principle which he would turn into a Presidential policy.

Immediately he was overwhelmed with memorials, with resolutions of commendation framed by some of the most worthy and admirable Christian and temperance organisations in the country. It was taken for granted that he would banish alcohol in every form from the 'White House. In simple honesty he had to tell all the reverend gentlemen that he had made no pronouncement with regard to limiting White House hospitality, that he had no desire to interfere with any normal man's personal habits and that as President he had no intention of trying to do so.

The truth is that he is a total abstainer because never in his life has he indulged in stimulants to any extent; they have no attraction for him whatever, and he found in those days that with so much dining out, it was wiser to decline all wines and liquors. Being naturally abstemious he has always rather objected to being given personal credit for such virtue.

It was about this time that I, too, got into trouble of a peculiar sort. In the mass of correspondence which began to roll in upon me as soon as my husband was elected, there were requests of every possible kind from all parts of the world. Among these came a letter from a society of women engaged in political and social reform work in one of the newer Balkan States, asking me to lend my aid in forming a similar society in the United States.

I declined with as much grace and courtesy as I could command and thought nothing more about it. Imagine my surprise to find almost immediately that my reply had been construed by its recipients into a sort of expression of personal interest in and sympathy for the people of their country in general. I was proclaimed the warm friend of the young State and an enemy to all her enemies. The incident became the subject of an exchange of diplomatic notes in Washington, and it took a bit of the suavity of the State Department to extricate me from the tangle in which my alleged active participation in the trouble in the Balkans had placed me. It taught me a lesson.

Throughout my four years in the White House my mail contained surprises every day, but I soon learned not to be surprised at petitions for assistance in various forms. It is extraordinary how

335

many of these a President's wife receives. The greater number came to me from small charitable organisations throughout the country. It seemed to me that nobody ever thought of organising a bazaar or a church fair without asking me for some sort of contribution, and holidays, especially Easter and Christmas, I was simply besieged. They did not want money ever; they wanted something that could be sold as a souvenir of myself. I never, to my knowledge, refused a request of this kind. Mrs. Roosevelt had used a photograph of the White House, and I decided, finally, to do the same. I chose a view of the South Portico eight by ten inches in size which I thought very nice, and asked to have it reserved for me. With my signature across one corner it became a most satisfactory souvenir. I hesitate to hazard a guess as to the number I signed and sent away, but, ordered by the hundreds, they didn't cost very much, so contributing them to good causes became a pleasure unmarred by a sense of unjustifiable extravagance. Handkerchiefs, too, were in great demand and I always kept a supply of them on hand.

I see I have wandered away from the receptions and dinners and my attempt to tell in some sort of consecutive fashion what a social season at the White House consists of, but remembering the crowds I lived in for four years it seems to me that everybody must know just as much about these things as I do. I have to keep reminding myself that I am not writing altogether for people who live in Washington, but for the people in the far places who have never been to Washington, but who have just as much of a personal property right in the nation's capital and just as much interest in the proper conduct of its affairs whether they be legislative, administrative, diplomatic, or merely social, as any President ever had.

CONCLUSION

OUR second summer at Beverly began with a call from Mr. Roosevelt. When the ex-President returned to the United States, on the 18th of June, 1910, after an absence of a year and a half, Mr. Taft sent two members of his Cabinet, the Secretary of the Navy and the Secretary of Agriculture, and his aide, Captain Butt, to New York to meet him and to extend to him a personal as well as an official welcome home. According to Captain Butt's Official Diary:

"Immediately upon the arrival of the S.S. *Kaiserin Auguste Victoria* at Quarantine the Presidential party scaled the sides of the steamer by means of a rope ladder and proceeded to the staterooms of Mr. Roosevelt where each member of the party greeted the ex-President. Then Captain Butt, who was in full dress uniform, saluted Mr. Roosevelt and presented to him the letter of welcome entrusted to his care by the President. Mr. Roosevelt read it and expressed his great appreciation of the honour of the receipt of the letter, as also for the ordering of the U. S. S. *South Carolina* and other vessels to accompany him from Quarantine to New York. Captain Butt also presented to Mr. Roosevelt a letter (from Mrs. Taft) supplementing the President's invitation to Mr. and Mrs. Roosevelt to pay them a visit at the White House now or at any time when it might be convenient for them to do so.... Mr. Roosevelt took occasion to send his sincere appreciation and profound thanks to the President by Captain Butt both for the official and personal welcome extended to him."

I removed the Presidential household to Beverly the week Mr. Roosevelt arrived and did not see him until after Mr. Taft joined me about ten days later. Again to quote from Captain Butt's carefully kept record:

"June 30—At 3:30 o'clock ex-President Theodore Roosevelt, accompanied by Senator Lodge, called to pay his respects to the President. He was met at the entrance by Captain Butt, who announced his arrival. The President immediately came out and greeted his visitor most affectionately, addressing him as Theodore.

"Colonel Roosevelt took both hands of the President, and said, "'Mr. President, it is fine to see you looking so well.' 'But why "Mr. President"?' laughed the President. "'Because,' replied Colonel Roosevelt, 'it used to be "Mr. President" and "Will," now it must be "Mr. President" and "Theodore."'

"The President conducted his distinguished predecessor to the side porch where they started into a series of delightful reminiscences of the past Administration.... Colonel Roosevelt remained two hours, during which he gave the President an interesting account of his trip."

I was present at this interview and remember it as being remarkably pleasant and entertaining. Everybody will recall that the question of Mr. Rooevelt's attitude toward my husband was even then a debatable one, but Mr. Taft had resolutely refused to believe that it could ever be anything but friendly. I did not share his complete faith, but I was glad on this occasion to find the old spirit of sympathetic comradeship still paramount and myself evidently proved to be unwarrantably suspicious.

Mr. Roosevelt had just been in England where he acted as the representative of the President of the United States at the funeral of King Edward, and that solemnly magnificent event seemed to have overshadowed in his mind every other experience he had had during his long absence. He described the stately ceremonies and the medivally picturesque procession in vivid detail and did not fail to emphasise their grave and reverential aspects, but he dwelt particularly, and to our great amusement, upon the humorous side of the situation in which he had found himself.

It will be remembered that among Kings and Emperors and Czars, and even lesser potentates, the rank of Presidents was a difficult thing to determine. Should minor royalties take precedence over the representatives of the French Republic and the United States of America, to say nothing of Mexico, Brazil, Switzerland, and all the other great and small democracies?

Mr. Roosevelt had great difficulty in finding his place. Then, too, he was constantly running into kings and other royalties to whom he, naturally, owed ceremonious respect. They were so numerous in London at the time that familiarity with them bred carelessness in one whose tongue had not been trained to the honorifics of Court life, and he found himself making extremely funny blunders. He told us many stories of his adventures with the world's elect and, with his keen appreciation of the ridiculous and his gift of description, gave us as merry an afternoon as we ever spent with him.

I dwell on the memory of this agreeable meeting with Mr. Roosevelt and the entertainment it afforded me, because by his manner he succeeded in convincing me that he still held my husband in the highest esteem and reposed in him the utmost confidence, and that the rumours of his antagonism were wholly unfounded. I was not destined to enjoy this faith and assurance for very long.

In mid-July of that year we started off for a short cruise on the *Mayflower,* the only one we ever made. It is not really possible for the President to have a vacation, but if he happens to be a good sailor I know of no better way for him to get short intervals of rest than by boarding the Presidential yacht and steaming away, out of the reach of crowds.

We had only a small party with us, my husband's brother, Mr. Horace Taft, my sister, Mrs. Louis More, Miss Mabel Boardman and the Assistant Secretary of the Navy, Mr. Beekman Winthrop, and Mrs. Winthrop; and Captain Butt, of course, was with us always.

We headed north for the Maine coast with Eastport as our first stopping place. The mayor of that interesting city of fisheries came on board as soon as we dropped anchor, made a felicitous speech of welcome and proceeded to lay out a programme of sightseeing and festivities which would have kept us there for a considerable longer time than we could stay if it had all been carried out, and this experience was repeated everywhere we went. We had to decline everything except a motor ride about town for the purpose of getting a glimpse of the weir fisheries and the sardine canneries, but a President doesn't visit Eastport very often, so the people thronging the streets made it seem quite like a holiday.

Then a committee from the Island of Campo Bello, which lies a short distance off the coast and which is a British possession, waited upon us with an invitation to come across and go for a buckboard ride around a part of the island. It sounded like such a homely and restful form of amusement that Mr. Taft was sorely tempted to break the unwritten law which decrees that a President may not set foot outside United States territory, but he concluded that he had better not. The rest of us, however, decided to go and we had a jolly, jolting ride which ended at the summer home of Mrs. Franklin Roosevelt.

Everywhere we went we were most delightfully entertained, finding beautiful homes and merry summer hosts at every port and town. At fashionable Bar Harbor we found a colony of friends whose winter homes are in Washington and Mr. Taft got some excellent golf. There were luncheons and dinners, of course, every day and everywhere, to say nothing of teas and large receptions, and Mr. Taft had to make speeches, too, and meet all the Maine politicians.

But there were the long restful nights on the *Mayflower*, steaming along among the crags and rocks of the broken, picturesque coast, or lying at anchor in some quiet harbour with only the soft water sounds to break the stillness, and it would not have taken much persuasion to have kept me aboard indefinitely.

The *Mayflower* is used ordinarily for official purposes in connection with naval reviews and other naval ceremonies, and at such times, with the President on board, there is a punctilious formality to be encountered which makes a mere civilian feel like a recruit under the eyes of a drill-sergeant. But it is very interesting. One gets so used to seeing everybody in uniform standing stiffly at attention as the President passes that one almost forgets that it isn't their natural attitude.

And then the guns. They shake one's nerves and hurt one's ears, but they are most inspiring. The President's salute is twenty-one guns. It is fired every time he sets foot on the deck of the *Mayflower*, or any other naval vessel, and when he passes, on the *Mayflower*, between the lines of naval vessels on review he gets it from every ship in the fleet, not one by one, but altogether, so I think I know what a naval battle sounds like.

Shortly after we returned from our little cruise on the Maine Coast we received a visit from the President of Chili, Señor Montt, and Señora Montt. He was on his way to Europe, having been ordered abroad on account of ill health. He stopped in New York at the request of his government, and at Mr. Taft's invitation came to Beverly to pay his official respects to the President of the United States. He made the trip to Boston by special train and was there met by the *Mayflower* and by Captain Butt.

President Montt was very ill indeed. On the way down to Beverly he had a heart attack which alarmed everybody and made it seem very probable that he would not be able to land. But he recovered sufficiently to become the most cheerful and confident member of the party and we found him and Señora Montt to be among the most delightful of all the distinguished visitors we had the pleasure of entertaining during our term in the Presidency. After the ceremonious presentation and the exchange of international compliments were disposed of they took luncheon with us and we spent several most interesting and memorable hours together. The members of his numerous *entourage* for whom there was no room in our modest summer cottage were entertained at luncheon on board by Captain Logan of the *Mayflower* and by Captain Butt. We were told afterward that they managed to create quite an *entente cordial,* toasting each other's Presidents and armies and navies and ministers and attaches and everybody else they could think of with great enthusiasm and gusto. Señor Montt died a week later just as he reached England on his health-seeking trip. In his death Chili lost an eminent citizen.

Mr. Taft remained with us at Beverly, playing golf, attending to routine business, seeing the never-ending line of visitors and preparing speeches until September when there began for him one of those whirlwind seasons, so many of which he had lived through. With a printed itinerary in his pocket he was off from Boston on the third of September to attend the Conservation Congress at St. Paul. With two speeches to be delivered, one at the Congress and one at the State Fair in Minneapolis, to say nothing of another in Chicago and numerous short speeches from the rear platform of his train, he was still back in Boston on the eighth to be present at an aviation meet where together we saw the performance of the best aviators of that day.

A short interval of rest and he was away again to New Haven to attend a meeting of the Yale Corporation, then out to Cincinnati to the Ohio Valley Exposition and back to Washington as quickly as a long programme of speeches and hospitalities could be disposed of.

The political skies were then beginning to cloud up in earnest; he had a Democratic Congress to prepare messages for, and I suppose the approaching winter looked anything but alluring to him.

For the first time in the history of the Executive Mansion it was turned into a bachelors' hall during my various absences. My husband always had one or more men staying with him, he would move his aides and secretaries into the White House, and so arrange things that my frequent desertions of him never weighed very heavily on my conscience.

When he arrived in Washington this time he organised a Cabinet House Party so that Washington and the newspaper correspondents had something to worry about for quite a while. He gathered all the members of his Cabinet under his roof and kept them there where he could have three Cabinet meetings a day besides the ones he called in the Executive Offices. People made wild guesses at all kinds of crises and at all manner of important disclosures to be made, but it was only a house party after all. There were a great many problems to be solved, proposed legislative measures to be discussed, and with every woman in the Cabinet off summering somewhere it was an excellent opportunity for the Executive branch of the Government to do extra work.

The distinguished gentlemen had to "double up" in rooms, too, so I have often imagined that they got very little rest at any time. The Secretary of State and the Secretary of the Treasury had the southeast room; the Secretary of the Navy and the Secretary of the Interior had the northeast room; the Attorney General and the

Secretary of Commerce and Labour had the northwest room; the Postmaster General had Robert's room; the Secretary of Agriculture had the housekeeper's room, and the Secretary to the President had my son Charlie's room. I think probably as a house party it was unique, but if there had been any more Departments of Government the President would have had to fit up a dormitory.

At this point in Archie Butt's record I find the note: "Mrs. Taft left this morning for New York to fit her son Charlie out in long trousers."

That brings up unpleasant memories. Like any sensible woman I never would admit that I had reached the high point in life as long as I had one son still in knickerbockers, but with one son at Yale, with a young lady daughter ready to be presented to society, and with Charlie going into long trousers I felt that the day was approaching when the unhappy phrase "getting on in years" might be applied to me.

The very rapid lengthening of Charlie's legs had been a subject of much discussion at Beverly during the summer and the necessity for bestowing upon him the dignity of man-style garments had been manifest to everybody sometime before I would consent to recognise it.

One day the telephone rang and Helen answered it. A voice at the other end of the line said:

"I'd like to speak to Master Charlie Taft, please."

"Somebody wants to speak to you, Charlie," said Helen. Then sister-like she stood by to see who it was and what he could possibly want with her unimportant younger brother. She was surprised to hear this half of a very earnest conversation:

"Who said so?"

"Certainly not!"

"Well, somebody has been giving you misinformation."

"An absolute denial."

"Well, if you want to quote me exactly you may say that

343

I said the rumour is false; wholly without foundation." "All right. Good-bye."

Helen was sufficiently startled to place Charlie under cross-examination at once. She had visions of grave complications wherein he played the unfortunate part of a President's son who had forgotten the rigid discretion exacted of him by the nature of his position.

Charlie admitted that it was a reporter who had called him up.

"Couldn't you tell that from the way I talked to him?" said he.

He had heard enough such conversations to have acquired the natural "tone," but he insisted that the subject of his conversation with his reporter was "purely personal" and had nothing whatever to do with his sister nor yet with any matters of high importance to the Government.

The question had to be referred to the President, his father, before he would admit that the reporter wanted to write something about his going into long trousers.

"And if that isn't a personal matter," said he, "I should like to know what is."

To his intense delight, his "absolute denial" to the contrary notwithstanding, I fitted him out, kissed my baby good-bye and sent a young man son off to school in his stead, feeling vaguely thankful that I should have until Christmas to get used to the thought of him before having to see him again.

Shortly afterward I returned to the White House and to the routine of a social season. The Cabinet officers having all gone to their respective homes we gave the Cabinet Dinner with all its accustomed formalities, then came musicals, luncheons, small dinners, teas and parties of various sorts until near the end of the year when I introduced my daughter to society.

Helen had gone out in Washington and had attended my entertainments during the winter of 1909 whenever she had been at home from college and when I was ill had even as hostess in my place at a dinner we gave for Prince and Princess Fushimi of Japan, but she had never "come out," so I gave two parties early in the winter of 1910 in honor of her debut.

We began with an afternoon At Home, for which, as my daughter says she "got all the flowers there were in Washington," and later I gave a ball on the night of December 30th, when the East Room was filled with hundreds of young people clamouring for "just one more dance" until two o'clock in the morning.

The New Year's Reception was followed in quick succession by the Diplomatic, Congressional, Judicial and other state functions; the winter passed like a dream; the Garden Party season was upon us; then came the greatest event of our four years in the White House, our Silver Wedding.

Twenty-five years married and all but a single year of it spent in the public service. It did not seem unfitting to me that this anniversary should be spent in the White House or that we should seek to make it an event not to be forgotten by anybody who happened to witness it. I thanked the happy fate that had given me a summer wedding-day because I needed all outdoors for the kind of party I wanted to give. That silver was showered upon us until we were almost buried in silver was incidental; we couldn't help it; it was our twenty-fifth anniversary and we had to celebrate it.

I am not going to try to remember or to take the trouble to find out how many invitations we issued. I know there were four or five thousand people present and that a more brilliant throng was never gathered in this country.

It was a night garden party with such illuminations as are quite beyond description. Every tree and bush was ablaze with myriads of tiny coloured lights, the whole stately mansion was outlined in a bright white glow; there were strings of bobbing, fantastic lanterns wherever a string would go; the great fountain was playing at its topmost height in every colour of the rainbow; while on the gleaming point of the Monument and on the flag stretched in the breeze from the staff on the top of the White House shone the steady gleam of two searchlights.

My husband and I received the almost endless line of guests under a large tree about midway between the South Portico and the fountain; the entire house was thrown open and was filled constantly with people seeking the refreshment tables laid in the dining rooms and vestibule. I have a right to be enthusiastic in my memory of that party because without enthusiasm it could not have been given at all. And why should not one be frankly grateful for success'?

With the passing of another season, in no way different from those that went before, I come to the end of my story. There is another story to tell, longer and fuller, but it does not belong to me. It belongs to the man whose career has made my story worth the telling.

After Mr. Taft was renominated, or rather after the second convention in Chicago when the Republican party was divided, I began to make plans for the future in which the White House played no part. I stopped reading the accounts of the bitter political contest because I found that the opposition newspapers made so much more impression on me than those that were friendly to my husband that I was in a state of constant rage which could do me no possible good.

Mr. Taft had never been subjected to bitter criticism and wholesale attack until his term in the Presidency and I suppose I had formed a habit of thinking that there was nothing to criticise him for except, perhaps, his unfortunate shortcoming of not knowing much and of caring less about the way the game of politics is played. Such criticism of him as Mr. Bryan's supporters were able to create for their use in 1908 amounted to nothing. His record of twenty years' uncriticised service stood, and he stood on it. I think we both avoided much perturbation after we became convinced of the unfairness and injustice of much that was said by hostile newspapers, by not reading it. Mr. Taft took much satisfaction from those words of Lincoln's which Mr. Norton, his Secretary, had photographed and placed in a frame on his office desk:

"If I were to try to read, much less answer, all the attacks made on me this shop might as well be closed for any other business. I do the very best I know how—the very best I can; and I mean to keep on doing so until the end. If the end brings me out all right, what is said against me won't amount to anything. If the end brings me out wrong, ten angels swearing I was right would make no difference."

I wanted him to be re-elected, naturally, but I never entertained the slightest expectation of it and only longed for the end of the turmoil when he could rest his weary mind and get back into association with the pleasant things of life. Fortunately we are a family that laughs. Both Mr. Taft and the children manage to get some fun out of almost everything, and I and my matter-of-factness have afforded them life-long amusement. They like now to tell a story about me which doesn't impress me as being particularly funny.

During the last campaign I was at Beverly alone a good part of the summer, but when Mr. Taft did join me for short intervals he brought Republican Headquarters with him, more or less, and a few political supporters were sure to follow for consultation with him.

There was one good old enthusiastic friend who had always supported him and who was then making a valiant fight in his behalf. And he had faith that they would win. He assured me they would win. He told me how they were going to do it, pointing out where Mr. Taft's strength lay and telling me how kindly the people really felt toward him.

"Mrs. Taft, you mark my word," said he, "the President will be re-elected in November!"

"Well," said I, "you may be right, but just the same I intend to pack everything up when I leave Beverly, and I shall take the linen and silver home."

At a dinner given by the Lotos Club in New York, just ten days after Mr. Wilson's election in 1912, Mr. Taft said:

"The legend of the lotos eaters was that if they partook of the fruit of the lotos tree they forgot what had happened in their country and were left in a state of philosophic calm in which they had no desire to return to it.

"I do not know what was in the mind of your distinguished invitation committee when I was asked to attend this banquet. They

347

came to me before election. At first I hesitated to accept lest when the dinner came I should be shorn of interest as a guest and be changed from an active and virile participant in the day's doings of the Nation to merely a dissolving view. I knew that generally on an occasion of this sort the motive of the diners was to have a guest whose society should bring them more closely into contact with the great present and the future and not be merely a reminder of what has been. But, after further consideration, I saw in the name of your club the possibility that you were not merely cold, selfish seekers after pleasures of your own, and that perhaps you were organised to furnish consolation to those who mourn, oblivion to those who would forget, an opportunity for a swan song to those about to disappear....

"The Presidency is a great office to hold. It is a great honour and it is surrounded with much that makes it full of pleasure and enjoyment for the occupant, in spite of its heavy responsibilities and the shining mark that it presents for misrepresentation and false attack.... Of course the great and really the only lasting satisfaction that one can have in the administration of the great office of President is the thought that one has done something permanently useful to his fellow countrymen. The mere enjoyment of the tinsel of office is ephemeral, and unless one can fix one's memory on real progress made through the exercise of presidential power there is little real pleasure in the contemplation of the holding of that or any other office, however great its power or dignity or high its position in the minds of men.

"I beg you to believe that in spite of the very emphatic verdict by which I leave the office, I cherish only the deepest gratitude to the American people for having given me the honour of having held the office, and I sincerely hope in looking back over what has been done that there is enough of progress made to warrant me in the belief that real good has been accomplished, even though I regret that it has not been greater. My chief regret is my failure to secure from the Senate the ratification of the general arbitration treaties with France and Great Britain. I am sure they would have been great steps toward general world peace. What has actually been done I hope has

348

helped the cause of peace, but ratification would have been a concrete and substantial step. I do not despair of ultimate success. We must hope and work on."

THE END

BIG BYTE BOOKS is your source for great lost history!